The Boys from Little Mexico

A Season Chasing the American Dream

Steve Wilson

BEACON PRESS
BOSTON

Beacon Press
25 Beacon Street
Boston, Massachusetts 02108-2892
www.beacon.org

Beacon Press books
are published under the auspices of
the Unitarian Universalist Association of Congregations.

13　12　11　10　　8　7　6　5　4　3　2　1

This book is printed on acid-free paper that meets the uncoated paper
ANSI/NISO specifications for permanence as revised in 1992.

Text design and composition by Wilsted & Taylor Publishing Services

Library of Congress Cataloging-in-Publication Data

Wilson, Steve.
  The boys from little Mexico : a season chasing the American dream / Steve Wilson.
    p. cm.
  ISBN 978-0-8070-2167-5 (hardcover : alk. paper)
  1. Soccer—Oregon—Woodburn. 2. Woodburn High School (Woodburn, Ore.)
3. School sports—Oregon—Woodburn. 4. Soccer—Social aspects—Oregon—
Woodburn. 5. Soccer players—Mexico. 6. Illegal aliens—Oregon. I. Title.
  GV944.U6W55 2010
  796.334'620979537—dc22   2009042841

To Cathy, Ben, and Nate

This is a true story; however, some names have been changed. Portions of the book that were not witnessed by the author were re-created through interviews with those involved and are subject to the usual frailties of memory, although every effort has been made to verify facts. The terms *Hispanic* and *Latino* are used interchangeably throughout the text despite the vagueness and inaccuracy of such labels.

CONTENTS

I carried my one-year-old son, Ben, across the springy running track —one of those made from recycled athletic shoes—heading toward a grass field where about two dozen boys ran back and forth, their attention focused on a black-and-white ball. Coach Mike Flannigan stood watching them, a tall pacing figure, face shaded by a dark baseball cap. He nodded at me as I put Ben down and turned his attention back to the game. The sun, blindingly bright, gleamed off a row of metal bleachers nearby.

For the next fifteen minutes, I alternately chased my son and watched the game. Even with my attention distracted, it didn't take long to notice a wiry midfielder with a pencil-thin mustache who had tremendous ball control. The ball left his foot, bounced around among the other players, and returned, almost as if it were on a string. Like the others that Mike coached, this kid was Hispanic; unlike the others, he played with focus and intensity, his face stern, almost grim. His teammates seemed to be enjoying themselves, but Mustache was locked in a fight.

I picked up Ben and walked over to Coach Flannigan as Mustache trapped a pass and dribbled around an opposing player.

"Who's that?" I asked.

"Oh, you noticed," Mike said. "That's Octavio. He's probably our best player."

He was clearly the best player in the group, moving around like a spider, the soccer field his web.

"Where's he from?"

Coach Flannigan glanced over. "You'll have to ask him," he said.

People from Woodburn can be reluctant to discuss their birthplace. With few exceptions, Latinos in Woodburn either were born in Mexico or are Mexican-descended Americans, and for those born in Mexico, legal status can be a touchy subject.

Sweat trickled down my forehead, and Ben struggled in my arms as something caught his attention. I put him down.

"Have you met Carlos?" Coach Flannigan asked. He gestured toward a nearby bench, where a well-built teen sat talking to a girl about his own age. Carlos turned and looked at us. His black hair was combed forward over his forehead and seemed to shimmer with either water or styling product.

"Hi," he said.

"How come you're not playing?" I asked.

"Injured," he said, gesturing toward a leg.

"Carlos is our keeper," Coach Flannigan said, his eyes still on the game. "He's probably the best keeper in the state."

Carlos snorted and turned back to the girl.

"These two guys are going to be the key to our next season," the coach said. "Hopefully, they can both keep healthy."

More sweat trickled down, and I removed my sunglasses to wipe my face. It was ninety-two degrees, the middle of August, and the temperature was forecast to approach one hundred—unusually hot for northern Oregon. The kids on the field were only a skeleton crew of the entire Woodburn High School squad, but here they were, playing an intense pickup game against another partial team at midday on a shadeless field while their coach stood watching, unpaid because it was summer.

Ben tottered off toward some football equipment and I followed, thinking, these guys sure take their soccer seriously.

. . .

I first heard of the Woodburn Bulldogs soccer team when I came across a newspaper article about a game between the Bulldogs and the visiting Lakeridge Pacers, from Lake Oswego, a town twenty miles north of Woodburn. I lost the article after I read it and never tracked it down again, but I recall the story, in a Lake Oswego paper, describing the Pacers traveling to a hostile and foreign land where Spanish was more common than English, and where, the article seemed to suggest, the visiting team was lucky to leave with their cars' windshields intact.

Lakeridge is one of two high schools in the town of Lake Oswego, the most upper-crust suburb of Portland, Oregon's largest city. It's a town where the wealthy live, which means almost everyone is white. Locals joke about Lake Oswego's lack of diversity by calling it "Lake No-Negro."

Woodburn, on the other hand, calls itself "The City of Unity" and may be Oregon's most ethnically diverse community. As of the 2000 census, Woodburn was 51 percent Hispanic, 49 percent Anglo. Even this is somewhat misleading, since about 30 percent of Woodburn's "Anglo" population belongs to a non-Latino group of immigrants, Russian Old Believers, large, sunburned men with long beards and women with scarf-covered heads, about ten thousand of whom fled religious persecution and ended up around Woodburn in the 1950s and 1960s.

The Woodburn Bulldogs and the Lakeridge Pacers don't play each other often. Because the teams are from different regional leagues, the only times they meet are in pre- and postseason matches. Both schools typically field very good soccer teams; beyond that, there are few resemblances. The two schools represent two completely different Oregons. One could say that they represent two completely different Americas.

Lake Oswego's population is about 90 percent white, and an average resident makes $75,000 a year. Lake Oswego's most notable feature is a privately owned lake surrounded by expensive homes. Woodburn, a short drive to the south, has a median income half that of Lake Oswego's. The most notable feature in Woodburn? The Mac-Laren Youth Correctional Facility.

The differences extend to the high schools. The students who attend Lakeridge, considered one of the best public high schools in the state, go to college: about 80 percent of Lakeridge grads attend a four-year university and 10 percent attend a community college. Only 5 percent of Lakeridge students are eligible for a free or reduced-price lunch. At Woodburn High, 75 percent of the students are eligible for a free or reduced-price lunch. Not long ago, a lower percentage of Woodburn students graduated high school than Lakeridge sent to universities. It's so rare that Woodburn's Hispanic students receive scholarships that the local newspaper writes profiles about the kids who do.

With all this in mind, it's not surprising that people from the two communities don't mix—usually when they do, it's because one is mowing the other's lawn. The one place the two communities come together on equal footing is on the soccer field. Not coincidentally, the two demographic groups represented on that field—upper-middle-class Anglos and working-class Hispanics—are also the two groups in the United States for whom soccer is a real sport and not a punch line.

At the time I first read about Woodburn's soccer team, I was still a new arrival in Oregon. Woodburn, I knew, had factory outlets—I had seen them from the freeway—but I lumped in Woodburn with dozens of other single-exit suburbs cluttering the hour-long drive between Portland and Salem, the state capital. I didn't know that at the town's Greyhound station, one could buy a one-way ticket to the Nayarit city of Tepic, or that downtown Woodburn had the highest concentration of taquerias in the state, or that for girls in Woodburn, turning fifteen was a really big deal. Visiting one weekend, I found that the single exit became a two-lane highway curving into Woodburn, with more traffic than the town deserved. Highway 214 was choked with trucks carrying agricultural supplies to or from the area's farms and nurseries. A distant line of green hills squatted beyond the town.

The residential neighborhoods looked like . . . well, pretty much every other small town in the Northwest: a combination of new and old architecture, lots of trees, pickup trucks, minivans, and a scattering of churches. But, one thing was different. In parks and vacant lots, in front yards and in driveways, I saw boys and men kicking around *la pelota*—the soccer ball. In Woodburn, on Saturday afternoons, the town's parks are crowded with Hispanic men's league games, and the high point of the town's biggest annual celebration, August's Fiesta Mexicana, is an intense men's league tournament. The men I grew up with spent Saturdays playing golf or tennis; in Woodburn, men play *fútbol*.

A month after I joined Coach Flannigan to watch the summertime pickup game, I tagged along with the team on their annual preseason beach trip. Flannigan and Assistant Coach Chuck Ransom planned to take on this trip the best two dozen players out of the hundred or so who tried out for the high school team. By the end of the day, the coaches would pick about twenty for the varsity squad. The rest would be given spots on the freshman, junior varsity, and JV2 teams.

At the beach, on a sunny and windless day, the kids did some bonding over lunch and were put through conditioning drills, including a race up the 250-foot-high, sand-covered headland at Cape Kiwanda. After their climb, while the coaches looked over the roster and grilled burgers, the boys played beach soccer. They stripped off their shirts and began to have the kind of fun that only teenage boys seem to have—lots of yelling and insults and playful physical abuse. They were the only Hispanics on the beach. In the middle of the game, a blond kid, probably about fifteen, walked up to watch them. A couple of the Woodburn players invited him to join the game. As the newcomer received a pass and rushed through the sand, Mike Flannigan turned to me, thrust out an arm, pointing, and spoke in a defiant tone.

"You see!" he shouted. "These are good kids!"

Adults in Woodburn are like that. After all, there are few phrases with worse collective baggage than *teenage Hispanic male*. Seen on the street, Woodburn's players are more likely to be identified as gangbangers, thieves, or slick Lotharios than athletes, loving sons, or good students. So the adults who watch over them are as much sheepdogs as teachers, simultaneously herding their charges while peering over their collective shoulders for lurking wolves.

Coach Flannigan's young athletes may have bad reputations, but the Bulldogs are known across the state as excellent soccer players. Through 2009, the team has gone to the state playoffs an astonishing twenty-four straight years. No other high school team in Oregon, in any major sport, has been so good for so long.

That achievement is balanced by the limited success of the Woodburn Bulldogs off the field. Nationally, only about six in ten Hispanic boys graduate from high school, and just over 10 percent end up with four-year college degrees. The Woodburn Bulldogs do better than the national average, but not by much. There are a lot of reasons for this: poverty, immigration status, language, and culture among them, which makes the few boys who do get a college education even more unusual, for they have triumphed over their environment.

This book, which follows the 2005 Woodburn Bulldogs team, tells the story of a group of young Latino men who are trying to succeed with the odds stacked against them, both athletically and academically. It begins with a game that has already become a legend in the town that locals call "Little Mexico."

The Field of Play

> Woodburn strong? Only on account of villainy. Everyone
> who has played Woodburn understands that they flop at
> every chance. The worst personal story I have is when they
> come to your field with a ref who speaks Spanish and the
> team and the ref converse and no one knows what is going
> on. Woodburn is not a legit team, they'll squeeze through
> any way they can.
> —Posting on Oregonlive.com sports forum

It was a cold, wet November day in 2004 when the white boys from
Lakeridge High confirmed everything that the Mexicans from Woodburn feared about themselves. It happened during a game of soccer, the one sport that Woodburn should dominate. Woodburn's
kids should be the best because they grow up with a *balón de fútbol* practically glued to their feet. They should frighten white boys.

But they didn't.

That afternoon, as the clouds piled up darker and darker, the
crowd standing three-deep at Woodburn High's backup soccer field
roared with almost a single voice, the voice of high school kids and
their siblings, parents, and friends. The beloved varsity field, recently
rebuilt at great expense, had flooded, so aluminum bleachers and a
portable scoreboard had been dragged to the old field, the bleachers
sardine-packed with family members, all of them bundled in thick
dark coats, their voices ringing in the crisp night air. In comparison,
the twenty-two soccer players on the field, breath fogging before
their faces, looked woefully underdressed in their long-sleeved shirts
and short pants.

Because this was a home game for the all-Latino Woodburn
Bulldogs, known locally as Los Perros, the fans were mostly black-
haired, brown-skinned people. The Lakeridge Pacer fans, blond and

brunette parents wearing stylish clothing, sat together, slightly uncomfortably, in one corner of the bleachers. Behind them sprawled the baseball field, a parking lot, and the looming shape of Woodburn High School.

Omar Mendoza, possibly the most dependable parent fan in Woodburn school history, sat in the bleachers with his wife, Pat, and their two daughters, Clarissa and Veronica. Omar kept his eyes focused on Carlos, the team's budding star goalkeeper and Omar's foster child. Across the field, standing near Carlos, Coach Mike Flannigan rapidly shouted instructions at the boys huddled around him. Assistant Coach Chuck Ransom stood by to translate for kids like center-midfielder Octavio, a recent arrival from Mexico whose grasp of English was still slippery during the excitement of games.

As the scoreboard's timer counted down toward zero, players from both teams began to retake the field, rubbing their palms against the cold and jogging in place to keep their muscles loose. They had already played a regulation eighty-minute game that ended in a 0–0 tie. Because this was a quarterfinal playoff, Oregon rules dictated that they play two mandatory overtimes of ten minutes each. Both overtimes would be played in full, regardless of the number of goals either team made.

Retaking the field with the rest of his team, Octavio felt nervous, wishing the game had already resumed. Octavio was an exotic-looking kid, not what most people would picture as a junior at an Oregon public high school or one of the best soccer players on one of the best teams in a very white state. He didn't even look particularly Mexican. With his wiry build, dark skin, and Asian features, Octavio could be something far different, like a Malaysian pirate.

Reaching his position near the middle of the field, Octavio waited impatiently for the game to restart, glaring at the players from both teams around him. Octavio's teammates may have liked him or disliked him, but they all agreed that his internal flame burned brightly. Octavio had *ganas*, an observer might say, a desire to achieve that fueled his flame and sometimes burned those around him.

Most of the other Woodburn Bulldogs rested on one knee. The

opposing players, all of them nearly half a foot taller than the Bull-dogs, stood in staggered formation on the other side of the field. The referee blew his whistle to start the first overtime, *la pelota* pinballed back and forth between players, and Woodburn took control.

The Bulldogs drove into the Pacer backfield playing the kind of possession soccer—short passes, lots of lateral movement—that the team was known for. About a minute into the first overtime, Wood-burn got the ball into dangerous territory near the goal and a Lak-eridge defender booted it out of bounds past the end line, setting up an early corner kick.

Octavio, already warm, had stopped thinking. He had been play-ing *fútbol* since he was waist-high to his grandma, so he didn't need to consider much on the field anymore. Instead, he reacted to the changing geometry around him—the ever-moving ball and the tu-mult of shouts and fast-moving legs—not with his mind, but with his feet. The corner kick was set up, he took his place among the crowd of players in front of the Pacer goal, and he saw the ball come soaring toward the middle of the field.

As he ran forward, Octavio watched the ball bounce between himself and his teammate Rommell, a Brazilian exchange student. Both were running fast toward the Lakeridge goal, only a couple of defenders in front of them. Octavio was dimly aware of the Wood-burn fans on the east side of the field leaping to their feet and begin-ning to shout.

Octavio reached the ball first, turned, and ran a couple of paces with the ball at his toes. He saw defenders rushing toward him, the goalkeeper crouched midway between the posts and a couple of paces in front, and pulled his right leg back. A longtime defender who had recently been moved to midfield, Octavio didn't get a lot of practice taking shots on goal, and he wasn't the most accurate striker on the field, but he knew that when an opening presented itself, you took it.

Octavio swung his leg forward and blasted the ball toward the upper-left corner of the Pacers' net. He saw the keeper leap toward it, the ball sailing past his outstretched arms, and the sudden tight-ening of the net as the ball sank deeply into it. Then Rommell was hugging him and people were jumping onto his back and he felt a joy that held his burning intensity at bay for the moment. His goal, the first of the night, had put the Perros up 1–0.

The Woodburn fans, bench players, and coaches leaped into the air and shouted; many of the players and family members, especially new arrivals from Mexico, prepared to storm the field, mistakenly thinking that the overtime had ended—as it did in college—with a Golden Goal. The referee stopped the clock while word was spread that in high school, soccer overtimes must be played in full. Finally, the crowd settled down and the game resumed.

Sensing the end of their season, the Pacers fought back hard, repeatedly pushing the ball into Woodburn territory through long passes that the shorter Woodburn players had trouble defending. Once the ball was on the grass, however, the Bulldogs' intense defense prevented the Pacers from getting scoring opportunities. The first overtime ended with no additional goals, and deep into the second overtime, the game remained in Woodburn's control. However, tempers flared as the game became more physical, and boys were springing up from fouls and squaring off as if to brawl.

Octavio watched Carlos angrily confront a Pacer player and then complain loudly to the referee, prompting a quick yellow card that sent Carlos off the field for a mandatory substitution. A couple of minutes later, as Carlos trotted back to his place in goal, the clock counted down to under a minute and the Woodburn reserve players, who normally sat on an aluminum bench across the field from the bleachers, all began to stand, sensing victory. Many of the fans also rose to watch the end.

With twenty seconds left in the game, a Lakeridge pass was called offsides near the Woodburn penalty box. Coach Mike Flannigan turned and high-fived his father, Brian, as the bench players behind him hooted and cheered. It was a devastating foul for the Pacers, and as the Woodburn fans screamed and pounded the bleachers with their feet, Carlos watched one of his teammates pick up the ball and place it on the field for a free kick. From his position in the Woodburn goal, Carlos could see past the players to the scoreboard, with its glowing digital clock and the glorious numbers 1–0.

The clock was stopped. This irritated Carlos. Although only a sophomore, Carlos was one of the most experienced players on the Woodburn side. Most of his teammates played three months of high school soccer every year and pickup games whenever possible. Some of them played on a local Hispanic men's league team, but these were games more suited to drinking beer and bragging than learning team discipline. Carlos was one of the few to play on a private club team, keeping him playing either indoors or outdoors nearly year round.

Because of this, Carlos had played in more games than most of the Woodburn seniors, and never had he seen a referee so clearly favor one team over another. Usually in soccer, the clock never stops, and a ref will add extra time at the end of the game to make up for the non-playing time used by fouls. But this ref had whistled and rolled his arms over each other so often that Carlos felt like he was back in middle school playing football, and it seemed to him that most of these fouls favored Lakeridge. Now, with less than a minute to go, the clock was again stopped in Lakeridge's favor.

Carlos tried to calm himself. As a transfer student to Woodburn, he was new to the team, but he felt that he was already one of the better players. He had been put in goal, but Carlos also played forward, a position that he preferred because it allowed him to be aggressive, to force the issue, to use the strength in his legs to dominate. He loved hearing the crowd cheer when he scored, although he got a similar rush from a spectacular save in goal. Some of his teammates thought that he made some saves look more difficult than they really were, just to draw applause, and Carlos didn't deny it. He soaked up positive attention.

He was frustrated, though, because of the clock, and because he had only just returned to the goal after his temporary ejection, he still felt edgy and angry. He focused on teammate Cheo, standing behind the ball. Carlos, and probably everybody else watching the game, expected one thing: Cheo would punt the ball downfield, the Woodburn midfielders and forwards would swarm around it, try to maintain possession, and kick it out of bounds if necessary. With about twenty seconds to go, the Pacers wouldn't be able to get themselves in scoring position again.

Then, as he watched, something strange happened.

The ref jogged away from the ball, blowing his whistle to resume play. However, several Lakeridge players lingered near the ball, clearly upset about the foul and the impending end of their season. One of them, Danny Connors, stood within a few feet of the ball, effectively blocking a kick. For some reason, the ref had not moved the Lakeridge players the mandatory ten yards away from the ball. Carlos watched Cheo stand uncertainly, turning his head between the Lakeridge defenders and his teammates. Then Cheo tapped the ball with his foot, intending to move it away from Connors.

Carlos ran forward. He wasn't sure why the ref hadn't cleared the Lakeridge defenders and he wasn't sure the ref saw what was happening. He recognized the clear threat that Connors represented, though, and because Cheo's touch made the ball live, he decided to pick it up, to stop play until the ref could move the opposing players away.

The referee, twenty yards away at midfield, blew his whistle, stopping time again, and called another foul. This time it was a handball on Woodburn. A newspaper report later described how the call set off bedlam: "Coaches were screaming, the fans were going nuts, and a general feeling of confusion seemed to fall over the proceedings."

On the sidelines, Coach Mike Flannigan began bellowing in rage. It wasn't unusual for the normally mellow and thoughtful coach to become angry and yell during games, but he had never lost his cool this badly. He wasn't alone. Even typically Zenlike Assistant Coach Chuck Ransom lost his temper as the ref approached and explained the call. They quieted down long enough for the ref to say that it was clear to him that Cheo's touch had been the free kick, and that the goalkeeper had simply lost concentration and picked it up. He ignored their rebuttals about the lingering Lakeridge players and the absurdity of *that* being a free kick, and trotted away, Coach Flannigan livid in his wake.

On online soccer forums, many Oregonians protest that Woodburn, an all-Hispanic team, tends to get leeway on foul calls because so many soccer refs are Hispanic. Woodburn supporters like Flannigan are sure that it works the other way: Hispanic refs are harder on Woodburn players to prove their neutrality, and white refs are sometimes just plain-old racists. This ref, he was certain, was one of the latter.

Flannigan paced back and forth on the sidelines, trying to control his thoughts. Like it or not, the game was going to continue. His counterpart, Lakeridge coach Paul Slover, had already shouted out a play and gotten his team ready for the free kick. Danny Connors, the player who had prevented Cheo from kicking the ball just seconds earlier, stood a few paces behind it, his face turned toward Carlos and the Woodburn goal.

Coach Flannigan watched helplessly as his players set up a defensive wall between the ball and the goal—the boys lining up shoulder to shoulder to prevent a direct shot on goal. He watched Carlos shouting at them, arranging them with waves of his gloved hands until he had the wall where he wanted it. The ref blew his whistle, restarting the game with only seconds to play. Connors ran forward and kicked, bending his shot over the wall toward the upper-left corner of the Woodburn net.

Connors later said, "I thought, 'I can't miss this.' Because that was the end of the game, really. I just knew I had to make it. I wasn't allowed to miss it."

Coach Flannigan could see Carlos jump and get his hands on the ball, deflecting it. But not far enough. Brushing past his fingers, the ball sailed on, hit the crossbar, and bounced in. Flannigan closed his eyes and grasped his head with his hands. He couldn't believe it. Lakeridge had tied the game.

After two overtimes, Oregon high school soccer games go into penalty kicks. Each team selects six players to go one-on-one against the opposing keeper by kicking a stationary ball placed twelve yards from the goal. All six players shoot. When all are done, the team with the most goals wins. If the game is still tied, the PKs begin to count individually. Miss one, let the other team make one, and you've lost.

Omar Mendoza, still sitting in the bleachers, knew this perfectly well. Omar, whose perpetual scowl, broad chest, and thick head of black hair made him look like a short and bad-tempered bear, had never played soccer. However, he had been coaching private soccer teams for nearly a decade, initially in an effort to strengthen Omar Junior's clubfoot. Soon enough, though, Omar found that a guy with a truck, some time, and an open-door policy was a sought-after commodity by Woodburn boys. His teams, and soon afterwards, his house, became the standby diversion for kids who often had little parental direction or involvement. Omar got into soccer as a way to help his son O.J. get healthy; he continued coaching to keep O.J. and all his friends from getting into trouble.

Omar watched the penalty kick setup nervously. He had faith in Carlos's abilities as a keeper, but he had noticed that the other goalie was no slouch either. Also, he had seen the tempers flaring earlier in the game and knew that the Bulldogs were frustrated and angry. They need to calm down and concentrate, he thought.

Omar watched the first three kicks go in for both teams. The fourth Lakeridge player tried a low blast to the left, but this time Carlos guessed correctly and smothered the ball before it could hit the net, causing a wild cheer to rise from the Woodburn bench and the bleachers. Omar shouted encouragement.

Cheo, the Woodburn sweeper, stepped to the ball. If he made the kick, he would put Woodburn up by 1, not a victory yet, but with only two players to follow him, possibly enough to make a difference. He took two, three, quick steps to the ball and hit it low and left. The keeper jumped right, getting his hands on the ball, but Cheo's shot slipped out of his grasp and shushed into the back of the net, putting Woodburn up by 1 and prompting another roar from the crowd. The noise died, though, as Danny Connors, the next Lakeridge player, also scored on an off-tempo, low kick to the right, tying the game.

The next two players, one from each team, failed to score, bringing forward Octavio, the final player to take a mandatory PK. Making the shot would advance his team to the semifinals, one game away from the team's first championship bid in five years. Many of the watching Woodburn players and fans—mostly Catholics—clasped their hands in front of their faces, mumbling prayers in Spanish while they leaned forward. For once, Coach Flannigan stood still.

Octavio watched the Lakeridge keeper crouching in front of the net and decided to aim for the low-right corner, the opposite corner from where he had scored Woodburn's only regulation goal. With all eyes on him, Octavio ran forward and kicked to the right. The keeper jumped left. The ball headed toward the right-hand post, then slipped past it, just outside, and a communal groan escaped from the Woodburn fans and reserve players.

With the mandatory six PKs completed and the game still tied, every kick now became a potential game-winner. Each team sent forward a player to take a PK in turn. If one scored and the other didn't, the game was over.

The seventh Lakeridge player went first, and scored, making the PKs 5–4 in favor of Lakeridge. Woodburn's Enrique, who had drilled the game-winning kick in the previous playoff game, strolled to the ball. If he scored, the game remained tied. If he missed, Woodburn's season was over. Enrique stood motionless, studying the keeper, trying to guess which way he would jump. The crowd silenced.

Taking two steps forward, Enrique smashed the ball toward the goal, dead on, and it barreled straight into the arms of the Lakeridge keeper. The small contingent of Lakeridge fans began to scream as their team ran onto the field, piling onto each other as if they had just won the state championship. The Woodburn reserves slumped back down on their bench as the players on the field fell to the grass or stood, heads down, stunned. Some of them wept openly. Shaking his head, Omar began to navigate through the murmuring crowd to the field.

Carlos rode home with Omar, not feeling defeated, but sick to his stomach. He had never been scored on like that shot from Connors, not a free kick that he had time to reach, that he felt hit his hands. And he had never experienced anything like that crazy foul call at the end. He replayed the final moment of the game as he brushed his teeth, and even as he lay in bed in the room he shared with his two half-brothers, Tino and Alex, and Omar's son, O.J. All four bitched about the game and the unfairness of the call, the lucky kick, and the inability of their best players to score on PKs.

Carlos obsessed about the game for months: how he shouldn't have picked up the ball, how he should have jumped a second earlier, or punched the foul kick over the net instead of trying to catch it; how he should have guessed better during the PKs. It had come down to him, he thought, all eyes had been on him at the end. His choices could have made him a hero instead of just another bitter loser.

Eventually, he viewed it with his typical fatalism.

"It was a pretty nice goal," Carlos said. "Right then I knew we were going to lose. It was meant to be. Stuff like that doesn't happen for the hell of it."

The handball call infuriated everybody connected with the Woodburn team and haunted the players afterwards. That night, Cheo saw the scoreboard in his dreams. Omar fumed for days around his home, complaining to Pat about the terrible referee. Coaches Flannigan and Ransom, and Laura Lanka, the school's principal, wrote letters of protest to the Oregon State Athletic Association. They never received much of a response and never learned what, if anything, had been said to the referee.

"Either he is incompetent, he got confused in the excitement of a playoff game, or it was intentional," Ransom commented. "We'll never know. Only he knows. But either way, it was a terrible call. It was the most horrible situation I've ever experienced with a sports team."

Octavio left the game in shock and didn't sleep much for three days.

"We thought we were in the other round. Just kick the ball and that's it. The game is over. Then I looked over and saw Cheo move the ball and Carlos pick it up. I didn't understand what was happening. You are fighting for eighty minutes of normal time. Then twenty minutes for overtime. Then you lose in the last few seconds. It's terrible. Sometimes I think about it and it doesn't seem real. We were so close to making history." As he so often would, he laid the blame on himself. "Then I missed the penalty kick and I . . ." He exhaled with a sound like, "Whooooo . . ." that shrank out of his mouth and died.

From the other side of the field, Lakeridge coach Paul Slover gave credit to his team and viewed the win from the perspective of the fortunate. In a newspaper interview, he said, "Basically for us it came down to determination and will. I think we shocked them a bit."

Coach Mike Flannigan took the loss hard, for despite the Pacers' skillful foul and penalty kicking, he had no doubt that the referee had given Lakeridge the game. The 2004 team had been a surprise to Coach Flannigan because the Bulldogs had graduated a lot of seniors in 2003. He had expected 2004 to be a rebuilding year, but Woodburn had taken second place in their league and won their first two playoff games, even with a sophomore goalkeeper and lots of new players.

Coach Flannigan didn't have much time to be upset, however. Even though the soccer season was over, he still had his Language Arts classes to prepare for, and the JV basketball team, which he also coached, was just beginning its season. Still, while the coach had experienced many playoff losses before, none had been quite as heart-wrenching as this one.

Ultimately, it wasn't the loss that upset him, that made him drive home angrily and reenact the moment to his wife for weeks, it was the feeling that something had been stolen from his team. He worried that this defeat would break some of his kids, cause them to quit pushing forward, either in sports or academics; he worried that they would take the experience as proof that in the game of life, the cards really were stacked against them.

On Monday, back at school, Octavio once again looked around at the new high school building, which still represented unimaginable wealth. He had arrived in the United States three summers earlier, moved in with an uncle, and that fall, started as a freshman at Woodburn High. He described his first class as "where you learn to say 'hello.'" Now, as a junior, he had signed up to take International Baccalaureate classes, having been told that the harder courses would impress college admissions officers. But some of the classes, especially one called Theory of Knowledge, baffled him. His Uncle Ricardo and Aunt Evelyna, with whom he lived, had left Octavio's hometown in Guanajuato, Mexico, with grade-school educations, and they were unable to help him with academic concepts such as rhetoric and semantics. So, stubbornly, Octavio sat up late trying to decipher what it was that he was supposed to learn in these classes.

With only a month left in the fall term, he was fearful of failing Theory of Knowledge. (Why is a chair called a chair?—it just didn't make sense!) After working hard to learn English and maintaining nearly an A average, that kind of academic insult hurt badly. Worse than that, it made him question his decisions.

Octavio had given up a possible career as a professional soccer player in Mexico to come to Woodburn at fourteen, leaving his family behind. At first, it had seemed like an adventure, but now, after two years of school and the struggle to learn English, he knew that he would not be happy if he failed to go to college. In Mexico, sending a child to college was all but impossible for poor families; he would have been fortunate to go to high school. But here, the rules were different. Everybody went to high school and successful people went to college. They studied, became scholars, teachers, architects. He saw how those people lived in houses that had two bathrooms, curving stairways, and perfect green lawns. He saw those things and he wanted them.

But these latest setbacks, the loss to Lakeridge and the poor grades, made Octavio wonder if college was in his future. He wondered if any college coaches would offer him a spot. As a junior, he was eligible by NCAA rules to be contacted; he knew he had talent and he was a disciplined student, but no coaches had come calling, and he had only one year left in which to impress the world with his skills. Octavio wondered if he should have taken the offer from Fútbol Club Atlas, a First Division team in Mexico, to return. If he did go back to Mexico, he could probably regain his old spot on the developmental team. If he stayed in America, what was his future? Taping and painting? Clearing weeds? It was such a strange country that seemed to both welcome and reject him, and for the moment, Octavio didn't know what to do about it.

Finally, Octavio told himself what players and coaches have told themselves at the end of every non-championship season since sports began. We've got a lot of good players, he thought. The sophomores and juniors will be bigger, faster, stronger. We'll learn from this experience. I'll practice penalty kicks. Just wait 'til next year.

PRESEASON

ONE

Steps to Success

Our guys rely a lot on talent and hustle, but when they need
that psychological element, that confidence, that invincibil-
ity, that ability to stay calm and to really believe that we are
going to win because we are better—I think that's a missing
piece of magic. I think the coach at Woodburn needs to
address that problem. He needs to give the kids a vision of
success.

—Coach Chuck Ransom

Coach Mike Flannigan, from behind a baseball cap and sunglasses,
gazed at the dozens of boys sprawled on the field before him. On
this sweaty day in late August 2005, the boys looked relaxed and un-
concerned as they peered back, leaning their faces into the available
shadows and occasionally shoving one of their friends for no reason.
The field they rested on was thickly packed with thin-bladed grass,
vibrantly green and surprisingly cool on the skin. Coach Flannigan
thought of this field as *the pitch*, using the British term for a soccer
field. Given the opportunity, he would quickly proclaim it the finest
soccer pitch in the state, and perhaps it was.

Mike Flannigan was tall and sturdy, with graying brown hair and
a body that was, at thirty-six, beginning to show the effects of the local microbrewed beers he loved. He wore a dark blue track suit, and
in his right hand he carried a metal clipboard, which he was known to
throw to the ground when angry. He had a charming lopsided smile
and a nasal tone to his voice, as if he was permanently congested. In
photos from a decade earlier, he looked like the actor Kevin Costner,
especially around his mouth and chin. The resemblance had faded
somewhat with his shaggy goatee, but it was still there.

Mike had his opinions, but he also could listen respectfully to
others. Off the field, he was soft-spoken, with a dry sense of humor

and a touch of melancholy. On the field, he became focused and often temperamental, making decisions quickly. Some parents and even
assistant coaches said that Coach Flannigan was unwilling to make
changes, that he ignored outside suggestions. Parents of his players
were sometimes dubious of his coaching skills, mostly because of the
lack of a state championship.

Sometimes Coach Flannigan thought the same thing. He wondered if he was the reason his team faltered in the postseason. He
worried that he was lacking something that good coaches have, some
instinct or insight, a better game plan, or some new training regi-
men. Year after year, he bought coaching videos and attended semi-
nars. Then year after year, his team played well, got into the playoffs,
and lost after one or two games. Coach Flannigan worried that other
teams didn't take the Perros seriously, and that he was letting down
the kids, the school, the town. He wondered if he needed to take
Spanish lessons.

All this was somewhere in the background of Coach Flannigan's
consciousness as he began to pace in front of the kids. Flannigan,
as his players called him, had never learned to remain still during
games, as if the movement of his players on the field created in him
some sympathetic motion. Even now, with all his players relaxed and
stretched out in front of him like a family of tired kittens, Coach
Flannigan walked back and forth, speaking in short sentences. He
saw kids he didn't know, freshmen mostly, and many he did know.
He saw many seniors. There was Betos, the reserve goalkeeper he
had called and convinced to play his senior year. There was Javier, a
stocky, hard-working kid who Flannigan sometimes saw taking or-
ders at McDonald's, and Ramon, a burly defender who Flannigan felt
was fearless.

On the adjacent practice field the grass was dry and sunburned.
Woodburn High was blessed with a large area of land for athletic
fields. Besides the varsity soccer pitch, there was a baseball diamond,
a football field, and four practice fields that went unwatered during
the summer, baking into a pale yellow by fall. The varsity pitch was
never allowed to dry out, but with school about to start, the practice

field was being soaked by enormous commercial sprinklers, pulled by a huge spool called the Water Reel. From where Coach Flannigan stood, he could hear the sound of pattering water and the mournful creak of the rotating Water Reel, like the call of a lonely humpback whale.

Behind Coach Flannigan stood Assistant Coach Chuck Ransom, also the school's assistant principal, and coaches Levi Arias, Dave Ellingson, and Mike Flannigan's adoptive father, his Uncle Brian. They coached the junior varsity, freshman, and JV2 soccer teams, respectively. The boys sitting in front of them, with the exception of two white kids and an Italian exchange student, were all Latinos. About half of the Bulldogs had been born in Mexico, although many came to Woodburn at such a young age that they had no memory of their homeland. One kid, Jovanny, was from El Salvador. Nearly all the others, born in the United States, had immigrant parents.

Many of the boys already knew each other, which simplified Coach Flannigan's first objective: creating an artificial family. He was a big fan of families, real and artificial, and began both his coaching season and his teaching season with the intention of bonding his charges together, the sooner the better. With that in mind, during the first week, he tried to have the emerging teams interact, scrimmage together, and train together before he eventually would separate them based on skill level and age. Although he already had a good idea of who his varsity players would be, for the moment, he kept them all together in front of him.

"All right," Coach Flannigan said. "You guys, especially you freshmen, need to know that Woodburn is a soccer town. And the high school has a proud heritage of winning. All right?"

He paced several steps to the right and stopped.

"Woodburn's varsity team has made the playoffs every year since 1986. People expect Woodburn to win soccer games. And if you guys don't screw it up, this will be our twentieth year in a row of making the playoffs."

Coach Flannigan stepped to the left, one, two, three steps, turned, stopped. The sun dipped behind his head and cast an oblong shadow across the field. In the distance, one of the regularly scheduled trains brayed its horn as it passed on the other side of the high school. The coach looked at his players.

"Most of you weren't even alive when Woodburn started going to the state playoffs, that's how long ago it was. So there's always a lot of pressure on the varsity guys. All right?"

He cleared his throat, stepped to the right, once, twice.

"A couple of years ago," Coach Flannigan began again, "we were in fifth place with a couple of games left. Only the top four teams from each league go to the playoffs, so we were getting on the guys on that team. We said to them, 'Are you going to be the first team since 1986 not to go to the state playoffs?' They rallied and got us there, so people are going to expect a lot out of you. They expect the best from Woodburn."

Pause, step, stop.

"If you are on the varsity team, know that you are one of the twenty best soccer players in the town in your age group, and one of the best in the state. All right? People expect you to go to the state playoffs, and they expect you to win it all. We have gone to the state championship three times, but we have not won it all. As much as we are proud of our record in the playoffs, we really want a state championship, and that's why we're going to work hard this week, next week, and every week, till the beginning of November."

The kids sprawled on the grass appeared to be listening, but nobody said a word. Their eyes followed the coach as he paced.

Coach Flannigan wondered what to say next. It was sometimes hard, these first few days, like the first few days in the classroom. It was hard to get everybody involved, to make them feel safe enough to talk in front of each other. In the classroom, he had exercises designed to break down barriers. Perhaps he should use some of them on the field. Was it enough to give the kids a sense of the team's history? Would they understand the expectations placed on them? He glanced at the boys through his glasses. Which one of these guys knew how to win?

"Okay," Coach Flannigan said, looking back at the other coaches. "Let's introduce ourselves. My experience. I started coaching here in

1994. To you that probably doesn't seem so long ago. To me it seems like a hell of a long time ago. As you get old, time goes by fast."

Pause, turn, step.

Mike Flannigan had stumbled into his head coaching job courtesy of his adoptive father, but he didn't explain that to his team. He didn't tell them much about himself, apart from his love of soccer, and they had probably already figured that out. Had he offered to tell them more, they might have been interested to know that Mike Flannigan was the beginning and the end of successful Woodburn High soccer, and most of the middle as well. Back in November 1986, a sixteen-year-old Mike Flannigan had been the starting goalkeeper on the high school varsity team's first trip to the state playoffs, and after graduating from the University of Oregon, where he met his wife, Lynn, and gazing at his navel for a while, he became part of the coaching squad for most of the Bulldogs' subsequent trips.

Young Mike had moved to Woodburn when he was ten, to live with his Uncle Brian, who would later adopt him. Mike liked to describe Brian as a product of the 1960s, the kind of guy who liked to live and let live. But Brian had come from a rough background in Spokane. He had watched his brothers go to jail, but he noticed that all the kids he knew who stayed out of trouble played sports. So he took up football. Brian's athletic talent took him to Gonzaga University, and after graduation, he began teaching and coaching.

Through Brian, Mike discovered soccer, and by the time he reached high school, Mike belonged to a group of boys who had played together for years on club teams that Brian coached. As juniors, Mike and his mostly-white friends pushed the Bulldogs into the state playoffs for the first time. Back then the team was ethnically mixed, half Anglo, nearly half Hispanic, with a few Russians.

During Woodburn High's first playoff game in 1986, young Mike was in goal. They lost 4–0 in the first round. During their second trip in 1987, with Mike now a senior, the team made it to the state championship, where they met the Jesuit Crusaders, a hand-picked team from one of Oregon's most prestigious private schools. The Crusaders, who were and still are Oregon's winningest soccer program, fielded a team with some of the best players from across the state, and they destroyed star-struck Woodburn. From his vantage point between the posts, Mike watched six balls zip past him into the net. Even with Mike's brother Timm playing forward—a kid who turned out to be a gifted striker—Woodburn couldn't score once.

Mike was upset, but he wasn't destroyed. His team had made it to the state championship after only one previous year in the postseason and had lost to Jesuit, that well-organized, highly experienced, and well-funded private sports juggernaut. Mike and Brian both felt that the Bulldogs were the best public school team in the state.

Following the 1987 championship loss, the team's coach, Greg Baisch, quit to become the school athletic director. Brian Flannigan, who had been coaching the Woodburn girls' soccer team, took over as head coach of the boys' team. Mike graduated and went to college. Brian Flannigan took the team right back to the state championship in 1988, where they lost 3–2 against Catlin Gable, a team from another private school in Portland. After Mike graduated from college, Brian talked him into helping out at a game, and Mike discovered that the knowledge he had built up as a keeper and as a coach's son translated to an understanding of directing players on the field.

A three-month assistant coach position didn't pay the bills, however, so after a few dead-end jobs, Mike decided to go back to school. Eventually he ended up teaching reading and writing at Woodburn High. He spent several years as his father's assistant coach, and then the two co-coached the team from 1994 to 2000. Together they took the Bulldogs to the state championship in 1998, losing 3–0 to La Salle, another private college prep school team. In 2001, Brian took over coaching the junior varsity team and Mike officially became the head coach of the Bulldogs varsity squad. In the nineteen years of playoff history preceding the 2005 season, the team took first place in their league fourteen times, made the state quarterfinals six times, and the state semifinals four times. And there had been at least one Flannigan involved in every one of those games.

When Coach Flannigan finished his introduction, Assistant Coach Chuck Ransom stepped forward. Coach Ransom was shorter and stockier than Flannigan, with dark hair and an unblinking stare. Ransom was a confident, almost polished speaker, who could talk off-the-cuff without the usual pauses, ums, and uhs that most people use. Along with coaching and his position as assistant principal, Ransom taught Spanish, so many of the boys already knew him, even if they hadn't played for him. Ransom had a reputation around the school as a man whom one could approach with problems, a guy who was willing to be discreet. Rumors swirled about his past, the most popular that Ransom harbored some secret professional or semi-pro team experience, possibly as a Second or Third Division player in Mexico.

The reality was that Chuck Ransom had been the child of two high school teachers with artistic dreams. Chuck's father, after graduating with a master's in fine arts from the University of Oregon, took a U.S. foreign service job during the Kennedy administration, eventually posting to Brazil, where five-year-old Chuck first encountered soccer. Returning to the United States four years later, Chuck then discovered that Americans didn't speak Portuguese.

After graduating from high school, Chuck traveled, following his father to Portugal and living there for several years and then going to college in Mexico before finally graduating from Portland State University. He found a job teaching at a private Catholic high school in Portland, where he also took on a position as assistant soccer coach. He later took over the head coaching position before leaving and moving to a country home not far from Woodburn.

He'd only been at Woodburn for a few seasons, but already it was Ransom whom many of the boys, including Octavio, turned to when needing adult advice. It was Ransom who calmed Octavio down when he got too upset to think during games, and Ransom whom Octavio approached with questions about classes or American culture. In turn, Ransom admired Octavio and his best friend, Cheo, for their drive and desire to overcome the difficulties of living in a foreign country.

"I've been coaching high school soccer for almost twenty years," Coach Ransom said to the boys on the field, "and I grew up in Brazil, so I've been around soccer my whole life. I love playing soccer, but

I think the next best thing to playing is coaching and helping young players develop. I'm excited to work with you guys this year and to help you win games and become better players."

When Ransom stopped speaking, the other three coaches introduced themselves. Levi Arias, the lone Latino coach, was in charge of the junior varsity team. Levi, who had the gentle handshake of a Mexican native, had come to the high school the previous season after coaching at a nearby middle school. Brian Flannigan, tall, red-cheeked and white-haired, ran the JV2 team as well as being director of soccer operations, which meant that Brian hounded kids to fill out forms, made sure that they met their academic requirements, and insisted they get health insurance. The final coach was Dave Ellingson, a science teacher who had been at Woodburn High for seven years. Dave, who coached the freshman team, liked to introduce himself to new students by saying that he too was an immigrant. Fair-haired and fair-skinned, he was known to the other coaches and to his players simply as "Canadian."

Introductions over, the coaches herded the boys across the parking lot toward the high school building. The players had recently received their class lists, and some compared schedules. Chuy, a junior who stayed out partying most nights, complained about the courses he had to take. When a teammate pointed out that he had chosen those courses, Chuy shrugged. "That doesn't mean I like them," he said.

As they entered the building, the boys walked past signs in English, Spanish, and Russian. Despite the smaller numbers of Anglos and Slavs, who combined made up 30 percent of the student body, the two groups regularly outperformed the majority Hispanics in test scores and graduation rates. In Woodburn, as in school districts across the country, educators had discovered that for some reason, they were failing to teach Latino kids successfully.

The boys filed into Canadian's biology classroom, chattering to each other. Despite the skeletons, skulls, assorted bones, and a human torso model with exposed organs and a green hard hat, the room was a conveniently large space in which to collect all the prospective members of the varsity soccer team. Flannigan's own classroom, the walls decorated with posters of Irish writers and projects written by students, was a third of the size.

Coach Flannigan moved to stand in the front of the room, Coach Ransom sat on a stool to Flannigan's right, and Coach Arias leaned against a sink to his left, arms crossed. The kids clustered around the worktables looking at a handout with a list on either side, "The Twelve Steps to Success" and "Characteristics of the Mentally Tough Competitor." The boys mumbled aloud as they read. The two white kids, Brandon and Kevin, sat together.

Mike Flannigan had created the handout years earlier to address what he considered his major hurdle as a coach: his team's mental state. He had seen it over and over in games and in the classroom. His teams had talent; what was holding them back was confidence. The Lakeridge debacle was an example. With the pressure on, two of his best players had missed their penalty kicks, missed the goal entirely. He saw it in his classroom every year as his sophomores prepared for the state's mandatory reading and writing tests. They expected to fail.

Coach Flannigan felt that he understood why. His students had no history of success. They had few positive role models. They grew up in homes with poorly educated parents who spoke little English; some of them did not have permission to be in the country. Most were poor. By the time they got to high school, they had figured out that the future of Hispanics, especially Hispanic boys, did not include wealth or fame. In the classroom, they stopped trying. On the field, they didn't give up as easily, or sometimes at all, but they died inside when they lost. A newspaper reporter pointed this out to Coach Flannigan once, saying that of all the high school teams he covered, only Woodburn's soccer players wept when their season was over. And the coach knew what he meant: losing a playoff game demolished his players. They fell to the grass, unashamedly sobbing; their heads and shoulders drooped; they looked as if they had lost a family member.

Flannigan knew that he couldn't change in three months what his kids' lives had created in sixteen years, but he at least wanted to make them think about their decisions. He wanted them to take responsibility for themselves. He wanted them to consider long-term consequences.

"All right," Flannigan began, "who can tell me who a good teammate is?"

Tony, a slim midfielder with a quick smile who had a hard time sitting still, blurted out, "Somebody who helps!"

Flannigan nodded, his tone respectful.

"Okay, somebody who helps. How do you help? What ways can you help your teammates?"

From around the room, words and phrases burst forth:

"Homework!"

"Have confidence in them."

"Be a good role model."

"Do their homework for them!"

Laughter.

Ignoring the last outburst, Flannigan continued.

"Being a team means working together, passing the ball. How can you individually be a good teammate? What do you need to do personally?"

"Have *huevos*!"

More laughter.

"What about outside the soccer field," Mike persisted, "off the soccer field?"

"Stay out of trouble!" somebody shouted, and immediately many of the boys began shouting Martin's name. Martin, sarcastic, rail-thin, with high cheekbones, accepted the judgment with a wave of his arm.

"Do your own homework!"

Flannigan nodded. "Thank you, yes. I would say that twenty-five percent of the people sitting in this room are on academic probation. That means the first game, we might not have four to five people. Is that being a good teammate?" He paused to let the boys think about this. "Being responsible for what you need to do to be on that field is being a good teammate. Getting your work schedule figured out so you can get to practice. Getting a good night's rest. Eating what you need to eat. Not getting girls pregnant."

"Carlos!" somebody shouted, and again the class tittered.

After a decade of coaching teenage boys, Flannigan knew that the laughter, the sexual innuendos, would always be there. He tried to ignore them. But this was important to him. Every year, a large portion of his team was on academic probation, which was frustrating. State rules required that students on high school athletic teams must have passed at least five classes their previous semester. Woodburn's own standards were even higher. If a student received a D or F the previous semester, they were placed on academic probation and were required to show up to a weekly study hall. If they did not, and if they did not make progress in their fall classes, they were not eligible to play.

The door to the classroom opened, and the boys turned to see Octavio and Cheo enter, smiling awkwardly. Both wore painter's white shirts and pants, sprayed and mottled with a Jackson Pollock splatter of colors.

"Octavio," Flannigan said, "you guys get run over by a paint truck?" Then, concerned that he might have hurt their feelings, he added, "No, good to see both of you. I'm glad you could make it.

"All right," Flannigan continued. "You should be able to get to practice on time, get your homework done on time, work hard at practice. That's part of becoming a man. You guys are one of the few successful teams in the school. There are some others, but not a lot. The school relies on you to be successful. You may think it's just a soccer team, but it's more than that. You guys represent the community, and you represent success in the community. That's a lot of pressure, but we do it every year, and those of you who make it onto the varsity team will need to make sure that you are good teammates by being responsible."

Back on the pitch, Flannigan had asked all the boys to share a personal goal and a team goal. He had been a bit surprised by the response, for although kids always got around to saying they wanted to win the state championship, it didn't often happen on the first day. Usually, in the early goal-setting talks, the boys were more focused on winning their league, being the best team out of eight, not the best team out of eighty.

He decided to address this.

"I heard a lot of you say your goals are to win a league title, win a state championship, go to the state playoffs. None of that can happen unless you are good teammates and unless we handle ourselves in a professional manner. That means, don't argue with the referee, don't get in fights with the other players, believe in your coaches. That's kind of what we want to talk about today."

As he did on the field, Coach Flannigan began to pace in a tight circle.

"Emotional control. I think that's one of the most important ones. Don't worry about the referee, don't pay attention to the other players, don't let that fan who's yelling at you get under your skin. This is important because if a guy knows that he can tackle you hard and get you angry, he might be able to get you a red card and kicked out of the game. If they think they can do that, they will. And that goes for the coaches, too. We were able to keep ourselves under control until the last game last year, and I'm not proud of losing control then. It just goes to show you that even coaches can make mistakes."

Coach Flannigan worried about some of the goals his players had put forth out on the pitch. It was nice to dream of the state championship, but Flannigan also felt that for a large number of his soccer players, the team and the field was a place to forget the tribulations of home life. He had players who had to work to help support their families, who were living with uncles or cousins, who barely spoke English, who came to school without breakfast and went home to no dinner. For these boys, he wondered if it wasn't enough just to enjoy the game and the camaraderie. Did the desire for state championship just set them up for disappointment?

One of Coach Flannigan's outside midfielders from the previous season, a senior named Noe, had approached him earlier to say that he wasn't sure if he would be able to play. His younger brothers had been taken away from his mother by the Department of Human Services, and he was needed to help translate. Flannigan hoped that Noe would be able to play at least a few games, to take his mind off home.

"Sometimes we get really caught up in trying to win a state championship," Coach Flannigan said once. "But I think that for a lot of these guys, soccer really gives them their first taste of success. Especially guys that have only been in the U.S. for a couple of years, having to watch their moms and dads work some crappy jobs, maybe working crappy jobs themselves. From that aspect it's great to see some of these guys get that success, to get some of the reason why they came to this country."

Assistant Coach Ransom took over, talking about goal-setting, and Flannigan turned to observing his boys. He knew many of them from the previous year, and as he looked around the classroom, he was aware that he had a strong team. In fact, he had an unusually strong team because a group of juniors had extensive club soccer experience, which was rare for Woodburn. They sat near each other in the front of the room: Tony, the fast little winger who had made the varsity team his freshman year; Juan, a handsome defender and midfielder Coach Flannigan planned to try out as a forward; Carlos, definitely his starting goalkeeper; O.J., a year younger than the others but fast and very experienced; and Martin, the team smartass, who had played well the previous year and who, rumor had it, had spent the summer training with a professional team in Mexico. Five club players on one team. They might be half his starting squad.

Amateur soccer teams in the United States come in many different flavors. High school soccer requires the least investment. Uniforms are provided, and the season lasts only a few months. In towns like Woodburn, high-school-age athletes who want to keep playing after the season ends join amateur men's league teams, which can range from an excuse for thirty-year-olds to run around on a Sunday afternoon to organized, competitive, well-coached squads full of young studs from local colleges and high schools, good enough to compete with professional minor league teams.

Playing in men's leagues is great experience for young soccer players, especially since they have to learn to hold their own against older players. But the real training ground for top-level talent is private club teams. Private soccer clubs play year-round, both indoors and outdoors, and many of them feature top-notch paid coaches and trips to out-of-state tournaments. Club soccer is considered so much more competitive than high school soccer that college soccer coaches schedule visits to troll the multistate club tournaments yet barely visit nearby high school games.

The problem with club soccer is the investment of money and time that it requires. For parents, a child being on a club team means thousands of dollars a year in uniforms, team fees, and travel expenses, not to mention the time invested in driving the kid to practices, games, and tournaments nearly year-round. So the vast majority of club soccer players are middle- and upper-class kids, meaning mostly white. Usually Woodburn had one or two club players, and those players tended to be some of the best athletes on the team.

But this year, Coach Flannigan was the recipient not only of the five friends who sat together, but also two freshmen with club experience. He had maybe the state's best goalkeeper, several highly talented defenders, and a couple of top-notch midfielders. The coach slipped this information into a mental equation alongside his knowledge of returning varsity players and decided that it could be the best defensive team he had ever coached. A solid team.

And yet something was missing. Looking over the boys in the classroom, he saw midfielders and defenders whom he felt good about. His forwards, however, were a question mark. Apart from Carlos, whom he needed at goal, nobody had shown him the confidence and selfishness that marked a good striker. Coach Flannigan looked at all the boys before him and wondered where he was going to find somebody who could score.

TWO

The Immigrants' Game

Sometimes players say things to get in our heads, call us
short, brown. This guy said, "You ain't nothing to me, man.
You're only to my waist!" I thought, "I'll take you, man."
They say, "Stupid Mexicans, go home, go back to Mexico."
If they do that, then one or two times in the half I don't go
for the ball but go for them.

—Angel

The Woodburn Bulldogs emerged from their bus and strolled toward Wilsonville's field. Their second preseason opponent, the Wilsonville Wildcats, represented a new community best known for a giant discount electronics store. Because of the town's fast growth, the Wildcats were moving up a division. The Wilsonville team viewed the game against Woodburn as a test of its abilities against a new, higher-level of competition.

The week before, the Bulldogs had beaten a bunch of big white kids from West Salem 1–0, and they had played three halves against three different opponents in a jamboree on a skinny field in the foothills of Mt. Hood, winning or tying each one without allowing a single goal. During the first of these, Octavio scored early on a PK, a sharp, accurate kick to the right side of the net that inspired Coach Flannigan to announce, "Last year is officially done now. It is officially behind us. We can let Lakeridge go."

Flannigan had also noted Brandon's play at left wing. Brandon, blond and pale-skinned, was the only white kid to make the varsity team, having moved up from JV for the jamboree. Flannigan knew him from the basketball court, where Brandon played point guard. But on the morning of the Wilsonville game, Flannigan's ideas of a two-pronged wing attack—Tony on one side and Brandon on the other—were upset when Brandon announced he was quitting.

The coach asked him why—was he having trouble making friends? Brandon said no, he had friends on the team. He just wanted to concentrate on basketball. He wasn't having fun playing soccer.

Flannigan suggested that Brandon might be bored because he had played only one game before moving up from JV. And nobody likes practice. Coach Flannigan suggested, why not stick around and play a couple more games before you decide.

But Brandon said no, he wanted to quit. Flannigan wondered about this. Over the years, the teams had become increasingly Latino-dominated, and he suspected that some of the white kids at the school felt intimidated or left out, and so they didn't try out for the team. There was another white kid in JV—a tall boy named Kevin whose brother had played for the Bulldogs a couple of years ago. With Brandon gone, Kevin would be the only Anglo on any of the teams.

As the Bulldogs walked toward the Wilsonville field, Flannigan was still trying to figure out who to put in at left wing. One possibility was Jovanny, a sharp-shooting freshman who had impressed him at tryouts but who had missed some practices. The last thing Flannigan needed was another kid without discipline.

The team walked in front of him, identical black backpacks on their shoulders, and two fair-haired boys about fifteen years old, dressed in their white home uniforms, stopped to watch. The two boys didn't move for a moment, and then one of them spoke without turning to his friend, his eyes still focused on the Woodburn players.

"Jesus!" he said. "Did you see how many Mexicans they've got?"

It wasn't a slur, but a gasp of astonishment and respect. Despite the negative characteristics some people ascribe to Hispanic teenage boys—violent, untrustworthy, lazy, stupid, drug abusers, illegal residents—one positive trait associated with them is skill with a soccer ball. Across Oregon's Willamette Valley, white boys have learned this through years of playing soccer against kids from Woodburn, some of them, like Octavio, born in Mexico, and some of them, like Carlos, born in the United States.

The discrepancy in skill between young Hispanic and young Anglo soccer players seems to be most pronounced in elementary and middle school years, when the extra hours of practice Hispanic kids get by playing informal games with friends and family creates sometimes comical mismatches. Often the boys from towns like Woodburn have so much more control over the ball, and so much better footwork, that the scores of young Hispanic club teams can be 12–0 over their Anglo rivals.

Everardo Castro, who graduated from Woodburn High in 1986, recalled coaching his nephew's club team, one of the first all-Hispanic club soccer teams in the state. For several years, his team dominated the state tournaments, their closest competition being another all-Hispanic team from another Willamette Valley town. "We'd go to a tournament," Castro said, "and it would always end up with us two at the finals. One of us would win and then the other would win."

Although such lopsided success ebbs by the late high school years, Hispanic soccer players in a mostly white state like Oregon are assumed to have rare and magical qualities. When Omar Mendoza coached club soccer, he would regularly receive phone calls from other coaches who wanted his help locating Latino players.

"They'd always say, give me some guys from Woodburn—they think all of them are so good. I'd say, 'I'm not an employment agency.'"

With so much emphasis on Latino soccer skills at the high school level, it would seem natural that colleges would also be full of Latino players, but that hasn't happened, probably because such a small percentage of Latino high school students go on to college. Even fewer Hispanic names are seen on the jerseys worn by professional soccer players in the United States, at either the minor or major league level. What happens between elementary school and high school? Why don't Latino soccer players continue to dominate at all age levels? Why isn't Major League Soccer (MLS) in the United States full of Arellanos and Romeros?

The path from youth prodigy to professional soccer player generally takes two different directions, depending on what country you live in. In soccer-focused parts of the world, such as Latin America, young, skilled athletes are scouted by Division One teams, which trawl for kids, often in impoverished areas, much in the way that prep schools in the United States scout talented players from the basketball courts of black neighborhoods. In countries from Sweden to Argentina, these young athletes, generally around thirteen or fourteen, begin to go to "soccer school," the first step toward making it in the big leagues.

Kids work their way through age-specific teams, then into the minor leagues of professional soccer, until eventually rising to the highest level of competition in their own countries. If they are really special players, they leave their home country to play in one of the world's elite leagues in England, Spain, Italy, or Germany. The players on teams in these countries are an international smorgasbord of talent. FC Barcelona, one of the world's most popular and successful teams, features players from ten countries, as far apart as Uruguay and Belarus.

In the United States, on the other hand, high-school-age standouts are scouted by college coaches during private club tournaments, soccer championships featuring the best non-high-school teams in the country. The best club players, if they also have good enough grades, go on to play for university teams, and from there to the U.S. professional leagues or even to play overseas. In other words, in the United States, guys who make it to the big leagues tend to come from money, while in the rest of the world, they don't.

Aware that a large number of the Latino immigrants and children of immigrants in the United States are skilled soccer players, and aware that these young men rarely make it to college, critics of MLS have for years complained that the league does little to tap into the vast resource of talented young athletes not playing for club or university teams. Underneath what these critics say is an unspoken theme: Professional soccer has failed to acknowledge the changing demographics of the United States.

In an interview on ThisIsAmericanSoccer.com, *Sports Illustrated* soccer writer Luis Bueno said that he felt MLS clubs need to work harder to find Mexican American athletes because Latinos tend to play in less-established, less-wealthy leagues.

"I have a cousin who's pretty good at soccer, I think he's fifteen," Bueno said. "I'm thinking, 'All right, is he going to have the chance to go to college?' Probably not. I'm just being honest. He plays on club teams right now. They're not the big club teams that the Sacha Kljestans played for and the [Jonathan] Bornsteins and the Benny Feilhabers. Those guys had the opportunities to play on those teams whereas someone like my cousin doesn't. Maybe he plays high school and then that's it. There are a lot of players like that, who for financial reasons just can't afford it."

Bueno, like other MLS critics, wonders if the coaches of MLS and U.S. national teams realize how much talent may be in their own backyard.

"We don't know," he said. "There could be the next Landon [Donovan] out here, the next [Jozy] Altidore. We don't know since it's something that's never really been explored."

In response to this type of criticism, MLS in 2007 launched a televised player search with a reality format called *Sueño MLS* (MLS Dream). *Sueño MLS* was shown only on Spanish-language television in the United States, running as a segment on Univision's popular *República Deportiva* show. While *Sueño MLS* was not open exclusively to Latino athletes, it was clearly aimed at them and at their television-viewing peers. In the program's debut year, Chivas USA, MLS's version of the wildly popular Guadalajara, Mexico, team, offered a slot on its roster to the best player out of two thousand applicants. Over several weeks, the contenders were narrowed down to one: Jorge Flores, a seventeen-year-old kid from Anaheim, California.

Born in the United States, Flores moved to Guanajuato, Mexico, with his mother when he was a year old. Flores remained there while his mother moved back to Anaheim and remarried. Jorge rejoined her as a teenager, moving into a strange home with a new stepfather in a country whose language he didn't understand. His skill at soccer helped him to make friends, and by the time he graduated, he was Anaheim High School's team MVP and team captain.

Flores hadn't heard of the *Sueño* tryout, and when his uncle signed him up, he didn't even make the initial list of two thousand. Instead, his name was put on the waiting list, one of four thousand additional young men who hoped for a last-minute phone call to come to the group tryout.

He got one.

After winning the competition by impressing coaches with his skills, determination, and shot-making ability, Flores was signed to Chivas USA's under-19 squad, and he was shifted to the regular squad soon after. In the 2008 season, coming off the bench half the season and starting the other half, Flores notched three goals for his new team. He also was selected to play on the U.S. National under-20 team. Since then, *Sueño MLS* has tapped three other winners, two in 2008 and one in 2009, all of them Hispanic.

Sueño's apparent success both in attracting applicants and finding quality players is not just a feel-good story for MLS to trot out for journalists. It's a necessary part of keeping the league alive, for although the United States has its white, college-educated soccer fans, their numbers pale compared to the number of Latino fans.

In 2007, the U.S. national team played the Mexican national team in the Gold Cup Final, an international tournament pitting teams from North America, the Caribbean, and Latin America against each other. The final was held in Chicago's Soldier Field to a sold-out crowd, but so many of the fans were supporters of the Mexican team that ESPN reported that "almost the entire crowd of 60,000 was wearing green." A total of 2.8 million households tuned in to the Spanish-language broadcast of the USA versus Mexico Gold Cup Final, making it not only the third-most-viewed Spanish-language broadcast to that date, but outdelivering all other broadcasts for the same time slot in Spanish or English. In comparison, the 2007 Stanley Cup finals in the National Hockey League was viewed in two million households. In other words, although Latinos are still a numerical minority in this country, soccer is watched by such a large Latino audience that it represents a gold mine to any professional soccer league or advertiser.

And yet, until recently, MLS has clung to the outdated idea that commercial soccer success will be driven from white, upper-class, educated fans, not the blue-collar ones who support the Almighty

THE BOYS FROM LITTLE MEXICO   *37*

triad of baseball-football-basketball. In 2002, the L.A. Galaxy, playing in a city about 50 percent Hispanic, did not feature a single Mexican player. In 2006, Houston, a town with the third-largest Mexican
American population in the country, named their MLS team the
Houston 1836, based on the year of Houston's founding. But 1836 is
also the year Texas gained independence from Mexico after a bloody
war, and the name rankled many of the city's citizens of Mexican de-
scent. The team soon changed its name to the Houston Dynamo.

During the past few years, however, MLS seems to be getting the
message. The league has started summertime soccer programs and
tournaments aimed at Latino kids. MLS Futbolito, a 4-v.-4 tournament, travels the country playing in MLS stadiums and is broadcast
on Univision. A brand new program called Distinguished Hispanics
aims to recognize Hispanic community leaders across the country,
no doubt hoping they will encourage their flock to watch their local
MLS team. In addition, through the Designated Player Rule, MLS
now allows each team to bring in one international star whose salary
will not affect the team's salary cap.

The Designated Player Rule, which began in 2007, has so far
brought in six international stars—two of them European, four of
them Latin American. In its first year, the rule forced soccer briefly
into the consciousness of average Americans due to the L.A. Galaxy's
signing of David Beckham, star midfielder and husband of former
Spice Girl Victoria Beckham. Because he is both good-looking and
married to a onetime pop-star, Beckham has managed to be the rare
soccer player Americans care about (or at least are aware of). His
signing was considered to be a coup, and many MLS watchers insisted that with Beckham playing, soccer was about to take off in the
United States.

It didn't. Soccer temporarily became popular, or perhaps more
accurately, Beckham's team, the L.A. Galaxy, found itself sucked
briefly into his orbit. Beckham's presence on the team did little to
help the Galaxy win games, however, and soon enough he became
just another celebrity living in southern California.

Far more important than Beckham's signing to many fans was
the signing of Cuauhtémoc Blanco, an aging Mexican star who was

brought in by the Chicago Fire. Moving to the United States at age thirty-four, Blanco became the league's second-highest-paid athlete, trailing only Beckham, yet his arrival was almost completely over-looked by the English-language sports press. For Spanish-language print and television in the United States, however, Blanco's signing was big news. Blanco is a popular and somewhat controversial star to Mexican soccer fans, a creative player from a tough Mexico City neighborhood who is prone to temper tantrums on the field. As an attacking midfielder with the Mexico City team, América, and as a member of the Mexican national team, Blanco was known as a pro-lific and aggressive goal scorer whose signature move involved grip-ping the sides of the ball with his feet to leap between two trapping defenders, carrying the ball with him.

Hispanic fans came out in droves to see him. When the Fire ar-rived in L.A. to play Chivas USA, fans bearing Mexican flags went to the airport just to see Blanco disembark. Mexican fans of Blanco were seen sporting Chicago Fire jerseys in Mexico—maybe the first time Mexican soccer fans held an allegiance to any U.S. soccer team. At home, the Chicago Fire's 2007 attendance soared 20 percent, and the team sold out six of its final seven home games.

Beckham and Blanco exemplify the bipolar nature of U.S. soccer. Beckham, a smooth, handsome metrosexual, stands in for the upper-middle-class soccer fan in the United States, while Blanco, aging less gracefully, prone to violence on the field, and reluctant to embrace his fame, represents the Latino immigrant fans. Ask the boys on the Woodburn varsity team who their favorite players are, and Blanco's name is in the conversation, not Beckham's. Ask the average Anglo sports fan to name an MLS soccer player, and Beckham's name would probably be the first, if not the only, name to spring to his or her lips. Cuauhtémoc Blanco? White guys don't even know how to pro-nounce that.

As it did against many all-white teams, Woodburn put on a ball-handling clinic against Wilsonville. Using the game as an opportu-nity to practice playing on artificial turf, Coach Flannigan had his boys focus on timing their passes. When the Bulldogs played their best Latin-style soccer, they used short passes, one touch per player, to rocket the ball around the field, like a colossal game of keep-away. When done right, the fast passes and quick ball movement are beautiful. But waiting too long to make a pass opens up chances for the opposition's defense. When Martin took too long to forward the ball, allowing it to be stripped by a Wilsonville player, Cheo began shouting angrily from his position at sweeper: "Sólo uno! Sólo uno!" Only one!

The Bulldogs kept control, but they couldn't score despite many chances. Juan's kick from in front of the goal just missed the left post. Vlad headed the ball over the net, then a few minutes later, kicked it wide right. Octavio tried a long shot that missed left.

After a scoreless first half, Coach Flannigan moved Carlos to forward. Although he felt good about his team's ball control on the fast, flat surface, he still didn't have a forward who wanted to score. He gave some brief directions to the team.

"Forwards, you need to run through if our outside mid has it. Everybody else, get the ball going across. Get it to our wings!"

Most of the boys didn't look at him, staring at the turf field instead.

"And c'mon," Coach Flannigan said. "Let's raise our heads up! Let's be positive!"

Coach Flannigan had not yet decided on his right-side midfielder. But his left midfielder, Tony, had solidified his starting role. Tony was a lean kid with an easy smile who tended to laugh when he missed a shot. He wasn't tall or strong, but he was quick. When Coach Flannigan told his boys to get the ball to the outside mid, he meant get the ball to Tony, who would dash up the left side, head down, dribbling the ball just inside the foul line, then briefly pause to let his defender go flying by before cutting inside with the ball for a well-placed pass to the middle.

Tony and Carlos were best friends who had played together for years, and fifteen minutes into the second half, Tony spun a pass to Carlos's feet. Carlos bullied his way past two defenders into the Wilsonville box where he was slide-tackled from behind, earning a penalty kick.

Taking his time, Carlos lined up his PK. He had seen the Wilsonville keeper in action for just a few minutes, but already he knew the boy's skill limit. I can take this guy, he thought. With both teams silent, Carlos casually bashed the ball past the keeper's left side and put Woodburn on top, 1–0.

However, three minutes later, Wilsonville returned the favor when two Woodburn defenders forgot who they were marking, allowing a quick Wilsonville player to slip a long kick in past Betos's fingers.

Betos shook his head as he bent over to retrieve the ball from the goal. A senior who worked at a car wash, he had almost not signed up for soccer. He was already looking ahead toward graduating, and planned to attend community college before transferring to a university. Then, just before school started, Coach Flannigan called him, asking him to play. Betos was touched by the gesture—he liked his coach—and he mulled it over. He had trouble with his ankles, and unlike many of his friends, he didn't hope to play in college or the pros. Thinking of that helped him make up his mind. This would be his last chance to play team sports, and he wanted one more year of feeling part of a group.

For a while, it looked as though the game would stay tied. Then, taking an indirect free kick from about midfield, Tony drove in an elegant, curving pass that dropped out of the sky right in front of Juan, who punted it in on the first bounce, pressing back the Wilsonville net for the second time and winning the game for Los Perros.

Coach Flannigan watched Angel shove the net bag of balls into the bus and climbed on afterwards. The engine rumbled to life and he stared back at the boys on the bus, already checking their cell phones for texts and plugging into MP3 players.

"We're hungry, Coach," somebody shouted.

"All right," Flannigan said. "Let's go get some doughnuts."

He considered the game stats. His team had controlled the game —the shots on goal proved it. Woodburn had taken fifteen of them, to Wilsonville's three. He was pleased they were taking shots, but why weren't they making more? The Wilsonville keeper wasn't that good—most of the balls had simply missed the net, going to the left, right, or most often, zipping by overhead as if on their way to the moon.

What he needed was another Carlos. Put one in goal and one in at forward.

A couple of players worried him. Chuy, a possible replacement for Brandon, was fast but easily distracted. Vlad and Martin, whom he hoped would score for him, were passing up shots that they should take. And Ramon. The year before Ramon had been the immovable object Flannigan sent against the other team's unstoppable forces. He was strong and stubborn—a perfect defender. But this year, Ramon was letting guys get by. Flannigan didn't want to bust him down to JV. Ramon was smart and hard-working—he was the 2005 student body president—and one of the few kids on the team whose future Flannigan was certain of. The coach had gone into the season assuming that Ramon would start as a marking back; now he thought that would never happen. Other coaches and Ramon's teammates were approaching him to say that Ramon shouldn't start.

Ramon was worrying, but nothing like Octavio. Along with Cheo and Cesar, Octavio had been voted in as co-captain by his teammates. Cheo seemed unfazed by the responsibility, and Cesar, one of the quietest young men on the team, accepted it, even though nobody expected him to suddenly start preaching fiery pep talks before each game. Octavio, on the other hand, had come to Coach Flannigan saying he didn't want to be captain. Not only that, he didn't want to play center-mid. He wanted to go back to his old position at sweeper, the position he had trained for in Mexico.

Flannigan didn't understand this. When he had played for the Bulldogs, Mike Flannigan had longed to be captain. In a small way, it was the equivalent of his boyhood fantasy of playing quarterback for the Dallas Cowboys. Even as an adolescent, Flannigan's gifts had been more cerebral than physical, but he took pleasure both in being the team's vocal leader and in preparing for leadership. He and Brian spent hours watching soccer games, the two of them learning strategy together. They would sit in their living room and quiz each other. "How do you prevent an offsides trap? How can you draw defenders away from the goal?"

Through those sessions, Mike began to think of the field and the players almost as chess pieces to be moved around, each with its own strengths and weaknesses. During games, he would call out directions to his teammates, moving them about the field. His teammates usually took it in stride, although one time a defender snapped back at him, "Man, you just never shut up back there, do you?"

Mike replied, "I can't, or you would never know where to be."

With his 2005 team, Coach Flannigan saw Carlos taking on some of the role that he had filled as a teenager. But Octavio was something else. The boy wasn't shy about expressing his opinion on the field—Mike could hear his high-pitched voice shouting throughout games, and Octavio always spoke to the team before a game, trying to get everybody fired up—and yet, he didn't want to be team captain.

When Octavio had told him this, Flannigan and Ransom had both tried to reason with the young man. Word had already spread through the team. Juan and Carlos had complained to the coaches about it.

"Look," Flannigan said. "Like it or not, the kids look up to you. They voted you captain. A lot of them are hurt that you don't want to be captain. You've been with the varsity team since your freshman year. You're one of our best players. Why wouldn't you want to be captain?"

And Octavio had no reply. He just didn't want to.

Most of the time, despite cultural and linguistic differences, Coach Flannigan thought he understood his players. He had been in their shoes and he had been around kids like them for better than a decade. But Octavio was a mystery to him. Octavio was the best player on the field, a smart, hard worker, and never got in trouble— he should be a perfect kid to coach. But Flannigan didn't know what to do. He didn't know who Octavio was.

THREE

Octavio

I was causing too much problems over there in Mexico.
I wasn't behaving. I would always disobey my mother, go
outside and play, don't do my homework, all that stuff.
My mom decided to call my uncles here in Woodburn and
have them come to pick me up. Since I didn't have any
papers, she told somebody to let me borrow papers that
would fit my age. We went to the airport. She told me that
I had to memorize the name so immigration can't stop me.
That's all she said.

—Manolo

The start of the 2005 season made Octavio feel like a teenage father, proud and terrified, excited for what was coming but sad about what was ending. The season—this final high school season—seemed to him to be the end of a journey he had started years before, when he first saw that his future, whatever it would be, lay in a road through *fútbol*. At first, he had thought that he might have the skill to become a professional soccer player in Mexico. Then, once he moved to Oregon, he had thought that soccer would pay for college.

Octavio paid attention. He saw how colleges wanted more Hispanics, both in classrooms and on the soccer field. He knew that if he played well, and if some college coaches got wind of him, he might be able to parlay his on-field talent for the college education that he could not otherwise afford. Octavio had the grades to go to college and he had the desire. What he didn't have was money and the right immigration papers. Without those things, especially without a soccer scholarship to help pay for it, college was just a fantasy.

During his final season, then, Octavio wanted badly to be offered a spot on a college team, and those offers were not coming. Not for the first time, he wondered if he should stay in the United States at all. His dilemma cut to the heart of his identity and that of many of his peers. He thought of himself as Mexican, as he was, both legally and culturally. Yet he had found a home of sorts in an Oregon town that allowed him to do the things he couldn't have done in Mexico. If he had stayed in Guanajuato, for example, Octavio would probably not have gone to high school because mandatory education in Mexico ends at eighth grade. At fourteen, Octavio would have had to leave home to attend school elsewhere, which would have cost money his family didn't have.

Beyond that, in Mexico, Octavio would not have the opportunity to learn English, or to make friends with white kids, or to experience all the things that one experiences when traveling, expanding one's knowledge of the world, understanding cultures in perspective, and seeing one's own life from a broad view. As a high school senior in Oregon, Octavio looked back on his life and saw crossroads. Looking forward, he saw yet another approaching: what would he do when he graduated?

Long before Octavio knew anything about Oregon, about brief daylight, endless drizzle, Douglas firs and Taco Bell, long before he had an e-mail account and went shopping at Wal-Mart, and long before he struggled with how to define himself, he was a spindly kid kicking a ball around on his family's farm in the highlands of landlocked Guanajuato, just southeast of Mexico City and one of Mexico's poorest states. Octavio lived in a concrete block house, one of six houses on a property that he described as "kind of like a little ranch." His extended family also lived on the *ranchito:* his grandparents, parents, uncles, aunts, four brothers, three sisters, and ten cousins, along with chickens, goats, cows, and a couple of dogs. The family farm produced milk, beans, corn, carrots, fruit, and tomatoes, but mostly sorghum, a drought-resistant grain used for making bread, porridge, and cattle feed. Octavio had grown up eating food from the farm, and years later, when he lived in the United States, it was the taste of home-grown guavas that he missed most of all.

On weekday mornings when he was young, Octavio would walk five minutes down a cobbled street, or sometimes dash across the field behind his house, to his village school, a single-story concrete structure that hunched its shoulders at the base of a hill as if bracing itself for violence. As Octavio walked to school, he kicked or carried a soccer ball, sometimes juggling it on his feet, knees, and head as he walked, sometimes passing it to friends before sprinting down the road to retrieve their passes. He was one of those kids who carried a ball with him everywhere, putting it under his feet in the classroom, bouncing it to friends at lunchtime, and organizing informal games after school. Back at home, he played two-on-two with his cousins, putting the ball down only to help his father repair the farm's irrigation system, to spread out fertilizer, or to tend to the cattle.

When Octavio was thirteen, a scout from Club Atlas de Guadalajara, a professional Primera División soccer team, spotted him playing in a multi-village tournament. The scout, a wiry guy in his forties, wore Club Atlas warm-ups and looked as if he might have been an athlete once. He approached Octavio's uncle, Pedro, the team's coach and tournament organizer, and spoke to him as the game continued. Octavio watched them out of the corner of his eye. When the game ended, Pedro called Octavio over and introduced him to the scout. At first, Octavio thought his uncle was teasing him. Then he saw the Club Atlas patch on the scout's blue jacket. Octavio stood there sweating on the dried-out, patchy *fútbol* pitch, heart pounding, and listened.

If Octavio wanted to play soccer professionally, the scout said, he could help. He could get Octavio a spot on one of Atlas's youth development teams in Irapuato. It would mean leaving his home and school, but if he had the talent and work ethic, he could move his way up through the system.

"He said I can make money if I have enough talent. I said, 'Yes.' I was very happy that I had an opportunity to play."

He wouldn't get paid, but the potential for wealth was alluring. Most of Guanajuato's residents make less than ten dollars a day, and more than one-quarter work in the United States and send money home, so the wages that an unskilled farm boy like Octavio could expect weren't high. As a professional *fútbol* player, however, Octavio might earn a high salary, possibly several hundred thousand dollars if he made it to a Primera División team, and at least decent wages if he played on a lower division team. The odds were stacked against him, just as the odds are stacked against kids shooting playground hoops actually making it to the NBA, but he figured that he had little to lose.

Octavio knew what he wanted to do immediately. His family was self-sufficient but poor, and Octavio saw this as a chance both to help his family and to do the thing he loved most. His mother was reluctant—she had always been reluctant to let him play, worrying about injuries—but his father was supportive. The teams need players, his father said. If it's what you want to do, you should try. After all, Octavio was thirteen, which, for boys in rural Mexico, meant that he was practically a man.

"My mom, she didn't like it when I played soccer, but I say if I don't play soccer, what am I going to do? Be in gangs? I always say that to her. What do you prefer? Be in gangs or play soccer? She has no answer for that."

Octavio had one more year of mandatory schooling to finish. Following that, his future was uncertain. His village did not have a high school, and although Octavio was bright enough (in fact, he had sometimes notched one of the top ten scores in Guanajuato on competitive state tests), he wasn't sure if his family could afford to send him to high school in another town.

So, in the fall of 2001, Octavio moved to Irapuato to live with his Uncle Pedro and to begin life at soccer school.

Octavio had been to his uncle's home before and considered the man rich. His house was bigger than any of the homes Octavio was familiar with. It had six rooms and housed only four residents: Pedro, his wife, and their two children. In his innocence, Octavio accepted Pedro's explanation that he could afford such a nice house from raising cattle. Octavio was given his own room, a luxury, and the use of his uncle's bicycle to ride to the stadium. The first day he arrived, he stood looking at the field, one of the most beautiful things he had ever seen. The grass was trim and lush and perfectly flat. It was like a blanket of grass and he wanted to lie down on it, wrap himself up in it. It was so exciting that he hardly slept that night.

Octavio's new schedule began at 3:30 in the afternoon, when he left his uncle's house after spending most of the day playing with his cousins. From 4:00 to 9:00, he practiced with about forty other boys on Atlas's 14-and-under team—the youngest players in the developmental program. He stayed four days a week in the city, scrimmaging, working on drills, and playing games. On Fridays, Pedro drove him back to his village, where they spent weekends. During one of these weekend visits, Octavio's father, Pepe, was preparing to leave for the United States, a journey he had made dozens of times before, beginning when he was fourteen, barely older than Octavio.

Octavio's father was unusual. He had very little education, but he was bright and curious about the world. He had applied for and received temporary amnesty under the 1986 Immigration Reform and Control Act (IRCA), allowing him to settle down in the United States if he wished, but he had not pursued permanent residency there. Instead, he continued to live in Mexico as much as he could, preferring the slower way of life and the presence of his family, travelling to *el Norte* as much to earn some extra money as to visit his brother Ricardo, who lived in the small town of Woodburn, Oregon.

Like many of the Mexican immigrants who gravitated to Woodburn, Octavio's father came because of geography. Oregon's Willamette Valley is a broad cleft running two hundred miles due south from the Columbia River, which forms the border between Oregon and Washington. The Willamette River drains north, merging with the Columbia about a ninety-minute drive east of the Pacific Ocean. On a topographic map, the valley looks a bit like a cupped left hand, the thumb forming the Oregon Coast Range, the twisted fingers and raised palm edge forming the Cascade Mountains. If it were a hand, Woodburn would rest on the crease of the middle finger joint farthest from the palm.

With streams feeding the nearby Willamette River from two parallel mountain ranges, with steady downpours from November to June, and with comparatively mild year-round temperatures, the low-lying Willamette Valley is an agricultural gold mine. The conditions are so right for plant growth that the Willamette Valley has become one of the world's centers of turf production, a place where people actually do watch grass grow. From Eugene to the south and Portland to the north, the Willamette Valley is dense with farms, orchards, and nurseries, with small and large towns dotting the valley to provide the supplies and people (mostly Mexicans, today) to work those fields.

The first large numbers of Latinos to work Oregon's fields came during World War II, as part of the now infamous Bracero Program, which provided temporary visas for single Mexican men for agricultural work. About 15,000 Braceros came to Oregon between 1942 and 1947, the majority to the Willamette Valley. Omar Mendoza's father, working for the U.S. military, drove one of the trucks that carried Braceros from the border to Oregon. The journey could take a week, the men leaving rural villages in some of the poorest Mexican states, like Oaxaca and Michoacan, and traveling by bus to the U.S. border, where they were sprayed with DDT before being shipped north to a labor camp. Typically, the Braceros lived in tents supplied with folding cots and blankets, sometimes with wood stoves, had their pay docked for petty or nonexistent offenses, received no health care, and worked long hours in unsafe conditions. Lee G. Williams, the U.S. Department of Labor officer in charge of the program, later described it as a system of "legalized slavery."

Although Oregon opted out of the system when World War II ended, the Bracero Program brought Mexican workers to an area of the United States that needed cheap, seasonal labor, and set in motion a human migration to the Willamette Valley that continues today. Michael McGlade, a professor of geography at Western Oregon University, believes that well over half the field laborers in the Willamette Valley today can trace their migration back to someone recruited from the Bracero era.

Agricultural work meant that by the mid-1960s, Woodburn was the second-largest town in Marion County and was already becoming a center of Hispanic activity in the valley. Until the 1980s, however, most of the Latinos settling in the area were *Tejanos* like Omar and his brothers, Mexican Americans looking for a better life than they faced within spitting distance of the border in south Texas.

Octavio's father came with a different wave of agricultural workers, Mexican nationals who headed north to look for work after the Mexican economy collapsed in the 1980s. The sudden, massive increase in Mexican immigration—the Immigration and Naturalization Service (INS) reported nearly 1 million undocumented workers from Mexico were being apprehended annually at the time—forced a national debate and a change in immigration policy.

IRCA penalized employers who hired undocumented workers, but more importantly to the future of Woodburn and towns like it across the country, it also offered amnesty to undocumented immigrants (mostly Mexican men who had left their families behind to seek work) who could prove five years of continuous residence in the United States. The combination of this new law and the Immigration Act of 1965, which gave priority to family members over national quotas, transformed Woodburn and America forever.

Octavio's father, living in Woodburn in the 1980s, applied for amnesty, as did his brother, Ricardo. But Pepe never completed his application. Ricardo did, and received his amnesty, becoming a legal resident and making his children American citizens.

The same sequence of events spread legal Mexican immigrants into areas of the United States far from the border states. Hispanics began moving north and east, sparking triple-digit percentage growth in parts of the country where Spanish used to be rare: South Carolina, Alabama, Wisconsin, Iowa. In Raleigh-Durham, North Carolina, the Latino population exploded between 1980 and 2000, growing from under 6,000 to over 90,000. In Atlanta, Georgia, during the same period, the Latino population grew from around 24,000 to almost 270,000. The Latino population in Woodburn rose from about 10 percent of the town's 11,000 people in 1980 to just over 50 percent of the 20,000-person population in 2000. It's estimated that, sometime in 2010, the town will have grown to 23,000 people, still over 50 percent Latino.

Octavio knew none of this on his weekend leave from soccer school in Guanajuato. He watched his father pack, as he had before, wondering what it was like in *el Norte*. How similar was it to the TV shows and movies he had seen? He was glad his father hadn't stayed in America. He had friends whose fathers had been gone for years, some of them with young brothers or sisters who couldn't remember what their dad looked like. To them, Dad was a voice on the phone, a signature on a letter. But Pepe only left when necessary.

Before he left, Pepe told Octavio to make the most of the opportunity he had, to play hard, and to listen to the coaches. He would be back when he could, and until then, Octavio needed to help his mother when he was home on weekends. He was a man now, out of school and finding his place in the world. Octavio returned to Irapuato on Sunday night, and by the next weekend, Pepe was gone.

Octavio and his peers played against the developmental teams from other professional organizations: Pumas, Tigres, Chivas. They played high school teams. Once, in León, his squad played against the local university, a bunch of teenage boys against men. Octavio saw the other team come out onto the field and couldn't believe how big they were. Octavio's team lost that game, 3–2.

Octavio mostly played defense with Atlas. He liked being a defender, the way you responded to the other guy, anticipated his moves. After six months with Atlas, the coach told Octavio that he was doing so well that they were considering moving him up.

"I was close to getting on the third division team, which is when they give a scholarship to you. They give you money; it's almost like being on the real team. It means you have talent."

Octavio felt simultaneously nervous and excited. It was a mark of his skill that he could move up, but the move meant that more would be expected of him.

About a month later, in a tournament game against another young squad from Cruz Azul, he was slide-tackled while running with the ball. Octavio's left foot was planted on the ground, his right leg pulled back to kick. The opposing player came in from the left and slightly behind. Octavio didn't see him. The defender's outstretched leg hit the ball, and his momentum carried him forward, his body slamming into Octavio's left leg. The plastic cleats of Octavio's shoe anchored his foot in the grass, so when he was hit, his leg was not swept out from under him. His leg bent at the knee, but not in the direction the knee was designed to bend.

At the moment of impact, Octavio felt an intense pain and heard a crunch that sounded like plastic snapping. He fell to the grass, thinking that he had broken his leg. He was sure of it; nothing else could hurt so much. He grabbed his left knee with both hands and rolled back and forth in pain. The trainers carried Octavio off on a stretcher. He was sent to a local hospital, where the doctors X-rayed his leg. As Octavio understood it then, the diagnosis was a meniscus tear. The meniscus is a layer of cartilage that prevents friction between the femur (thigh bone) and the tibia (shin bone). When a piece of meniscus breaks off, even a tiny piece, it irritates the knee joint. Because most of the meniscus has no blood flow, it cannot repair itself. The usual medical technique is to open up the knee and remove the torn piece of cartilage. He would need surgery and eight to nine months of rest.

Octavio returned home, trying not to cry. His mother and grandparents hugged him; his cousins asked him what he would do next. His father was still working in Oregon, and when Octavio reached him on the phone, his father tried to calm the boy, told him that it was okay, that he could start again. Octavio, his father told him, you always think that the world is coming to an end.

Octavio spent the next few weeks in bed reading and watching TV. His mother and grandparents babied him, bringing him food and telling him how happy they were that he was home. They also told him not to listen to doctors. Like many rural Mexicans, his family preferred home remedies. Octavio's mother and grandmother believed that his injury was caused by the local nerves having been shifted out of place. The solution to this problem was a movement therapy similar to chiropractic medicine. Every day for two months, his mother and grandmother worked his knee with their hands, forcing blood through the muscles, trying to push the nerves back into place.

After a while Octavio was off his crutches, and a few weeks later, he walked the uneven dirt road to school, his knee still aching every time his foot shifted on a rock or turned in a divot. In March, Octavio tried to rejoin his class, but it was too far into the school year. He would have to wait until the following September.

Octavio spent the next couple of months at home, helping on the farm, watching TV, hanging out with friends. His leg healed slowly, although he still couldn't play soccer with it. He felt bored and wondered what to do.

At the end of spring, Octavio's Uncle Ricardo returned from the United States for a visit. He made Octavio a proposal. They could return to Ricardo's house in Oregon together. Octavio could see his father, and if he wanted, stay and work or go to school. Octavio was curious about the United States. He had heard stories about beautiful places and unimaginable wealth. He had seen it on TV, and he had seen the men who returned from *el Norte* in brand-new pickups, who spent money as if it could be plucked from the sky. But he also knew that moving to the United States was not like moving to Irapuato. If he left, he would not be able to come back on the weekends and possibly would not be able to see his family for years.

Maybe it was the time he had already spent away from home that made him feel comfortable going abroad. Maybe it was the chance to see his father. Maybe it was the opportunity to get a good education, or the chance to make some money. Maybe it was some kind of redemption, as if his failure at a professional soccer career made it mandatory to succeed at something else. For all these reasons, and at the same time, for not quite any of these reasons, Octavio accepted Ricardo's offer and left Mexico for a land he didn't know.

"I thought about it and I decided that I would go. I'm not sure why. I think it was just to see that it was like. I had never been to America and I was curious."

FOUR

Water on Stone

The scholarship [gave him] an opportunity for him to go to
college. But he couldn't see the end result being better than
a job at Winco stocking shelves at night. Why pass that up?
Why make those decisions?

—Marty Limbird

Coach Flannigan paced back and forth on the artificial turf in front
of the Bulldogs' bench, talking to the referee in a loud, aggrieved
voice, throwing his hands up in the air, and then lowering his voice to
question the ref's abilities. He yelled to his players, "C'mon, Tony!"
then mumbled under his breath, "What the hell was that? Pass the
ball . . . ," or stopped briefly to point out a movement or play to his
bench players. Sometimes, too far away for anybody to understand a
distinct word, he could be heard murmuring to himself in tones of
annoyance and dismay.

High above Coach Flannigan, the lights of Jesuit High School's
outdoor stadium hummed a song that nearby insects could not ignore; the bugs forming a whirling cloud above the red track that en-
circled the pitch. The sixth and final preseason game matched the
Bulldogs against the Jesuit Crusaders, the state's premier high school
soccer program, which had played most sports at such a high level
for so long that coaches around the state sometimes referred to it as
Jesuit University.

From the sideline where Flannigan stood, Jesuit's beautiful artificial turf pitch stretched out in front of him, as smooth and green and
perfect as a billiard table. On the far side of the field sat fans of both
teams, including Omar and Pat Mendoza. To his right, Flannigan
could see Carlos standing in front of the Woodburn goal, raising an
arm and shouting out directions in Spanish. To the right of Carlos,
the scoreboard told the story: Home 1, Visitor 0.

It wasn't a bad score, especially when it was still the first half and when the opponent was the most successful high school soccer program in Oregon. But Flannigan worried about his team's state of mind. When Jesuit's goal had come, and when the Bulldogs, as a team, turned and watched that single upright digit appear on the scoreboard, like a finger flipping them off, many of the players seemed to deflate.

Coach Flannigan liked to win as much as anybody, and he wanted to beat Jesuit more than any other team. It was the unfairness of it all. Jesuit, a private prep school, got to cherry-pick their teams from players around the entire state. The coach had seen it happen at Woodburn when Ricky Chacon, a kid with good grades and exceptional soccer skills, was snatched away from them by Jesuit. He knew it was good for Ricky, Jesuit was an excellent academic school, and Ricky eventually went to Duke, but it still pissed him off.

The two teams had met in the playoffs three years earlier, in 2002. That year, the Bulldogs moved to a new division—from 3A to 4A—as a result of the school's population growth. The team had such a hard time finding 4A teams to play them in the preseason, though, that they ended up scheduling mostly their old competitors from 3A. Even though the Bulldogs had finished first in their 3A league thirteen out of fourteen years, it seemed that nobody at 4A took them seriously.

That postseason, the Bulldogs' second playoff game was against Jesuit. The private school was highly favored. They had won the last two state championships and were undefeated that season. The game took place at Woodburn High School, and to almost everyone's surprise, it resulted in a deadlock, taking the two teams into mandatory double-overtime. The first overtime ended with no score. Then, with only six minutes left in the second overtime, a talented Woodburn forward named Henry tapped a shot into Jesuit's net, and the Crusaders were never able to catch up.

It was the most satisfying win that Coach Mike Flannigan could remember. It also changed the way that other teams viewed Woodburn. Suddenly, coming into their new division, they had a target on their back.

The game impressed Jesuit coach Dave Nicholas, an Englishman, who immediately began to schedule preseason games against the Bulldogs, games that he believed were good for his team. "They give us a different look than anybody else," Nicholas said. "The number one emphasis for their game is skill, whereas the American players are big and have such tremendous physical capabilities. So we like playing against Hispanic players because they are full of tricks, they're very creative, and I think to play against them defensively, you've got to be very good and you've got to be a thinking player."

As the half ended, many of the Woodburn players jogged off the pitch looking as if they had just been grounded. Chuy, who tended to droop when the ball was stripped from his feet or when one of his passes went wide, hung his head, looking at the turf and his shoes as he came off the field, shoulders rolled forward and down. Octavio and Carlos ran in angrily, Carlos tearing off his gloves and slamming them onto the bench. Carlos had kept the game close through a series of athletic saves.

"Dammit! Nobody is helping me! Our defenders are doing nothing!"

Octavio, standing by the cooler with a cup of water in his hand, red-faced and blaming himself for everything, took this as an accusation. As a freshman, he had played on the 2002 team that shocked the Crusaders, and he had learned to judge his team by the yardstick of playing Jesuit.

He snapped at Carlos.

"What could I do?!"

"Why can't we score?!" Carlos retorted.

Carlos stalked off a few feet down the red track, turned, and walked back. Above him, a cloud of insects whirlpooled around one of the stadium lights. Carlos jabbed ineffectually at the track surface with his cleats, turned to glance at the huddle of Jesuit players twenty yards away, sighed, and walked back to the turf where the coaches were standing.

Coach Flannigan watched the two boys. He identified with Carlos, a young man whose life oddly paralleled Flannigan's. Both had been foster children, and both had moved to Woodburn to live with men who were focused on keeping the boys around them out of trouble through sports. It was probably coincidence that both had become goalkeepers.

Coach Flannigan and Assistant Coach Chuck Ransom herded the team into a rough half-circle on the turf, where most of the boys sat, still stewing or bitching at each other. They knew what Flannigan was going to say. It was obvious when Mike Flannigan wasn't happy, and he willingly admitted that he could become "more intense and pessimistic" during games. Sometimes he apologized for it, said it was his Irish nature, but tonight, he just looked disappointed. He looked down at the boys' faces, beginning to pace within his usual arms-length circle, always facing the players. When Flannigan began speaking, most of the kids stared straight past him. He spoke sternly but calmly, his voice pitched just above a conversational tone.

"If I was scouting Woodburn, you know what I'd tell my players? I'd tell them, go in hard on a couple challenges, they'll get hurt, they'll go out and have to pull from their bench. All right? I mean we have four guys out right now from injuries. Are they that much stronger? Are we that much weaker? Maybe. Maybe they drink their milk and we don't. But the fact that they have had to make one injury sub and we've had to make four . . . I have some issues with that, guys, I really do. I have some serious issues."

He tried to look each player in the eye briefly and then move on, but many weren't even looking at him.

"To me, that tells me that you're scared, and you're thinking that if you're not on the field, it's not your fault if we lose or tie. That's what it's telling me. Anyone who says soccer is not a tough man's sport, all right, they never played the game. So you guys need to get a little more mental toughness. I mean, if you're really hurt, you're really hurt. But sometimes bruises happen in this game. All right? So get tough. I guarantee you, every team that we play, every game that means something, they're going to try to knock you."

He took two steps to the right and the list of places where the team needed to improve came tumbling out: We need to defend better. We need to win balls in the air. We need to pass to the feet. We need to take more shots on goal. Of all his team's problems, it was still the lack of an aggressive striker that concerned him the most. Nobody except Carlos had that killer instinct, and he couldn't pull Carlos from goal against Jesuit. Betos, the backup goalie, was good, but not that good.

"Listen," he said to the boys stretched out in front of him. "We need to take more shots. You guys get up there and act like you have all day. We talked about this the first day of our practice, all right? Strike fear into your opponents by shooting the ball anytime from anyplace! You guys think you have to be five yards away from the goal to shoot it."

He clapped his hands as if trying to wake them up.

"And c'mon, guys! Get your heads up! This isn't going to be the only time we're behind at halftime this year. I guarantee it!"

He gave them one last look, turned, and stepped back.

If only his guys had the money. If only their parents had the time. If only he could get all his guys to play club soccer . . .

In Coach Flannigan's dreams, his entire team would be made of club players, and then, he thought, with the combination of year-round club experience, innate talent, and playground creativity, the Woodburn Bulldogs would be unbeatable.

But how to create the club team? Flannigan wanted the parents to put together a club soccer team that all the Bulldogs could play on. It would make such a difference. His guys played maybe twenty-five competitive games all year; nearly all the kids from Jesuit played one hundred fifty. Flannigan had considered organizing and coaching the club team himself but was wary of the time and devotion necessary.

"It's hard to balance a life and try to win a state championship," he said. "I don't know if I would want to do that to my wife."

At the whistle, he watched his boys jog back onto the field and take up their customary posts, all but Carlos kneeling on one knee. Flannigan told himself to concentrate on the second half. They wouldn't face Jesuit again until the playoffs, if they faced them at all.

So far, the preseason had unfurled about as he had expected. They had played five games and an informal jamboree, and had not lost once, had given up only a single goal until Jesuit's shot. And although it was still just the preseason, he was already getting a sense of the other teams in their league. The Bulldogs were up there with the best, he knew. But from the records he had seen, at least two teams in their league—Tualatin and McMinnville—were competitive with Woodburn.

When the regular season began in a few days, all three teams would probably be tied for first based on their preseason records. Then there would be eight regular season games—such a short season; Mike wished they could play each team in their league twice—and then the postseason. Hopefully the Bulldogs would get there, and they would deal with Jesuit then.

And now? He wondered if his team could score in the second half. They were so strong defensively—it had been a very nice shot that got past Carlos—but in their other preseason games, the Bulldogs hadn't scored many goals and had ended up tied against some teams they should have beaten. In practice, the forwards did so well, made beautiful chip shots over the keeper's head, smashed the ball accurately into corners, and passed it crisply. But in games there were always one too many steps, a second too long of hesitation, and a pass when there should have been a shot on goal.

The boys on his team were like the boys in his classroom, who never raised their hands and were reluctant to voice an opinion. They were afraid to fail. They were the first generation, or immigrants themselves, and they were supposed to make everything better. By winning the championship. By learning English. By graduating from high school. By going to college. By making a good living. His guys were supposed to break the pattern, and they knew it and it weighed on them.

The game resumed with Jesuit in control, the Bulldogs passing up opportunities to attack, playing it safe. Ten minutes in, Juan and a Jesuit player collided, going down in a heap. Both of them sprang to their feet angrily, saying something indecipherable as they stood chest to chest. Teammates ran forward to separate them.

A few minutes later, an aggressive Crusader tackled Octavio, spilling him face-first onto the artificial turf, where he lay clutching his knee in pain. It was the right knee, the same knee he had hurt earlier that summer in a men's league game, not the knee he had injured in Mexico. When Octavio didn't stand up, the referee halted play and two Bulldogs carried him off the field. Laurie, the team's shy trainer, diagnosed a hyper-extended knee and shrink-wrapped a bag of ice to it while Octavio sat looking glum.

His mood was mirrored by his coach, still not seeing the fire he wanted his players to show. When Jesuit won an airball, he said, "This is killing me. Every ball in the air they win. Every ball. I know we're better than that—Corvallis was tall and we got some of those. We're just not playing Woodburn soccer. This is the sort of stuff I see in middle school!"

For Mike, the one bright spot was Carlos, who saved a barrage of shots by diving, leaping, and punching away the ball, all while shouting out advice and encouragement to his teammates. And, to be fair, Vlad, a short, beefy kid who tended to blush and smile when put on the spot, had almost evened the score with less than two minutes to go, heading a cross from about ten feet out that just skimmed the upper surface of the goal's crossbar. A foot lower, and the Bulldogs might have left the game with heads held high.

Instead, the game ended 1–0 to Jesuit, and the Bulldogs came off the field snarling at each other. As they gathered their gear and drank water from the big cooler, Tony tried to put a positive spin on the game.

"We win as a team and we lose as a team," he said. "C'mon, guys, let's move on. We've got to play Newberg on Thursday."

Tony smiled at everyone, but the team looked beat up as it limped off the field. Octavio dragged his leg along like a wounded soldier. O.J. hung off two friends to keep his weight off a twisted ankle. Many of the boys stared at their feet as they trudged toward the parking lot. Taking up the rear, Coach Flannigan joked with Angel, who was once again carrying the ball bag.

"We need to get a freshman on the team to help you!"

"I know!" Angel said. "I thought that I only would have to do this stuff last year."

Carlos walked toward the parking lot with his friends Tony and

Juan, complaining about the game. Carlos didn't like to admit defeat
—or at least, he didn't like to take responsibility for it. A win might
happen because of him, but a loss happened *to* him. He could be
cocky, too. One time, trying to describe his role at the high school,
he simply said, "I'm the King, man!" He leaned back in his chair and
repeated the phrase. "What can I say? I'm the King!"

Walking toward the team bus, Carlos was complaining about the
team's lack of scoring. Juan, perhaps defending his own lack of goals,
said, "But Octavio doesn't pass the ball! I get open and he won't pass
the ball!"

"Don't give it to him," Carlos suggested. "You guys have got to
score."

That included his friend Martin, he thought. Martin was such
a liar, claiming he had practiced with Chivas in Mexico during the
summer. If he had, then why couldn't he score?

"It's all good," said Tony. "We won't see these guys again till the
playoffs. They can't beat us on our home field."

"Nobody can beat us on our home field," Carlos agreed.

They climbed aboard the bus. Carlos expected the team to make
it through the regular season in first or second place, and he thought
they would do well in the playoffs. But he had gone into the Jesuit
game feeling more confident than he left it. There was something
about this team's desire that was missing. Last season, he had felt the
team's need to win almost as a physical urge, a collective drive to beat
the other guy.

Carlos thought that he still had that drive, but he wasn't sure
about the others. Did they think that it was just a game? That they
were just there to have fun?

Coach Flannigan was having similar thoughts, staring out the
window at the lights of cars and buildings as the bus drove south
to Woodburn. This team needed something. Not just scoring. It
needed to fight. It needed to want to fight, to go down swinging. He
wasn't sure he could get that from his players. Octavio had the desire,
but it was so strong that it seemed to paralyze him. Where would he
find his fighters on the field? Where was the toughness he had seen

before from Ramon, where was the intensity from Vlad, where was the desire from Martin?

He would have to find a way, he thought. He would need to light a fire under his boys, make them angry, give them a reason to fight. They had so much talent! If he could get his team focused and hungry, he thought, they could beat anybody in the state.

Coming down from the stands, Omar and Pat Mendoza each had a different reaction to the game. Pat, a cheerful stoic, concentrated on the positive. The boys were playing hard. Carlos had made some nice saves. Omar focused on the negative. The defenders were stabbing at the ball, the forwards looked scared.

Like many of the first Latinos to settle in Woodburn, Omar was a Texan. Growing up in the 1960s, just a stone's throw north of the Mexican border, Omar had started working in elementary school, shining shoes at nightclubs in Edinburg, helping his parents to pick fruit, or going door to door selling bags of vegetables.

The vegetables were just one scheme of many that his father came up with to make a living. His father would buy veggies in bulk, rebag them, and send his twelve children out to sell the small packages. Omar hated hawking veggies door to door. He felt small and ashamed of his poverty, as if knocking on doors were begging. As an adult, it was still sometimes hard to think about. He once said that he came from a family of panhandlers.

Omar first saw Oregon from the bed of a pickup truck. It was 1969 and he was six years old, packed in the back with nine brothers and sisters among the blankets and clothing and cooking equipment like the leftovers from an unsuccessful garage sale. His family had learned about Woodburn after years of doing migrant work in California, and Omar's aunt and uncle had already settled down in the town.

The trip from south Texas had taken a week, during which time Omar had slept in city parks and learned that in some parts of Texas, a Hispanic boy could buy food only from the back door of restaurants. On the trip, he and his siblings had counted cars, cows, and billboards, and as the truck slowed down in Woodburn, he stood up and poked his head out of the back of the tarp roof and looked through the drizzle at the greenest land he had ever seen.

The Mendoza family made arrangements to work the fields for a man Omar called Farmer Joe. They stayed in a couple of small plywood cabins equipped with bunk beds and wood stoves, and in the daytime, while his father and the older siblings worked, Omar and his brother Meme roamed the fields and small patches of forest. The tall, thick trees and lush undergrowth tickled his imagination. To the six-year-old Omar, Farmer Joe's land seemed like wilderness, a jungle full of creatures and adventures. He and his brother Meme lost themselves in their imaginary games, and then, as the months passed and the land grew more familiar, Omar found himself captivated by other pastimes, such as hunting the pheasant that scattered as he stalked through the woods.

For the next six years, the Mendozas traveled every spring to Oregon, until enough of Omar's elder siblings had dropped out of school and started working to make the family less desperate. One of them, Ernie, settled in Woodburn, marrying a local girl whose own family had come north from Texas in 1952, one of the first Latino families in the Willamette Valley. After 1975, the Mendozas expanded their work migration to include the Midwest.

Omar graduated from eighth grade in Carlyle, Indiana, while in nearby fields his mother and father picked tomatoes that were destined for ketchup bottles. Because he had missed so much school over the years, he was fifteen when he became a high school freshman back in south Texas, and he struggled to keep up. Interested in auto mechanics, Omar found a part-time job at a gas station, inspired by his older brother Johnny, who raced hot rods at an Edinburg track. By the end of his freshman year, Omar had dropped out of school and was working full time.

As Omar grew up, and after he married and had a child, Woodburn remained in his memory as a nearly mythic place of plenty far from the struggles of south Texas. And so, after losing his mobile home to Hurricane Gilbert and feeling fed up with the life he knew in south Texas, Omar convinced his wife, Pat, to give Oregon a try. It was 1988.

They arrived broke. Omar had become a skilled forklift mechanic by that time, Pat a prodigiously organized office manager. Together with daughter Veronica, they moved into a small mobile home and started rebuilding. Several years after moving to Woodburn, Omar had a broken arm and couldn't work for a few months. That was when debt collectors tracked him down, demanding the rest of the money owed on the mobile home that had been destroyed in Texas.

The debt collector wanted nine thousand dollars. Omar told him the truth: he had no job, and only two hundred dollars in savings.

"I said, 'You want me, come and get me. Come and arrest me. I'm not doing anything else right now.'"

The debt collector budged a little, but Omar stuck to his story: $200 was it. Over the next week, they talked numerous times, and although Omar never raised his price, he also never hung up on the debt collector. He just kept talking, telling the guy about his life, explaining that he would pay if he could. He kept the guy engaged, and eventually, they agreed on a price: 486 bucks, every cent Omar had or could borrow. During their negotiations, the debt collector had called Omar a "stubborn asshole." But after their agreement, he softened.

"At the end of it, the guy said, 'It was pretty good working with you, Omar.' He turned out to be a pretty nice guy. He even told me that they had bought the loans for two cents on the dollar."

It was the way that Omar dealt with problems in life. He was direct and he didn't quit. He was water dripping on stone. With Omar, eventually, obstacles just wore down.

SEASON

FIVE

A Lush and Level Field

I bet they just see us as a lot of troublemakers here and see Woodburn as a bad place because there's a lot of Mexicans. I've heard stories like, "Oh Woodburn. They're bad, they're bad kids." I hear that from people at school. Like our teachers, they tell stories about other people saying, "Why do you want to teach at Woodburn, it's all gangster kids." They tell stories like that. That's how people see us, I guess.

—Chuy

Before the first regular season game in 2005, the soccer team room was clean and the smell inside was still far from the wet-sock stink that would soak into the concrete by season's end, when rain fell on every game. The soccer team room—a fancy name for a square concrete bunker lined with blue lockers—was far too small for all the members of the varsity team to fit comfortably, so the group of eighteen young men on Coach Flannigan's final roster fitted themselves into the room wherever they could, standing against the lockers, sitting close together on aluminum benches, even lying on the floor. They talked, but not so loudly as to cover the rhythmic *cumbia* that chattered from tiny speakers connected to Juan's MP3 player. Juan had become the momentary center of attention since arriving with his new hairstyle, completed the night before by his mother. The ends of the black hairs atop his head were bleached golden and brushed upward, like the fur of a Rhodesian ridgeback. The hairstyle was that of his favorite player, Ronaldo, the Portuguese striker playing for Manchester United, and Juan's teammates alternately complimented and teased him about it. Juan ducked his head, an embarrassed smile on his face, waving an arm at the others as if swatting away a fly.

Sitting near Juan, Octavio draped his arm over the shoulders of

Betos, the backup goalkeeper, talking to him in a low voice. Angel and Luis sprawled on the floor, heads on backpacks, side by side like two shoes in a box. After a while, somebody turned off the lights and closed the door until only a sliver of white was visible along the door-frame. During the first few games of the preseason, the team—apart from Carlos, who said it was "retarded" and "gay"—spent the last minutes before the coaches' arrival with the lights off, packed to-gether into the small room like rabbits in a den. They claimed they were visualizing the game, yet the steady stream of music, laughter, and occasional shouts coming from the darkened team room sug-gested otherwise.

Carlos pushed the team room door open, bumping it against somebody's foot, then spun around and walked back out. Carlos had a hard time sitting still. When he talked, he constantly swiveled his head, shifted his eyes, looked at everything around him.

"I can't stand it in there," he muttered. While the others lounged inside, Carlos paced back to the wide hallway between the toilets and the showers, a space the size of a small bedroom. One wall was domi-nated by a massive semicircular sink with a mirror mounted above it. Carlos admired himself in the mirror, wet his hands at the sink, then slicked back his hair, turned to see his profile, adjusted his shirt, wet his hands and slapped water on his face, turned his collar up, looked at his reflection, then turned the collar down, tucked his shirt in, then untucked it. Stubbornly, he was wearing the away jersey, blue with white stripes, while everybody else was wearing the home uniform, white with blue stripes.

A few minutes later, the door to the coaches' room swung open and Mike Flannigan and Chuck Ransom strode purposefully toward the team room.

"C'mon, Carlos," Flannigan said.

Carlos took one last look at himself in the mirror and turned to follow the coaches.

"All right," Coach Flannigan said. "Let's get started. Juan, will you shut that off?"

Ransom stood in the doorway as if he planned to block anyone from leaving, while Flannigan wrote out the names of the starting players in their positions, diagrammed on the white board. The Bull-dogs used a 3-5-2 scheme: three defenders, five midfielders, and two forwards. Flannigan liked this because it clogged up the middle of the field and allowed his team, which depended on skillful ball handling rather than brute force, to control the game's tempo. The coach looked around. Three of his best players were injured and doubt-ful for the game. He was glad it was against the mediocre Newberg Tigers.

Mike Flannigan's pregame speeches were marked by pauses as he gazed about the room, deciding if he was understood. He almost spoke in essays: his introduction, usually a reminder of recent focuses in practices; the body, explaining any particular problems the Bull-dogs would face against their current foe; and the conclusion, which he often left to Ransom.

This pregame speech was short. In recent practices, the Bulldogs had worked on one-touch passes, just like the pros did, meaning that when the ball came to a player, he needed to know already where to send it, as if that player were simply a relay. It made for a fast game, the ball moving very quickly from foot to foot, and if done right, could tire the opponent and get the Bulldogs in position to score. Flannigan touched on this.

"All right. I know a couple of years ago we had some forwards and you thought, well coach, I give him the ball and I won't get it back. All right? But we don't have that this year. So there's no reason not to make that quick one-touch pass and get your guy the ball. All right. Then we go into running our offense. Get the ball to our forwards' feet, look for our outside mids, and off we go. Also, we need to attack that open space. If it closes in the middle, send it outside. If they're defending well on the outside, send it in the middle. All right?

"Defenders. Remember if your forwards check into space, check with them. All right? Go with them. We do those things, we will win this game."

As he spoke, the boys watched him or the board or the floor. Although the team had its cliques—the juniors tended to hang out together, as did the sophomores—there were enough interrelation-ships to rival a TV drama, and most of the boys knew each other off the field. Carlos, a junior, lived with O.J., a sophomore, and played on a club team with O.J., Martin, Juan, and Tony. O.J. was friends with sophomores Luis and Angel. Angel's teenaged aunt Veronica was also Jovanny's aunt, and she was also dating quiet senior Cesar, who was good friends with Betos, who had played middle school soccer with Edgar and Ramon. Jovanny's father and O.J.'s father once coached a youth club team together. Luis, Angel, and Vlad had been playing together for years. Even Manolo, a freshman defender who was a recent arrival from Mexico, knew somebody—he had played on a club team with Jovanny.

On any given Friday night, you might find half the team hanging out at O.J. and Carlos's house. Go downtown and sit in Luis's Taqueria for an afternoon, and after paying the guitar player to go away, you might see the other half coming in for burritos and *sopes*. Coach Flannigan cleared his throat.

"All right," he said. "I was telling Coach Ransom the other day, and I didn't want to say this too soon because I think your heads are going to get too big, but I think this is one of the best teams we've had at Woodburn High School. I won't live by those words till the end of the year when you guys have proved it, but I honestly believe that defensively we are one of the best, and offensively we're developing that way. And that says something, because, as you know, we've been in the state playoffs for nineteen years, we've had three teams make it to the state championships, you know, four teams get to the semifinals. That's not just a 'so-what, that doesn't mean much,' that means a lot. Now you guys gotta go out there and prove I'm right. This should be a win, gentlemen. Remember, this is a league game. All these games count. All right! Get a good warm-up, then take care of business."

He turned away, glanced at Ransom, who shook his head.

Carlos, who had been bouncing his knee up and down, jumped to his feet and shouted: "Qué le vamos a hechar, cabrones?"

"Huevos!"

It was a joyous shout. A sexual innuendo is always good for teenage boys. They stood up and gathered their gear.

Carlos, again: "What does Angel like?"

"Huevos!"

Angel took up the cry: "What doesn't Juan have?"

"Huevos!"

As the group broke down in laughter, Flannigan turned and asked Octavio to suggest a more appropriate word for the team to go out on.

"All right," Flannigan said, and stuck out an arm. The players shifted to make room as everyone extended an arm toward each other, like spokes toward a common hub.

"What do we got, Octavio?"

"Perros," Octavio said.

A shout: "PERROS!"

They marched in a ragged double-file line down the short hallway, out the blue door, across the grass, then onto the parking lot, the clop clop clop of their cleats as hard as horse hooves. It was a warm and pleasant September evening with a couple of hours of daylight still left. As they walked out, members of the football team headed in from practice. Tony wandered over to joke with some of the football players. For all that Woodburn was known as a good soccer school, it was also known as a bad football school. The team hadn't won a game in 2004 and wasn't looking ready to win any in 2005. Despite the record, the football team got a locker room twice the size of the soccer team's—a regular point of contention to the varsity *fútbol* players.

The Bulldogs walked past a light blue building that housed the groundskeeper's equipment, the trainer's room, and a snack bar. As they approached the soccer pitch, the entire team turned to glance at the junior varsity game still being played on the pitch Mike Flannigan was so proud of.

The varsity players continued past the pitch, dumped their backpacks along the tall, chain-link fence surrounding the baseball field, and began their warm-ups. Octavio and Cheo, two of the three team captains, led the team in a jog across the outfield. Cesar, the third captain, usually avoided leadership. They stretched in a wide circle, then wandered over to the balls spread out near the infield and began passing them mildly back and forth.

When the JV game ended, Flannigan herded the boys into a single-file line and marched them across the pitch toward the home team bench. Once again, they dropped their backpacks and headed onto the grass to start exercises: passing, keep-away, shots on goal. A dozen or so local kids, younger brothers and their friends, hung on the chest-high fence surrounding the pitch watching them warm up. Brian Flannigan, his white hair poking out from under a baseball cap, arrived in a green electric cart bearing ice and water, and began to straighten the backpacks into a neat, black row. JV coach Levi Arias hung around to chat with the Flannigans.

The first of the adult fans to arrive was Omar, already sitting on a bench low in the stands watching the boys warm up. Ramon's father sometimes showed up for games, as did Jovanny's, but Martin's parents never watched him play, nor did Chuy's. A few older siblings began to arrive as well, mostly ex-Bulldogs like Luis's two brothers, Francisco and Juan-Carlos, and his cousin Henry, who had scored the Bulldogs' single most famous goal against Jesuit a few years back.

They wandered near the field, stopping to chat with Omar, entertaining themselves by watching the high school girls. Henry and Francisco, aggressive forwards when they had played for the high school, had made some attempts to continue their soccer careers, heading down to L.A. to try out for Chivas USA. The two young men were regulars to home games and enjoyed telling the younger boys how much better their teams had been.

As the young men walked away, Omar turned his attention back to the field, as motionless and focused as a linesperson in tennis. He had a way of seeing what was not in front of him, not seeing boys chasing a black-and-white ball on a wide expanse of grass but rather gangs and drinking and teenage pregnancies. When he watched the team warm up, he saw sixteen-year-old kids with hard cocks and no plans for the future, and in many ways he felt that it was his job to protect them: Omar Mendoza, Woodburn's own Holden Caufield.

Omar obsessed about the boys he knew staying out of trouble, and to keep them that way, he seemed to be everywhere, watching them at high school games, coaching them on club and men's league teams, driving them home, taking them to appointments, and leaving the door to his house unlocked, so that any kid, at any time, could have a place to go.

Years earlier, when Omar had paid off the debt for his hurricane trailer, he had felt a weight lift off his shoulders, and after his arm healed, he found a job. Pat worked temp jobs, moving from place to place. They pinched their pennies, fixed up their mobile home, and sold it to come up with a down payment for their house in downtown Woodburn.

They owned the house, but sometimes it didn't seem like theirs. Omar had come home more times than he could count to find friends of his children sitting on the couch eating his food and drinking his sodas while none of his own kids were present. He had come home to find boys playing soccer inside the living room. He had fed almost all his teams after games at his house, and nearly all the Bulldogs spent the night there. Half the team he had coached: Tony, Martin, Juan, Angel, Luis, Jovanny, Manolo, his son O.J., and Carlos. He knew their parents, their friends, their girlfriends, knew what kind of food they liked to eat and what kind of trouble they got into. He knew about their limited foresight and about their grades. Knowing all these things made him frown.

For the past ten years, because of these kids, Omar had become immersed in soccer. He coached it, talked about it, watched it on TV, despite having never played the game. He was probably a bigger fan of drag racing, but he never took his own dragster to the strip any more. He was too busy keeping boys focused and out of trouble. Soccer was just a tool. If knitting had the same effect, he would drive his truck around with balls of yarn in the back.

Like most parents, Omar had his ideas about why Woodburn had never won the state championship. To the team's coaches, the discussion always centered on experience. When Flannigan or Ransom thought about the loss to Lakeridge—and they did often enough—they chalked it up to lack of club soccer experience.

Omar knew this was a factor, but his own ideas about why the Bulldogs couldn't win it all had little to do with soccer. He felt that the Bulldogs' major weakness was a lack of killer instinct, a missing drive to succeed. He felt that the kids in Woodburn needed to be convinced that they were good enough to win.

"I think Flannigan's a good coach," he said, "a real good coach, but I also think that he needs to get out in the community some more. He needs to know these kids better, know them outside of school. He's a good coach. I was impressed when I saw O.J. go in with him last year. I watched him and I thought, He knows what the hell he's doing. Ransom is another, they are equal. But they are three-month coaches."

What Omar felt the Woodburn coaches did not understand was how to get inside the kids' heads.

"My way is, I'm not going to teach them how to dribble a ball, or do tricks, but if you listen to me, I will make you play like a man. It's a mental game, that's all it is. And playing like a man is the biggest thing that's going to get you into college. At their age, right now, they're kids. You go out there, you see my players, they play with passion. They go out there with desire. You see these other kids, they don't. I don't care about the score, just don't give up. It burns my butt when they give up."

Kids giving up made him angry, but if there was anything that really set Omar's ass on fire, it was the attitude of parents. He was sometimes angry at parents for not showing up to games, angry at parents for not pushing their children, angry at them for letting the school make decisions. When Omar's eldest daughter, Veronica, was in middle school, he attended a school meeting to talk about the town's gang problems. There were parents, teachers, families from Mexico, city commissioners, Latino groups from Portland, local police officers, the sheriff. About halfway through the meeting, the mother of a student stood up and began complaining in Spanish about not getting enough help from the school. "If the school would send a police officer to our house to give us a ride to school," she said, "maybe we could deal with these kids."

The statement made Omar snap. He leaped to his feet and demanded of the woman, "Where you come from, would you ask the cops to drive you to school? No, you wouldn't, because cops would probably beat the living crap out of you! Where you come from, you probably drive a horse and buggy! Do you drive here? No, because you don't even know how to drive! We live here in Woodburn with the freeway going right past, hundreds and thousands of cars going by every day, people getting off the freeway, coming here, and doing who knows what! And we've got ten to fifteen cops to take care of the whole city. They don't have time to take care of you. What you need to do is take your kids in the back and beat the shit out of them to teach them a lesson, then walk to school and deal with it! That's where the problem is! That's why, in this town, nearly every kid, you don't even know where they are at night, what they do and where they hang out! That's the problem! It's not the cops' responsibility! It's your responsibility!"

He repeated what he had said in English and sat down, barely able to control himself. Later that night, he stood up again and apologized for shouting. But he never apologized for his opinion. He was a kid who had dropped out of school after eighth grade, grown up in the deepest poverty, picked crops in the fields, and he had never received help from anybody outside his family. He knew what it was like to struggle, but he refused to turn the responsibility for that struggle's outcome over to another person. Seeing somebody else do so could set him off in an instant, and he was old enough to know why.

"It's ignorance," he said. "I cannot tolerate ignorance. That's why I push my kids to get an education, because I'm ignorant."

Mike Flannigan shook hands with the Newberg coach, spoke with him for a while, then strolled back to his bench. After a conversation with Octavio, he decided not to play his talented midfielder, whose knee was still sore. Flannigan watched the Newberg team warming up on the opposite end of the field and made his assessment. "2–0," he said. "Really, it should be 3–0, but without Octavio, it will take us a while to score. Probably win 2–0, but that will probably end up being one–nothing."

In the early evening's waning light, the shadows long and the soft edges of summer finally retreating, the Woodburn pitch looked as green and inviting as any Irish patch of clover. It was a big field, one of the benefits of not sharing grass with a football program. Unlike football, with its requisite 100-by-50-yard field, soccer pitches vary in size. They must be between 100 and 130 yards long and between 50 and 100 yards wide, so soccer fields can range from long skinny rectangles to perfect squares. Pitches for international games such as the World Cup tend to be uniform, about 115 yards long and 75 yards wide. The Woodburn field, at 112 yards long and 70 yards wide, was the biggest high school field in the state, much larger than most high school soccer fields, which are usually modeled with football in mind.

The varied sizes of a soccer pitch give an extra advantage to a home team, and grass does as well. Flannigan liked to keep it slightly long, to slow the ball down more than other teams were used to, with their fast-reacting turf fields, so that a pass would die before reaching its intended foot. Until the twenty-first century, professional soccer was all played on grass fields, and most professional soccer teams, as well as most college teams, still play on grass. Many high schools, however, and an increasing number of college and professional teams, play on artificial turf, which although costly to install, requires far less maintenance. Because the Bulldogs played on grass, they were at a disadvantage on artificial turf. They mistimed passes, aimed too far ahead, didn't expect the ball to bounce quite as high. Moving from field to field was in some ways like moving from country to country: new laws applied, new customs needed to be learned, and if your learning curve was too slow, then you lost.

Assistant Coach Ransom spoke briefly with his son, Kane, who played for the Newberg team. Early attempts to have Kane transferred to Woodburn had failed. "He's a good kid," Ransom once said. "If he was a troublemaker, they would have let him go easily enough."

When games started, Ransom planted his legs a few paces from the noisy bench and rarely moved, while Flannigan paced back and forth, yelling at players and referees and occasionally at the ground. In the minutes before the Newberg game started, both stood near the midline watching their team take shots on Carlos and occasionally turning to observe the Newberg team.

With both squads on the field, anybody in the stands would have noticed several immediate differences. Most obviously, the Newberg team was nearly all white, while only the coaches on the Woodburn side were. But the Newberg players were also larger—and this was not an especially big team, not like senior-heavy Corvallis, whose squad looked as if it came from a nearby university. In this game, like most of them, Los Perros had four or five players the height of Newberg's average-height players, then four or five guys shorter than any on Newberg's side. Newberg also had four or five guys taller than Woodburn's tallest player.

In soccer, height is less of an advantage than speed, although it was one reason Woodburn often had a hard time winning airballs and one of the reasons why Coach Flannigan tended to rely on Luis, his tallest player at five foot eleven, and Cheo, who had springs for legs, in critical airball situations, such as a corner kick in front of the opposing goal.

With five minutes left before game time, Flannigan and Ransom called the team in. The players trotted off the field and drank water. They listened to a last short speech by Flannigan, and then collected in a huddle, arms around shoulders, heads bent forward as if in prayer. In the middle, Octavio began his usual rapid-fire speech. Transformed from his quiet and shy off-field self, he gave his pre-game speeches at a breathless pace. Cesar, one of the two other captains, never talked much before games, and Cheo's role seemed to be to support Octavio with a few added comments.

"*Vamos cabrones* . . ." Octavio began. "We have to play hard, play fast, play as a team, play *con huevos, con ganas*, give it everything!"

"Let's bark!" Angel suggested.

"No, fuck that, *güey*," said Carlos. "Let's just shout."

"PERROS!"

The reserves headed for the bench. The starters took the field, several of them snatching a few blades of grass with their fingertips as they stepped onto the pitch, tossing the grass into the air almost immediately, and crossing themselves with the other hand. In the moments before the game began, after they found their place on the field, the Woodburn team went down on one knee, a tradition whose origin was a mystery to the coach but was brought on by the influence of televised Mexican *fútbol* matches, the kids imitating the actions of their heroes. Juan, taking his place at center-mid, rested both knees on the field, placed his palms together at his chin, and shut his eyes.

A whistle. The game began.

Right from the start, Woodburn pressed forward, the midfielders and forwards passing the ball crisply. Flannigan had started Chuy at left wing, and early in the game the ball found him, chest high. Chuy beat his defender down the sideline, putting on a burst of speed near the end line to get some room, then crossing the ball into the middle. Ransom had been working with Chuy on his crosses, and it showed.

The ball found Martin sprinting ahead of his defender to tap the ball in for the first goal. Seconds later it was called offsides, but Flannigan didn't complain. His team now knew they could score.

Martin seemed to have figured something out, making himself open at just the right time for the next few passes. He took one shot from twenty-five yards out that went wide of the right hand post, and minutes later he missed again from inside the penalty box. He trotted back shaking his head. Why am I always missing to the right? he thought.

Midway through the first half, Tony tried a long shot on goal that bounced off a defender's back right to O.J., whose low roller edged past the keeper's arms and into the net, putting Woodburn up on the Tigers, 1–0.

Ten minutes later, Tony got tangled up with the Tigers wing player, a small redhead. In a battle for the ball, both boys went down, the redheaded kid first, Tony falling on top of him. On the ground, the redhead kicked his legs violently, in what looked like an effort to remove Tony. He probably thought Tony had tripped him deliberately.

Tony got up thinking that the kid had tried to kick him in the head. A few minutes later, as both leaped in the air for a ball, Tony positioned himself behind the other boy and swung out his right foot, kicking the redhead in the small of the back. Although he hadn't seen the kick, when the Newberg player went down grabbing at his back, the ref ran up holding a yellow card out in front of Tony's face.

Tony turned and jogged straight to the sidelines, slapping out-stretched palms as he made his way past the bench, stopping at the water bucket.

Down the bench, freshman coach Dave Ellingson beckoned him over. Tony loped along, nodded his head a few times as Canadian spoke to him, and then trotted back to his spot on the end of the bench.

"He told me that he would have given me a red card," Tony said with a smirk. "But I don't care. Nobody kicks me and gets away with it. I don't care whose son he is."

The Newberg player wasn't Ransom's son, and Ransom, who listened to Canadian explain what had happened, refused to be upset by it. He knew that these sorts of little vengeances happened on the field regularly; he had done them himself as a player.

At halftime, Woodburn was up 1–0. Flannigan's halftime speech focused on improving crosses. Accurate crosses, where a player passes the ball from near the sidelines into the center of the field, usually while running with a defender hot on his heels, are difficult. But in a system like Woodburn's that emphasizes moving the ball back and forth across the field as the team advances, an inaccurate cross can negate all the work that got the ball up the field. It was one of the reasons that most of the players up front hesitated before taking a shot on goal. If they missed, the team would have to start all over again.

Two minutes into the second half, freshman Manolo, playing out of position at center-mid, sent a beautiful pass ahead to Martin, who jumped to meet it just a few feet in front of the goal, heading it in.

"Yeah, Martin!" Flannigan shouted. The bench leaped up.

With the score 2–0, Flannigan decided to give Carlos some time at forward. Although principally a goalkeeper, Carlos was also a strong player on the field, with the physical gifts and mental focus to be a good striker. Carlos preferred playing forward, but he wanted to stand out to college coaches, and he figured that he would stand out more as a goalkeeper.

When playing for one of Omar's club teams years earlier, Carlos had been used as a secret weapon. After one particularly grueling game against the state champions, when the first of two overtimes found the game still tied, Omar pulled Carlos out of goal and put him in at forward. With fresh legs, he had little trouble knocking in the winning goal. Mike Flannigan had a similar role in mind for Carlos this year.

O.J. and Luis, sitting beside each other on the bench, watched Carlos race through the Newberg midfield, the ball at his feet. Carlos was more physically developed than the rest of his teammates. He had the stocky, muscular build of a physical laborer, the body of an adult. In the goal, he had the quick leaping ability necessary for a good keeper and what Ransom sometimes called an EPL (English Premier League) leg. From the middle of the penalty box, he could kick the ball out past the midline. But he had an ego that sometimes got on the other players' nerves. Now, watching Carlos dribble between two defenders, Luis observed, "He can do everything."

"I know, his name is always in the paper," O.J. said.

"He's the star goalie."

"He always wants his name in the paper, that's the thing."

"Who wouldn't want that?" Martin asked.

The one-sided attack continued. Manolo took a shot from twenty yards out that barely missed the left goalpost. Martin's shot was blocked. Cesar's shot went directly to the keeper.

Each time, Flannigan commented out loud. "Good idea, Manolo, good idea!" Or to Ransom, "As much as we give Martin a hard time, we are getting better." And to Ransom again, "Cesar's getting more attack-minded."

With fifteen minutes left in the game, Flannigan sent Vlad in to substitute for O.J. With only ten minutes left a Newberg player broke free and took a shot on the goal. Betos, playing keeper, blocked it but couldn't hold onto the ball. It bounced out, allowing the Tigers to take a second shot that deflected off the right goalpost and back to another Newberg player. As Betos picked himself up off the grass, he watched as the ball was kicked toward—and right over—a wide-open goal.

It was Newberg's best shot of the night. Five minutes later, Carlos passed the ball from the right corner of the penalty box to Vlad, standing alone ten feet in front of the goal. Vlad kicked with his right foot, hit awkwardly, and the ball bounced off his left leg and skipped by the keeper into the goal.

Woodburn 3. Newberg 0. The game ended soon after. The Woodburn players jogged across the field in a line toward the fans climbing out of the bleachers, and back to their bench, showing a white gleam of smiles. The Tigers walked away with their heads down. They had a long season ahead with few promises of victory.

"All right," said Flannigan after his team had gathered on the grass around him. "First league game. First league win. Give yourselves a hand."

As he walked back to the locker room, the boys already changed and gone, one part of Mike Flannigan's brain was occupied with thoughts that had nothing to do with soccer. The school district had recently announced that Woodburn High had once again not met achievement goals set by George Bush's controversial No Child Left Behind law. And although they faced no imminent danger, administrators at Woodburn School District were aware that, should they fail to get their kids to pass more tests, one possible future was the district's takeover by the state.

For several years, Principal Laura Lanka had been keeping an eye on a growing reform movement called Small Schools. Small Schools is based on the idea that kids learn better when they are part of a community small enough for everyone to know everyone else's name. Numerous studies have shown that keeping high schools under four hundred students creates that sense of community, and the Small Schools philosophy had been adopted by the Bill and Melinda Gates Foundation, which by 2005 had delivered over $700 million to high school reform, going to about 1,500 high schools. The Gates Foundation funds early-learning programs, high school reform, charter schools, and college scholarships.

In 2002, Lanka started a ninth-grade pilot program to see if Small Schools was something Woodburn might be able to do. "We had a hard time convincing teachers," Lanka said. "They said, 'teach only ninth-graders all day long?'" However, Lanka did convince four teachers, one in English, one in social studies, one in science, and one in math, to give the "small learning community" a try, and the results had convinced her that it was worth applying on a larger scale. She began the Gates Grant application.

At about the same time, Lanka was pushing for a bill that would allow nonresident graduates of Oregon high schools to attend state colleges for in-state tuition. In the midst of that, she discovered that she had primary bone cancer, diagnosed in only about a hundred Americans every year. As a result, Lanka abruptly left the high school in March 2003. In the hasty transition, the paperwork from the Gates Foundation was set aside. While sitting in for Lanka, Acting Principal Hank Vrendenberg, the onetime athletic director of the high school, rediscovered the grant proposal and, with Assistant Principal Tom Gazzola, threw together the paperwork and sent it off.

There were eight high schools applying for four grants, and with the last-minute application, it seemed that Woodburn may have waited too long, missed some detail. Instead, the Gates Foundation gave everybody a grant, in Woodburn's case, close to a million dollars to begin their changes.

The money began to arrive in the summer between the 2004 and 2005 school years. Soon after, school administrators and teachers began their planning, including Lanka, who was back to work after her successful chemotherapy. While the idea behind Small Schools is simple—a school with under four hundred students should be more of a community than a school of three thousand—the practical mechanics of dividing a previously large school into four small ones, and the ways in which the small schools are run, create a host of problems. For example, without additional funding, Small Schools often have a single administrator, rather than the two or three running a comprehensive high school. Also, splitting a large high school into several smaller ones does not mean class size gets smaller. In fact, class size may increase. There are fewer student activities and unless organized well, less time and money for special education. So, from the fall of 2004 to the spring of 2005, Principal Laura Lanka, Assistant Principal Chuck Ransom, and several teachers made trips to over a dozen Small Schools from Florida to Seattle, trying to figure out what worked and what didn't.

In the summer of 2005, before school started, Mike Flannigan and several other teachers had crafted a proposal for one of the future Small Schools, one of nine proposals that the school board was going to vote on the night of the Newberg game. Flannigan's proposal was for a sports school.

"That doesn't just mean we watch sports and play games," he explained. "It's a way for us to keeps the kids interested. And sports are big business now. With a sports school, you can read quality nonfiction, essays, and short articles, you can learn about the business of sports, about management and promotion, you can study biology and fitness."

He closed up the locker room and headed toward his car, wondering about the school board's vote. He felt confident. It was good to begin the season with a win.

SIX

El Norte

> I remember being in the van, crossing the border during
> the night. It was crowded. I remember it was dark. We
> were walking in the desert. We just traveled in single file.
> My parents were carrying packages. Mom would carry me
> sometimes. I got tired—I must have been tired. When we
> got into the van, I was all the way in the bottom. There
> were all these people on top of me. They were very heavy.
>
> —Edgar

Octavio and Ricardo flew from Léon to Mexicali, a border city on the
edge of the Sonoran desert, where they were met by two coyotes—
human smugglers—to whom Octavio's father had promised several
thousand dollars. They arrived in Mexicali in the early afternoon,
then for over an hour they rode a rickety yellow bus to a town called
San Luis Rio Colorado. In the 1700s, steamships sailing from the Sea
of Cortez up the Colorado River used San Luis as a port, but by the
beginning of the twenty-first century, the mighty Colorado, having
been diverted, drained, and tapped through the American Southwest,
barely turned the earth into mud.

From the bus, the four men walked across several blocks of in-
dustrial wasteland, the sun beating on their backs. Octavio stayed
near his uncle and rarely spoke. One of the coyotes was dressed like
a gangster—baggy chinos and an oversized white T-shirt—and when
he spoke, Octavio thought he heard a Sinaloan accent.

After a while they reached a concrete warehouse with a large rolling metal door. The sun had baked the building, once red, into a pale
pink, and as they walked inside, Octavio smelled grease and body
odor. They entered through a side door, going from bright sunlight
into cool darkness, and before he could see, Octavio heard several
subdued conversations. As his eyes adjusted, he saw that about thirty

people were already in the building. Like him, they wore their best blue jeans or cleanest skirt, and like him, they looked dark and poor.

Besides the coyotes and the other campesinos, there was an old woman who drifted in and out of a small kitchen like a ghost, setting out plates of tortillas and *carne asada*. The other travelers clung to their small groups, mostly clusters of two or three young men, sitting on the concrete floor or resting on small mats made of foam and covered with food stains.

Octavio and Ricardo ate some food, leaning their backs against the cool concrete wall. Octavio wanted to know if this was what his uncle's previous crossings had been like, and Ricardo described some of them. He had walked all day and all night one time, he said, and they had almost run out of water before making it to the van in *el Norte*. Several other times, the trip had been simple: crouch at a fence, wait until dark, run. Ricardo had never crossed at this location before.

After a while, Octavio felt the need to pee. The warehouse's single bathroom was occupied, so he walked cautiously to a door and peered outside. The gangster coyote was leaning over near a chest-high cement block fence, bringing his nose down to the top of the fence, one finger pressing a nostril closed, as if he was going to blow out some snot. Instead, he breathed in deeply through his nose and moved his head a few inches across the top of the fence, then straightened up and looked around him. He saw Octavio standing in the doorway.

"What do you want?"

"I need to use the bathroom," Octavio answered.

"Go over there," the coyote said, pointing at a dirt strip near the back of the warehouse.

When Octavio returned to the warehouse, he told Ricardo what he had seen, and his uncle told him not to mention it again. They are using *drogas*, he said. This was exciting to Octavio. He had never seen anybody use drugs before. For the rest of the night, he kept an eye on the gangster coyote, although he always pretended to look elsewhere when the coyote turned his way.

For several hours the coyotes came and went, always bringing new and often wide-eyed campesinos with them. Then, at about midnight, the gangster coyote strode toward Octavio and the other three dozen people waiting in the back of the warehouse. He stopped before them, lifted an arm, and brought it down quickly, as if chopping off a man's neck with his outstretched hand.

"The people on this side of the room stay here," he said. "You," he said, motioning toward the second group, Octavio's group. "You come with me."

The group of campesinos split up between an old orange truck and an even older white van. Octavio and Ricardo ended up in the middle of the white van, crammed in with the others like cigarettes in a packet, unable to even see out the windows. The van swayed and jerked as they drove through town, and Octavio could feel shifting pressure on his hips and shoulders as they cornered. Nobody spoke but the coyotes in the front seats.

After a while, maybe half an hour, the road grew bumpier, and the van began to lurch forward into hidden potholes, rattling and bucking like a small boat at sea. They were going slowly now, and over the sound of the motor, Octavio thought he heard the crunch of tires on gravel or sand. Finally, the van stopped and the lights were switched off. He heard the passenger door slide open and followed his uncle into the cool night.

The moon was not quite full, but there was enough light for Octavio to see the shapes of his fellow travelers, the two vehicles they had come in, and the straight, slightly lumpy lines of cabbage, or some other ground-hugging vegetable, vanishing into the darkness as far as he could see.

"*Mira!*" one of the coyotes said sternly. "Everybody get into a straight line. Don't talk. If you need to pee, tell me. If you fall down or get hurt, tell me. Don't ask questions."

They formed a line. Many of the campesinos wore small backpacks or carried a jug of water and a plastic bag full of belongings. Octavio, on his uncle's advice, carried nothing, not even a clean shirt and a toothbrush. He had no wallet, no identification, and no money.

The group began to march across the vegetables. Octavio couldn't tell what the plants were, and as the walk dragged on, its novelty

wearing off, he became more and more interested in trying to figure them out. Cauliflower? Lettuce? He wished he could see better.
Uncle Ricardo slowed down to walk beside him.

"How are you doing, Octavio?"

"Fine," he said. "Is it always like this? I thought people ran
through the desert."

"It's different every time," Ricardo said.

After walking for about an hour, they left the vegetable fields and
reached a sandy plain, dotted by some bulbous, waist-high bushes
bearing the fruit of windswept plastic bags. The group was told
to rest, sleep if they could. They would be staying there until the
morning.

"Won't la migra see us in the morning?" somebody asked.

"They are out there right now," the coyotes said. "But the people
who work at night will stop working in the morning, and they will go
back to their office before the next shift starts. That's when we will
cross. Right now you are safe. We are still in Mexico, and la migra
cannot drive here."

Octavio sat up for most of the night, looking north toward the
glow of an American city. He didn't know which one. Several times
he saw or heard la migra, usually hearing their radio before seeing the
black Border Patrol SUVs scuttling across unseen roads like enormous beetles. One drove by about a hundred yards from the group,
Octavio's heart thumping as it came closer. He and the others lay flat
on the ground while the coyotes hissed at them not to move. Voices
crackled from the car's radio in indecipherable English. The SUV
turned gently and slowly and veered away from the group, taking
with it the exotic monotone radio voices.

Octavio lay down and tried to sleep. He had expected the crossing to be long and dangerous. He had heard stories of people walking
in the desert for ten hours, twenty hours, three days. He had heard
about people dying in the wilderness. He had not expected agricul-
ture and rest stops. It felt to him almost like nighttime in his pueblo,
as if they were a bunch of children playing a game in which the goal
was not to be caught by other children. He wondered if they would

make it, and if they did, what the place was like where his father and uncle lived.

Octavio woke up to see a brightening sky. The coyotes were standing looking north, toward the lights that Octavio had seen the night before. He sat up and looked for any signs of la migra. Nothing.

The group was again organized into a single-file line and began their march north, more quickly this time. After about half an hour, they stopped, and one of the coyotes began to run. The other told them all to follow, and the group began to run.

Octavio, who spent hours running daily on the soccer pitch at home, found the pace easy, but Ricardo labored, his heavy breath coming in gasps. Once the coyote who stayed with them shouted for them to stop and hunker down behind some bushes. Crouching on the sand, Octavio felt his heart beating fast and heard the sound of people panting. His knee began to throb.

"¡Vámonos!" the coyote shouted, and they began to run again, this time coming almost immediately to the edge of a great sand dune that led down toward the biggest freeway Octavio had ever seen. The freeway had three lanes going in either direction and a constant stream of fast, shiny new cars and enormous trucks. He could see the lead coyote at the base of the sand dune, climbing over a tall chain-link fence and looking intently at the traffic. Octavio felt a surge of adrenaline as he watched the coyote suddenly dash across the free-way, pause for a reconnoiter in the median strip, then bolt through the far lanes toward what looked like a small park—what Octavio would later learn was a highway rest stop.

The two dozen campesinos bounded down the dune, sand spray-ing up from their feet, arms spread wide for balance. A boy of about Octavio's age fell down headfirst in the sand, and at the fence, a middle-aged woman lost her grip near the top and fell backwards to the sand with a cry.

Octavio paused at the side of the freeway until his uncle arrived, and together they raced through a break in the traffic, following the lead coyote, who had jumped into a large yellow van. A second, waist-high chain-link fence slowed them down on the far side of the freeway, and a boy about Octavio's age tried to leap it, but his shoelace caught in a top link and brought him crashing down on the garbage-strewn no-man's land between the freeway and the rest area. The American drivers and passengers at the rest stop, now aware of what was happening, had all stopped to watch the campesinos dash across the freeway, and stood motionless in disbelief. Octavio ran past one middle-aged woman standing like a statue near her car, her mouth dropped open, her hand clutching her jaw as if to keep it from falling off.

Somehow all two dozen campesinos crammed themselves into the yellow van, which jerked into reverse and peeled out of the parking lot as the American spectators pressed cell phones to their ears. Inside the van, people were panting and shouting, as if they had just won an important game. Octavio, face pressed against a window, saw his first American road sign: Yuma, Arizona.

And so, despite the multibillion dollar Homeland Security budget, despite twenty thousand border agents with their night-vision goggles, black SUVs, and high-tech video surveillance, despite the Minutemen and their fences, despite laws and oh-so-many hours of political rhetoric, despite the love of his mother, the comfort of the farm, the pleasures of playing with sisters and cousins, despite his uncertainties and his ambitions, on a warm night in May 2002, Octavio and his uncle simply jogged north across the dirt and sand, climbed into a waiting van, and drove into Arizona, leaving the border and Mexico behind.

"It was so short," Octavio said. "It was a fast crossing. Maybe because of that, it wasn't scary to cross. It was just exciting. You don't know anything; you just know why you want to go. I was going to the United States to see my father. It was my first time and it was exciting."

Octavio might have had an easy trip across the border, but even his nighttime jaunt was significantly longer and more expensive than his father's first trips to the United States, back when the border was as easy to cross as a suburban street. The increased security that the

United States had imposed since September 11, 2001, means that kids without Octavio's access to cash could face days of desert travel, the immigrants poorly prepared for the changes in temperature and the lack of water. Hundreds of immigrants die every year making the crossing, a number that is increasing as the United States grows more nervous about its porous southern border.

Because of the increased danger and difficulty, the cost of hiring a coyote has also shot up, and these things combined—danger and cost—have the ironic effect of making undocumented immigrants in the United States more permanent. People who in the past might have traveled back and forth across the border to visit relatives at home before returning to work in the United States now stay in one place.

One of the big changes is that kids now are more likely to travel alone because the cost of being smuggled across the border is so high—paying for one person is hard enough, but paying for two can be impossible. Mexican children who enter the United States as Octavio did, without parents, often without even close family members, can land themselves in a situation with a particular set of problems. Relatives in the United States who may have paid thousands of dollars to coyotes are often afraid to claim their children when the kids are nabbed by authorities. And while federal law requires apprehended children of most countries to be placed with their nearest relation on U.S. soil (if there is one) or kept in a federally funded shelter for minors until their immigration status can be determined, Mexican children are simply turned back across the border.

In 2002, when Octavio crossed the border, the U.S. Border Patrol apprehended more than 86,000 children. By 2006, that number had grown to over 100,000. Some minors go through hell to get to the United States, traveling through Central America and Mexico while dodging corrupt police, gangsters, and bandits. When *L.A. Times* journalist Sonia Nazario researched her book, *Enrique's Journey*, she found a river of children moving north through Mexico as vulnerable as baby turtles, and almost as likely to be swallowed up by predators.

Compared to these kids, Octavio had been lucky. He had traveled with an older relative, knew his destination, crossed Mexico by plane and hired experienced coyotes to help him slip across the border. He was the recipient of decades, even generations of cross-border wisdom accumulated by people from his village. He traveled well-worn pathways.

The yellow van parked in the garage of a Yuma home and the sore campesinos wearily stepped out of it and stretched. Each traveler in turn was brought to a telephone in the house until Octavio was motioned forward. A coyote dialed the number and gave the phone to Octavio.

"Tell him you are in America," he said.

After briefly greeting his father, Octavio told him that they had crossed the border, and the coyote took the phone away, spoke into it, and told Octavio to sit down and wait.

After a while, the other coyote returned to the home with bags of McDonald's hamburgers and Octavio realized that he was starving. He unfolded the paper wrapper and while others around him started eating, paused.

The limp, round bun on top was as smooth as paper. He lifted it and saw the thin hamburger patty, the smear of ketchup, the forlorn pickle.

"What is this?" he asked his uncle.

"It's a hamburger. It's beef."

Octavio lifted up the patty to investigate, then rebuilt the burger and ate it. He decided that he liked hamburgers.

After lunch, the coyotes loaded everybody back into the old yellow van and they drove straight to Los Angeles, five hours crammed in the rattling old van without a pee break. Some of the campesinos became angry.

"How much longer will it be?" somebody asked desperately.

One more hour.

But that was what they always said. It's one more hour. The van drove on and on toward the sun, the campesinos growing increasingly uncomfortable with every pothole.

In L.A., they pulled into another garage and were given the chance to rest in another house. Octavio and his uncle settled in, eating the pizza and burgers that the coyotes brought them, listening to Spanish radio, and watching sports on English-language television. Octavio practiced saying the one phrase he knew in English: "Thank you." He called his father again.

People started to leave from the L.A. house, one by one, driven away in the van, until, after two days, only eleven campesinos were left, all of them headed to Oregon.

The trip north took place in a newer, gray passenger van with deeply tinted windows. The coyotes took turns driving for about twenty hours. The van stopped in rest areas for the campesinos to pee, and at gas stations the coyotes returned with junk food: Doritos, Gatorade.

It was the first time that Octavio got a chance to look out of the window and see the new country around him. The freeway itself amazed him. As they left L.A., the road was sometimes eight lanes wide, and still that didn't seem to be enough to contain the amount of traffic speeding along in every direction. The bridges were bigger than any he had imagined, the trucks longer and larger and shinier.

As I-5 took them out of the valley and began the ascent into the mountains of northern California, Octavio saw trees unlike any he had imagined. Trees like arboreal gods whose heads scraped the sky. Everywhere he looked, he saw houses that only wealthy people could own, and new cars, and everything was so clean! It seemed as if everybody in America was rich. He saw houses that would only be in the wealthiest neighborhoods in Guanajuato, where doctors and lawyers lived, the neighborhoods Octavio had only seen from the far side of a metal fence. But here, they were everywhere.

The van pulled into Woodburn in the middle of the day. Following his uncle's directions, the coyotes drove the van through the town of Woodburn to a small farm. The van humped over some bumps on its way to a cluster of small houses. His father was at work, but another uncle came out to greet him.

The next day, Octavio, his father, and uncle went to Wal-Mart to buy some clothes. When Octavio saw the size of the store and the number of goods inside, he didn't know how to react. He walked through the place without speaking, staring at . . . everything. Not just the number of items for sale, but the variety. Twenty-one brands of dishwashing detergent! Seventeen kinds of toilet paper! A dozen different types of blue jeans! And it wasn't just varieties of things. In Wal-Mart, Octavio saw for the first time a remarkable variety of people. The store was full of Anglos and Hispanics, which he had expected, but there were also Asians, Indians, and African Americans. Many of these people were enormous.

Octavio tried not to stare too much at all the people. It didn't seem polite. But he couldn't help gawking, like a village child in his first trip to a big city. He had thought that he was fairly worldly; after all, he had traveled around Mexico playing for a big-time soccer team. But Wal-Mart, of all places, taught him that he still had a lot to learn about the world.

After a few days of inactivity, Octavio began to feel bored. When he was bored, Octavio would shut off the TV and cruise the edges of the fields, stopping to speak with Uncle Ricardo. Octavio enjoyed the agricultural rhythms of early morning labor, gurgling generators, muddy boots, dirty shirts, and people coming home hungry and tired. He was eager to see the town beyond field and store, but he was afraid to walk into town on his own, worried about getting lost in a country where only the visitors spoke his language, and worried about being stopped by police, arrested, and deported. He was sure the police would know he had no papers if they asked him a question and he wasn't able to respond. Sometimes he watched network TV, trying to wrap his mind around the fast-paced English words he wanted to understand and couldn't. During afternoons, Octavio and his cousin played some one-on-one, or took the .22 to shoot cans and bottles.

Accompanied by family, he began to go into town. He learned that his father and uncle were not alone. In Woodburn, Salem, and other towns in the valley there were dozens of families from his village, people he had known as a child now living and working in the United States, sometimes working skilled jobs and speaking English. Speaking English!

For the next five months, Octavio's routine revolved around the nursery and short trips with family around the valley. He did some minor chores for his father's boss. For the first time in the United States, he felt relaxed, both because he was with his family again, but also because they were living in a turf nursery. He could walk around the acreage without fear of police.

Octavio was mesmerized by the turf, which, reaching its peak at springtime in Oregon, was thick and lush, the grass of wealthy people. Although the grass was more lush than he had thought possible, and although he was still aware of being in another country, living in the nursery felt comfortable to Octavio—the quietness and rural nature of the farm, the familiar people, it all felt like home.

The feeling made *el Norte*—such a strange and wonderful place— seem less foreign. It gave him touchstones to compare his new home to his old one. Even the turf reminded him of the soccer stadiums he had recently played in. But those memories reminded him of the distance he was from familiar things, and although it was wonderful to see his father and to experience life in another country, he became very aware of how far he was from home.

Then one day Ricardo spoke to him.

"Listen," he said, "you could stay here, not be like us. Look at us, your father and me, we work hard for little money. You are smart. In this country, the way ahead is through education. You could stay here and study, get an education here, maybe go to college, so you don't have to work hard labor all day the way that we do. Here we have opportunity, and if you don't try to be different, you'll be the same as me and your father."

Octavio was taken aback. He had come to the United States to see his father, and he planned to leave the United States with his father. When he had said goodbye to his mother, his grandparents, his sister and brother, and his cousins, he had assumed he would see them in six months or so. But now Ricardo was talking about staying permanently. His father was going back and might not return to the United States again. He might not see his parents or siblings for years. At fourteen, Octavio was facing the third major decision of his life.

Staying in America was exciting—he liked the idea of going to school, but he wasn't sure about leaving everything behind. Without immigration papers, he wouldn't be able to visit his family at Christmas, and depending on whether he could ever get his own papers, might not see them for years. Staying in America meant giving up things: he wouldn't return to Club Atlas; he wouldn't see his girlfriend; he would lose his friends. Staying in America meant leaving behind all the external parts of his identity. If he stayed, could he ever really go back?

Another part of him thought, "Do I want to go back?" He wondered if returning home after seeing so many new things would leave him hungry. It was like playing for Atlas—seeing how the professional athletes lived, seeing and feeling and running on the perfectly groomed, lush, green fields in enormous stadiums, visiting other cities —and then returning to his village to kick a ball around on the scruffy schoolyard dirt patch. He realized that his wider horizons made the decision harder.

Octavio spoke with his father, who told him that his home was in Mexico, but that he was a man and would have to decide for himself. His father, finally reunited with Octavio after so many years, was reluctant to encourage him to stay.

Back in Mexico, Octavio's father had recognized his skill at school from an early age and had pushed him to do well. When they had debated whether he should join Atlas, his father told him that if he didn't play soccer, he should stay in Irapuato and go to high school, maybe even college.

Octavio had said to him, "Okay, I'll do it. I want to do it. But how are you going to pay for it?"

"I can sell this tractor," his father had said. "I can sell acres of land."

The offer broke Octavio's heart. His father couldn't sell the tractor, couldn't sell their land. There were six other kids; there were his cousins and grandparents. All those people would suffer, would have to get along with less just so that he could have more schooling? He told his father no, he couldn't do it that way.

Now, in the United States, with the chance for Octavio to get an education, his father was torn between his son's future and the family's loss. Ricardo worked on Octavio's father, making the same arguments that he had made to Octavio himself, knowing the father's desire for his son to be a success. Reluctantly, his father agreed that Ricardo's argument made sense.

One day in August, Octavio's uncle and aunt came into the house and made an announcement: they had enrolled Octavio at Woodburn High School. Unless he made efforts otherwise, he was going to school in the United States.

Then, almost as an afterthought, Ricardo said, "I also signed you up for the soccer team."

"They have a soccer team?" Octavio asked, intrigued.

"Yes, they're very good."

That was enough. He decided to stay.

A couple of weeks later, Octavio followed his cousin Everardo to the fields behind the school, where he saw a beautiful emerald pitch towered over by enormous lights. The field reminded him of the ones he had played on with Club Atlas, the perfect fields at college stadiums or the impeccable, short, stiff grass in the professional stadium in Irapuato, grass as fine and polished as a silk shirt. The field at Woodburn wasn't as nice as that in Estadio Jalisco stadium, but as soon as he saw the Woodburn pitch, he knew a field that nice meant the school truly cared for soccer.

On the field, about seventy other boys were milling around, talking and joking, their eyes on the coaches. With Everardo translating, Octavio went through the tryouts: distance running, sprints, lots of scrimmaging. At first it was awkward. He hadn't brought cleats from Mexico, and he kept falling down. He had to borrow cleats to come back the next day.

"I didn't know anything about varsity or JV," he said later. "So when the tryouts finished, they said, 'You're playing varsity,' and I said, 'Varsity? JV? JV2? What does that mean?'"

After his cousin had explained to him the breakdown of levels—varsity first, junior varsity second, JV2 third, and freshman—Octavio still wasn't sure what it signified that he, a freshman, was to play on the varsity squad.

"So I asked, 'What does that mean?' and they said, 'You play good!'"

Back home on the turf farm, Octavio saw his future roll out in front of him like a red carpet. He would stay in the United States, play soccer, get a college scholarship, and get a degree. He would be an architect or a teacher. Skill on the soccer field would bring him all those things his family didn't have. He would change his life, set it on a new road, and bring his family along with him.

SEVEN

Carlos

The best thing that ever happened to me was coming to
Omar's. You have no idea how I felt moving in and getting
unpacked. When I was cleaning my room the next day,
stress released from me. I just felt like a new person, rejuve-
nated or something like that. I felt so good. I was just thinking, my life is going to start from here on out.

—Carlos

Omar arrived at the slippery field in Silverton shortly after the
team bus, carrying two boxes that had been delivered to his house:
a goalie jersey for Carlos and a pair of shoes that Chuy had ordered
online. He walked toward the Woodburn players, who were milling around uncertainly while the Silverton football team grunted and
tackled each other fifty yards away. The Bulldogs had done better
than Coach Flannigan expected against Newberg, and going into
their second game of the season, they had a combined preseason and
regular-season record of four wins, three ties, and the one loss to
Jesuit. Silverton, a town of seven thousand surrounded by farmland
and a state park, had a weak soccer team, and most of the Bulldogs
already etched a W onto their mental scoreboards before climbing
on the team bus. Silverton would later gain national fame as the town
that elected the nation's first openly transgender mayor, who would
run on a pledge to keep the conservative town's population small; in
2005, though, the town was simply quiet, rural, white.

A light mist, what Oregonians call "liquid sunshine," spattered
Omar and his two FedEx packages as he strode across the wet grass,
the front of his boots darkening with moisture. He spotted Arianna,
Carlos's girlfriend, standing under the outstretched arms of a ce-
dar, trying to keep dry. His mouth briefly tightened. Despite Coach
Flannigan's rule forbidding girlfriends on the team bus, Arianna had

become a regular at the team's away games because she was the only reliable person the coach could find to run the video camera. Ever since the humiliating loss to Lakeridge, Flannigan had been determined to record all the games. He watched the films to educate himself and occasionally showed some of them to his players, but mostly the tapes seemed to be a form of insurance that the team would never suffer such an injustice again.

Omar tossed one package to Carlos and stood still for a moment, looking for Chuy. A backup winger who had rarely played organized soccer, Chuy was a gifted athlete. He spent a lot of time in the gym, and in the winter he was on the wrestling team. Despite standing only 5-foot-3, he recorded the team's fastest forty-yard-dash time, and had the kind of muscular, ripped body that you see on action movie stars. Walking through the corridors at school, girls sometimes told Chuy that he had a nice butt.

Chuy might have also been the worst student on the team, the kind of kid who didn't do homework, who skipped class, who drank and took recreational drugs, and who didn't care about the consequences. Teachers at Woodburn all had Chuy stories, like the time he left one of the classrooms in a temporary building to use the bathroom, decided that he didn't feel like walking all the way to the regular school building, and walked around the classroom to pee in the bushes. He didn't realize that everybody in his class could see him out of the room's rear windows.

Like a couple of other members of Los Perros, Chuy had grown up in a bad part of Los Angeles, in a neighborhood full of gangs. His parents, Mexican immigrants, worked long hours, so Chuy and his older brother spent their afternoons and evenings in the street, committing minor acts of vandalism like stealing road signs and throwing eggs at cars.

When he was eleven years old, an uncle who lived in Woodburn came down for a visit. Before returning to Oregon, the uncle invited Chuy and his brother to come along, to spend the summer far away from the big city.

There wasn't much to do in Woodburn, but the threat of violence that hovered around him in L.A. was gone. Not that Woodburn lacked crime—Latino gangs from California had pushed their territory into Oregon a decade earlier—but it was nothing like Los Angeles.

A bit dull, maybe, but neither Chuy nor his brother wanted to go back home. They moved in with their uncles and in September started school in Oregon. Chuy's parents didn't move to Woodburn for another year.

By his junior year in 2005, Chuy's relationship with his parents had deteriorated. They were thoroughly traditional Mexican immigrants, spoke only Spanish, and were insecure in their new country. Chuy was American, English-speaking, a skate-rat who liked hip hop and spent weekends partying with friends. His parents didn't come to his games, and Chuy didn't like going home.

Chuy also didn't have a job, and because he had little pocket money, he had been playing with a pair of loaner cleats since the preseason. On a recent Saturday, Chuy had gone to work with his father picking blueberries and made enough to buy his own cleats, which had been delivered to Omar's house.

Chuy pulled them out of their box and showed them around, gold Nikes that shone in his hand like slivers of the sun.

"Size six," he said. "I got them cheap and I'm not going to use them. I'm going to sell them on eBay and make some money."

"No, *güey*," replied Martin, gazing at the shoes. "You need to wear those."

Chuy was still deciding when Coach Flannigan called the team over, gave them a brief speech, and sent the starters out on the field. Chuy slipped the shoes back into the box and tucked them under a backpack to protect them from the rain, still wearing borrowed cleats.

As expected, Woodburn scored their first goal within the opening minutes, and after their second goal, Coach Flannigan decided to give some of his bench players extra time, substituting Ramon and Javier early, while Cheo clowned on the bench. The third goal came soon after. Chuy passed to Cesar, who passed to Martin, who scored and then ran around, delighted.

Coach Flannigan turned to the bench. "See what happens when we play Woodburn style? Look what happens when we play the way we practice."

Coach Ransom, standing beside him, commented, "What I've learned from coaching teenage boys is that you have to teach them the same lesson over and over."

Flannigan put Betos in goal and Carlos at forward. Carlos headed in the fourth goal on a corner kick from Tony, sending it into a hole between the keeper's outstretched hand and the crossbar. Woodburn finished the game up 7–0, and the boys were laughing as they climbed aboard the bus.

Carlos and Arianna snuggled together on one of the front seats. Although Omar could have given O.J. and Carlos a ride home, Coach Flannigan liked his players to travel to and from games together. As the bus pulled out, a small convoy followed. Omar would pick the boys up at the school parking lot.

Carlos and Arianna had been going out for three months. Carlos found it difficult to be serious when speaking about her to others. He said he loved her, then took it back. Omar was nervous about their relationship. Early pregnancy loomed as one of the worst possible events that might sidetrack one of his charges from getting out of high school and into college.

Omar knew that Carlos was sexually active, had been for years. He had started with a girl in junior high, a dead ringer for the tiny D-list celebrity Tila Tequila. They started dating when Carlos was in seventh grade, and after about a year together, she told him that she thought she was pregnant.

It scared Carlos badly. He lay awake the next night thinking about the reality of being a parent.

"I mean, you think about it," he said. "I've heard kids say, 'Oh, it's going to be fun, having a kid'—kids that I was friends with said that—they can't wait. But you sit there and think about all the things that a kid needs to be taken care of in a proper way—I mean, that's a freaking pain in the ass! I mean, it might be fun when you get older and have money to do it, but man, doing it young and on welfare!"

Four months later, the girl still was not showing any belly bulge, and Carlos decided that she was lying and broke up with her. Wanting to talk to somebody, some adult, he settled on Omar, his club soccer coach. Carlos first met Omar in eighth grade when he tried out for a Woodburn club team that boasted many players who would become Bulldog starters: O.J., Tony, Martin, Juan. Omar needed a goalkeeper, so one of his players brought Carlos, whom he knew from the middle school at Gervais, a tiny town outside of Woodburn. Carlos was overweight and not very good in the net, but Omar had no other options and had already proven himself to be unable to turn away a kid who needed a father figure.

They spoke about the pregnancy in Omar's truck one late afternoon. Carlos had called him up from his Gervais foster home, and Omar had gone driving over there, not sure what the boy wanted. They drove away, and Carlos began to explain what had happened, or might have happened.

When he finished, Omar asked him what he was going to do about it.

"I don't know," said Carlos.

"It's up to you," Omar said. "You make these decisions. You don't use protection, that's what happens."

Over the years, Omar came to feel very protective of Carlos and thought that soccer was necessary to both keep him out of trouble and give him a reason to go to college. Carlos often infuriated him—the boy thought with his dick too much, Omar said—but Omar loved him anyway. Not for the first time, he wondered if the boy might be better off living with him.

Carlos was five when representatives of the state of Oregon took him away from his mother for the first time. He had woken up that morning on the floor beside his younger half-brother, Tino, and turned his head to see a German shepherd bouncing on his mother's bed. Two men stood in the bedroom with the dog. They were tall and wore black clothing, black bulletproof vests, and black balaclavas over their faces. One of these men wrenched the mattress off the box spring, slid it onto the floor, and watched the dog sniff the box spring.

Carlos turned his head and saw another black-clad police officer standing near his mother, Beth, his grandmother, Cerise, and Tino's father, Alejandro, the most recent and longest-lasting of Beth's boyfriends. Carlos's own father was in prison. All three were seated on the flowery second-hand couch in the living room with their wrists handcuffed in their laps, as if they were patiently awaiting a platter of hors d'oeuvres, or, judging from the looks of concern, anger, and fear on their faces, perhaps praying. Behind them the apartment door was open, and sunlight warmed the carpet near Carlos's face. He didn't see Alex, his baby brother.

As he looked around, Carlos saw more cops—maybe six in all, plus a couple of women with stern faces. One cop in particular caught his attention. He stood in the small kitchen opening cabinets, yanking out colorful boxes of breakfast cereal and pouring the cereal into the garbage before reaching into the empty boxes. For a moment, Carlos might have wondered what he was going to have for breakfast. Another officer went through the refrigerator, tossing opened cans and bottles of beer onto the vinyl flooring. None of the cops' faces were visible, and they moved through Carlos's apartment like large masked monkeys, turning over and opening anything and everything that caught their attention.

Later, Carlos would realize that somebody in the apartment complex must have called the police, probably on his behalf. His mother and Alejandro didn't hide their addiction well, and when Carlos was older, he would see them snort what his social worker called crank, become momentarily bright and animated, then gaze at the walls without speaking before falling asleep. When Alejandro and Beth fell asleep, he and Tino would flee the apartment for the parking lot outside. Those were the best times of day for the young boys.

A woman in a skirt spoke to Carlos, who sat upright and unsure beside his brother. His mother started to cry, and the woman in the skirt led Carlos and Tino outside, the other woman following with baby Alex in her arms. The boys were placed in a white van and driven across town. Carlos could see out the windows as they drove. He watched the passing trees and people and buildings and gave short answers to the social workers in the front seats, who asked about sports and TV shows and smiled a lot.

When they reached the Department of Human Services, the boys were led into a bland room where they waited until a white couple arrived. Carlos did not know what was happening or why. The foster parents spoke soothingly and looked tall. They talked with the social workers about things he didn't understand. Then they took the boys to their home, out in the country, where Carlos found sunshine and a swimming pool and a yard big enough for a boy to run forever. He cried as he realized, even at six, that if he and his brothers were going to be safe, he was going to have to be in charge.

"One time I recall clearly. Tino was in the swimming pool and their dog went in with him. The dog scratched his back real bad. Tino tried to get back inside the house but they wouldn't open the door. The dog wasn't hurting him anymore, but Tino was scared. They wouldn't let him in because he was still wet from the pool and they didn't want him to get the floor wet. He just stood at the door and cried."

The white couple spent most of their time watching television, ignoring the foster children. When Alex cried, Carlos gave him a bottle and changed his diaper. The three boys stayed close, and after about a month, they were brought back home. The apartment had been cleaned and the adults hugged the boys and cried. Then their new caseworker took Carlos and Tino into their bedroom and showed them a present: new bunk beds.

After dinner, the boys went to their room and climbed all over the beds, pretending the structure was a castle, a mountain, a fire station. They were so excited that they stayed up far into the night playing.

The second time that Carlos was taken away from his mother was a warm day in early August. Carlos's grandmother, who still lived with them, had cashed her disability check and given Carlos and Tino their allowance for the month. They were playing in a friend's apartment when the cops and social workers arrived; Carlos learned they were there when two girls ran into the room and started shouting, "You guys are going to leave! You're going to leave!"

Beth had recently given birth to another boy—his brother Jonathon—and most likely DHS had received copies of his mother's blood tests, indicating her return to drug use. Jonathon was Beth's sixth child.

Startled and frightened, Carlos and Tino dashed back to their home, saw the police, the white van, and the women in drab skirts. Carlos recognized one of them, the family's head caseworker, and when he saw her, he started to cry. Beth was already crying, and soon after, his brothers joined in. His caseworker walked up to him, knelt down, and tried to soothe him, but he knew what was going to happen and was inconsolable.

"They didn't really say anything to us. They didn't really talk to my parents. They just wanted us to pack our stuff, but we didn't want to pack our stuff."

Carlos slumped to the floor, refusing to leave until the social workers packed a bag for him and, holding his hand, guided him out the front door. Carlos envisioned another stay at the white couple's home, another lonely month away, only this time he was ten years old, the eldest of six kids, including a newborn.

Since the first time he was taken away, Alejandro, Alex and Tino's father, had been deported. Carlos had followed a girl out of his school bus and kissed her behind a building. He had moved several times and was attending his third elementary school. Carlos and Tino had started playing basketball at the parks when their mom was asleep. Alex, who had been a baby the first time DHS came, was almost ready to attend kindergarten.

The boys sat in the DHS office for about an hour before they were met by an elderly Hispanic couple. When Carlos saw them, he felt some relief. "They seemed nice," he said.

The nice older couple led Carlos, Tino, and Alex outside, where they met one of the couple's grandkids, Jorge, a boy about Carlos's age. The other three boys went off with another family and Carlos never saw them again. Later, he heard they moved to Mexico.

The older couple's home turned out to be a double-wide trailer on the end of a dirt road in the don't-blink hamlet of Gervais, ten miles south of Woodburn. Carlos and his two brothers moved in and lived with the couple's two grandchildren, Jorge and Emilia, a girl about four years older than Carlos.

The town was much smaller than the boys were used to, a quiet, dusty island in a sea of farms. Narrow roads, no sidewalks, and dried-up stores and shuttered doors along the two blocks of downtown. Near his home was a Christmas tree farm. Lining the road to Wood-burn were flat oceans of agricultural fields—trees, shrubs, cauliflower, berries.

His new foster parents were not like the first ones. Nobody was locked outside or injured, but it didn't feel right, and after a few months, Carlos realized why. His foster parents were just go-ing through the motions. At some level, he thought, they viewed him and his brothers as a meal ticket, to be protected and properly taken care of, but not to be loved. He came to hate the house and the flower garden that his foster parents tended. They spend so much time giving affection to the flowers that Carlos decided the yard at his house—whenever he got a house—would be all dirt.

"They looked like nice people, but they were assholes. I haven't gone back to see them at all. They gave us some good times, but man, they put us through hell."

He hated the way that the couple treated their grandchildren bet-ter than their foster children. When the granddaughter threw a shoe at his head, he was the one who got in trouble. When an argument broke out between his brother and the grandson, it was Alex who was sent to his room. Carlos and his brothers had bedtimes; the grand-children didn't. They had to do more chores. And the foster parents didn't come to watch Carlos play soccer.

Carlos kept busy in Gervais. He played soccer in sixth grade, football in seventh, and basketball all the time. He spent a lot of time at Omar's, hanging out in the living room in front of the big-screen TV with all the other boys on Omar's club team. They would come in the door and head straight to the fridge, where the one inviolable rule was always to leave at least one Coke for Pat.

Omar's house was comfortable and full of life. They played soccer indoors sometimes, pushing the furniture out of the way. During one game, they broke a small *quinceañera* statue, and not knowing what to do, fit the broken pieces back together and replaced the statue in the hope that neither Pat nor Omar would notice. But the boys didn't use glue, and when Omar came home and strode past the statue, it crumbled to the floor. He instantly knew what had happened—which was why he had told them not to play soccer in the house that evening. Omar yelled and grumbled about responsibility, and a kid named Ivan took the blame. Ivan bundled up the statue, promising to fix and return it. But he never did.

They also played video games—O.J. usually won—and waited until it was late and Omar offered to drive people home. Sometimes Carlos slept over.

Once, when the room was full of his friends, somebody mentioned how Carlos spent more time at Omar and Pat's than he did at his foster home.

"Yeah, Pat," Carlos said, serious but not wanting to sound serious, "I'm going to come and live with you!"

"You should!" Pat replied, and the guys all laughed. Carlos joined them, but he was watching Pat and wondering.

EIGHT

Adjustments

I had a kid who got marked down on his test because he
had never heard of a country club! He's from a farm in
Michoacan! Why in the world should we expect him to
hear of a country club?

—Coach Mike Flannigan

Following the win against Silverton, Carlos was put back in goal for
the next match, a home game against the Tualatin Timberwolves, a
very good team that the Bulldogs had traded wins and losses with for
years. It was another game that highlighted the team's strengths and
weaknesses. Time and time again, the Bulldogs drove through the
Tualatin defense and took a shot, but each time, the shot failed to find
the back of the net. Midway through the first half, Octavio got an
open look and kicked the ball over the crossbar. Chuy's shot from the
right sideline soared straight to the keeper. Octavio's foul kick was
too high. With four minutes left in the first half, the Bulldogs finally
scored on a penalty kick.

For the rest of the game, the score stayed 1–0 as Woodburn's
defense stopped Tualatin's star player, Reid Phillips, and Woodburn's offense seemed to stop itself. Coach Flannigan became more
and more frustrated with each goal attempt that went high, wide, or
directly to the keeper. Following one kick, he turned to the bench
and snapped:

"You guys just kick it away like it doesn't mean anything."

The comment was uncharacteristic for Coach Flannigan, who
typically reserved his vitriol for the referees and opposing coaches.

The bench players looked at each other and rolled their eyes.

"*You* kick it away like it doesn't mean anything," one of them said
under his breath.

Flannigan called for a substitution, and O.J. came trotting off the field, ripped his shirt off as he reached the sideline, and threw it to the grass. He hurled himself onto the crowded bench and began complaining to his teammates.

"What's wrong?" Coach Flannigan asked, turning to face O.J.

"It's Octavio!" O.J. shouted. "He doesn't pass it to anyone! I've been open and he won't pass me the ball!"

The coach nodded. "I'll talk to him. But you need to put your jersey on right now or you're out of the game."

O.J. jerked up out of the seat and went to retrieve his shirt, pulling it on over his head.

"What's his problem?" O.J. asked aloud.

Octavio's problem was ambition. As the season progressed and the team proved itself poor at scoring, Octavio decided that the Bulldogs were going to screw up his chances with college coaches.

"Here they play for fun," he said stiffly. "But I think we can play better. I have in mind to play soccer as a way to improve yourself, to be better every day. They play here because they like to play. When you play *to be* somebody, you play different. You have opportunities when you play good, you get scholarships."

Coach Flannigan saw Octavio's actions but didn't understand them. Coach Ransom did. He saw a kid who had organized his entire future around being noticed in high school soccer games. As a junior, Octavio had been more relaxed on the field, and because of that, he was a better athlete. Ransom worried that as a senior, Octavio was getting desperate.

With less than a minute left in the game, Tualatin got the ball downfield and crossed it into the penalty box. One of the Timberwolves captured the contested airball, knocking it to the feet of Reid Phillips, who blasted a perfect shot toward the top of the Woodburn net. Carlos got his hand up, felt it deflect the ball, but knew it wasn't enough. The ball hit the underside of the top post and ricocheted in for a 1–1 tie. Coach Flannigan ripped off his hat, spun around, and threw it. It twirled and helicoptered through the evening air, over the fence behind him, and settled in the dirt of a new housing complex. Forty seconds later, the game was over.

The Tualatin players trotted together as happily as if they had just won the state championship, while the Bulldogs swooned as if all their girlfriends had broken up with them at once. They formed a huddle for the traditional postgame shout of the opposing team's name, but it came out weak and defeated.

"C'mon," shouted Carlos angrily. "Do it again!"

"Tualatin!"

He came off the field and slumped onto the bench, stripping off his gloves.

"Goddammit," he said. "Goddammit. Right in the box. How come we're not scoring more goals? These guys talk a lot . . ." He looked around at the forwards, Martin, Vlad, O.J., Juan, as if hoping for a response. None of them looked at him. Then, with less conviction, he said again, "Goddammit."

Following the tie with Tualatin, Mike Flannigan decided he had to make changes. He wasn't upset with Carlos; it had been a very good shot. He was upset that his team couldn't get the ball in the back of the net more often.

Flannigan told Martin and O.J. that they would have to earn their starting positions. O.J. sulked a bit. Martin felt angry and sad. He still wasn't sure why he couldn't score. This wasn't the way the season was supposed to go.

Like Carlos, O.J., and Tony, Martin had played club soccer for years and was a very experienced forward and midfielder. In middle school, Martin had been his team's leading scorer, but in high school, he had struggled.

To improve his skills, Martin had spent part of the previous summer in Mexico, playing with a youth team connected with the popular Guadalajara club Chivas. His father had once played for a Chivas semipro team, making the trip from L.A. to Mexico for the soccer season, and Martin hoped to follow in his father's footsteps.

Martin took the trip to Guadalajara with his godmother, who left him with members of her husband's family, people Martin had never met before. He hadn't visited Mexico since he was a child, and instead of the friendly, soccer-crazy country he had imagined, he found dirty streets, packs of roaming dogs, open sewers, and entire families begging on the sidewalk. His Spanish was good enough, but it marked him as an outsider, and he didn't understand most of the slang.

The guys on his youth team called him *Pocho*, an unflattering term for somebody born in the United States to Mexican parents. His teammates were all older than Martin, young men who had grown up in poverty and who drank beer before practice and made crude jokes that he didn't always understand. Instead of hanging out with them, Martin retreated in the afternoons to his relatives' house to listen to music and kick a ball around with his younger cousins, who were so in awe of him that one even requested his autograph.

Although he had been lonely during the Mexico trip, Martin thought that he had played well, had scored goals and improved his skills. He had returned to Woodburn confident, feeling that he would dominate the league as a forward. It hadn't worked out that way. Instead of scoring at will, he seemed unable to find the back of the net, his shots skipping past the outside of the goalposts, as if drawn there by invisible magnets.

He blamed Flannigan, who clearly expected Martin to play better. The constant nagging from the coach had been bad enough, but now, having the starting position taken away from him . . . Martin considered leaving the team. Maybe, he thought, it would be for the best. He had injured his knee the previous year, and it had started hurting him again, enough that he spent free time at home massaging the tendons around the joint the way that his physical therapist had taught him. If I quit, Martin thought, at least my knee will heal for next summer's trip to Mexico.

Before the next game, against tiny, rural Dallas—a team that rivaled Silverton for poor soccer—the school board's decision on the Small Schools proposals was released. The Woodburn school board ended up taking nine proposals and fitting them together to create four Small Schools: Wellness, Business, and Sports; Science and Technology; Art and Communication; and International Studies.

Flannigan was happy that his proposal made the cut. Hopefully, he thought, I will get to teach there.

With the planning out of the way, the coach had little to do with the Small Schools until they were implemented in 2006. Coach Ransom, however, having already traipsed across the country figuring out what kind of school would work best at Woodburn, now had to spearhead the transition.

Ideally, each Small School would be housed in a separate building, each with its own cafeteria and athletic department. But Woodburn couldn't afford to build four entirely new high schools. Ransom had to figure out how, within a budget, to keep the different student bodies separate while still sharing some of the same building space.

The sports teams, too, had to be figured out. Would they invite all four schools to play on one team, keeping them competitive against larger schools? Or would they drop down to a division for genuinely small schools? That would probably mean some of the new Woodburn high schools would field certain teams while others would field none. It was a headache.

One thing that Ransom was fairly certain of, though, was that the curriculum at each of the Small Schools was going to change. He and Principal Laura Lanka had talked about it at length. Ransom had looked at a lot of schools and read a lot of studies, and to him, one thing was clear: the schools that were a making a difference among large Hispanic populations spent a lot of time on the three Rs. In the new and improved Woodburn High, it would be back to basics. Ransom and Lanka planned to increase the time spent on reading and writing, even if it meant doubling up on class time for those topics and dropping the number of electives.

The boys on the soccer team were vaguely aware of the Small Schools changes, but none paid them too much attention. Before the vote results were announced, almost all had decided to join the sports school, even if none of them knew exactly what that meant.

Against Dallas, Flannigan started Juan and Vlad at forward. Martin and O.J. watched from the bench. By halftime, Woodburn was up 4–0 and the bench was getting giddy. Following a header by Cheo that went over the crossbar, the bench said:

"Head it!"

"*Cabeza* it!"

They burst into giggles. Coach Flannigan had to turn around to quiet them, worried about how the other team might feel. Freshman Manolo came off the field complaining about a Dallas player who had kicked him with no foul being called. He spoke loudly in Spanish to Ransom, who held his hands out, palms down. Forget the ref, he said.

"But it's not the first time he's kicked me!"

"Forget it."

At halftime, following Octavio's usual attempt to fire up his teammates, several of the players who stayed on the sidelines began to imitate him. Play hard, play *con ganas, con todo*, play hard, they said in high-pitched voices. In Octavio's brief time on the field, several of his teammates did their best not to pass the ball to him, worried that they might not get it back.

The team scored easily but also made stupid mistakes. Chasing the ball in front of the Dallas goal, Juan and Vlad tangled their legs and fell to the ground, missing a scoring opportunity. Alone in the penalty box, Cesar collected a pass from Tony and booted it five yards to the right of the net. And one goal was a mistake: the ball bounced off Juan's leg, off a defender's back, and in. Fortunately, their opponent was in worse shape. The keeper was slow and the defenders were easily faked by Woodburn's superior ball control. Woodburn won 6–0 and moved into second place behind undefeated McMinnville, a team Woodburn was scheduled to play the following week in what most local papers figured would be a battle for league champion.

A few days after the Dallas game, the Bulldogs played Forest Grove, a good team with a significant number of Hispanic players. Los Perros scored quickly, Cesar blasting in a cross from Chuy within five minutes, and moments later, Vlad tapped in a pass from Juan. Tony banked one in off the post, and O.J., looking to regain his starting role, knocked in the fourth goal late in the first half. For all the bungling that the team had struggled through against Dallas, at Forest Grove, they had looked crisp and in control.

For once, Octavio also seemed to master his desperation. Halfway through the second half, he made a run down the left side, outdistancing two Forest Grove midfielders, slowing slightly, then tapping the ball through a defender's legs and racing around the other side to recover his own pass. He ran several steps before sending the ball far forward to a wide-open Juan, who unfortunately was whistled off-sides. Later he sent another pass ahead of Juan that was intercepted by the goalkeeper, who smacked the ball out toward midfield. As the keeper turned and sprinted back toward his undefended goal, Octavio tracked down the ball and from about forty yards out, placed a perfect two-bounce long shot that whizzed past the retreating keeper into the middle of the net for Woodburn's fifth and final goal.

Cheo left the game early with a pulled hamstring, which didn't stop him from singing most of the bus ride home from his usual perch next to Octavio. On bus rides, Cheo's natural cheerfulness usually found an outlet in song, and with his friend nearby, Octavio's taciturn nature eased and he became talkative and outgoing. As the Woodburn bus trundled away from Forest Grove, the friends sat happily together in the back, content with the evening's victory.

In front of them, Betos and Cesar joked loudly with Tony and Juan. They watched the cars driving by and teased each other about the women driving them.

"Hey, is that your girlfriend?"

"Look, here comes my ride!"

"She's the one for you, *güey!*"

Behind them, Cheo sang.

As a freshman, Cheo sat in the back of the Newcomer class while Octavio sat in the front. They first talked during an in-class assignment, when they discovered that they had grown up within sixty miles of each other. At first they didn't talk outside of class. When Octavio saw Cheo with his cousin and his cousin's friends, he looked at their baggy clothing and assumed that Cheo was a gang member. A few days later, Cheo came across Octavio juggling a soccer ball in the fields behind the school and joined him in a pickup game.

Through their freshman and sophomore years, the two boys settled on a distant friendship, nodding to each other in the hallways. In their junior year, Cheo joined the varsity soccer team and they recognized in each other a similar ferocity as players. Octavio, who had a weekend job at a vineyard, heard that Cheo was looking for work and invited him to come along. They soon spent so much time together that kids at school called them twins and, sometimes, lovers. To Octavio and Cheo, it was almost true. They felt like twins and loved each other like brothers. Sometimes it amazed them that they had to move two thousand miles away from home only to become friends with somebody who grew up a hundred miles away.

"When I got to know him," Octavio said, "I felt like we were the same. You know. He was responsible and hard-working and good at soccer. Just like me."

"He didn't just want to party," said Cheo. "He wanted to be somebody. He was ambitious."

Back in 2002, Cheo's father received his U.S. residency papers while living in Woodburn. He phoned his family, still living in Mexico, and told them to get ready. They were moving to Oregon. It happened quickly: packing, a bus to the border, a second bus to Woodburn, and then the house that Cheo Sr. shared with his brother.

For as long as Cheo could remember, his father—who was fourteen when he first came to the United States—had spent nine to ten months a year working in the United States. Living in Woodburn was the first time Cheo's entire family had been together year-round.

"My parents said that it was very important for us to come, to study and to be educated," Cheo said. "I wanted to come. But also, I didn't know. I had to leave my friends, my team, my school. It was a hard decision, but I wanted to come."

Within two weeks of his arrival, Cheo was working in the fields near Woodburn with his cousin. It was his father's idea. Cheo Sr. wanted his son to experience the low-back pain, the long hours, the poor wages, the shirt sticking to his back in the sun. He wanted to give Cheo some motivation to do well in high school. This is your opportunity to get a good life, he told Cheo. You have to work hard at school.

Back in Guanajuato, Cheo had heard that you could make a lot of money in the United States. He had seen men return wearing new blue jeans and fine-looking cowboy boots, often driving new trucks—men who had money to spend around town. But in the fields around Woodburn, Cheo saw Mexicans working hard for little pay and felt the dirt dry under his fingernails and the rain soak his pants cold against his legs. By the end of the first day, Cheo agreed with his father viscerally.

"I don't like that kind of life," he remarked. "I want to be educated and to have something better."

Cheo and his cousin spent the summer working at farms and nurseries across the Willamette Valley. Most of the time he planted grass sprigs, which meant lying face-down on a sled pulled behind a tractor, poking the plugs into the earth every few inches. It made his shoulders cramp and burn. Once he went over the mountains to Madras in a large van packed with other young Hispanics, to plant trees. He worked in Madras trimming newly planted grass the day before he started high school.

At the beginning of Cheo's sophomore year, his cousin took him to the high school soccer tryouts. In Mexico, Cheo had played *fútbol* and volleyball and was a thousand-meter runner. He was strong and limber and could flip himself from a prone position onto his feet without using his hands, the way martial artists do in fight scenes in the movies. He was a gifted athlete, and Coach Flannigan was impressed by his speed, skill, and intensity right away, starting him on the JV team.

When Cheo made varsity, Coach Flannigan used him as a marking back, a defensive position, although Cheo was used to playing right wing, a natural role for a distance runner. He played alongside Octavio, who as a junior played sweeper, the last line of defense before the goalkeeper. During substitutions, when Octavio was moved to the center-midfielder spot, Cheo took over the sweeper position.

Coach Flannigan loved Cheo's speed and single-mindedness. He was catlike in his quickness and focus on the ball. Cheo liked the responsibility of sweeper, liked stripping other players and denying them their shot on goal. He liked Flannigan's emphasis on quick passes and ball control, even if he would at times lose patience with the coach, who could seem more intent on giving everybody a chance to play than on winning every game. It was a complaint that a few other kids had, especially around playoff time, when some of the players felt that Flannigan gave too much time on the field to his seniors, even if they weren't the best players at their position.

Cheo did well on the field and, a bright kid, he also got good grades in his Spanish-language classes. But learning a new language did not come naturally to him. He spent a lot of his freshman year not understanding what he was being asked to do, so he developed a strategy for new classes. He would sit next to another Hispanic—it wasn't hard to find one—and ask him to interpret the assignments. Sometimes other students helped, but sometimes they said that they didn't know or simply would not answer. He tried asking teachers, but only some were bilingual.

"That just meant an F on that paper," he said.

Part of Cheo's problem learning English was the limited amount of practice he got. His family spoke Spanish at home. Around town, it was easy to get by without using much English. The ground floor of the old Mason's Lodge, for example, now houses Lupita's Mexican Panadería, a bakery. Across the street, in a brick building that once held a bank, is a discount store, Tienda Lucero, and down the street are Novedades Mantalvo, La Caseta Telefónica, the Fiesta Boutique, and Mendoza's Panadería. Around the corner are a *tienda de música*, a *carnicería*, a *peluquería*, and a bench-strewn plaza often filled with men wearing stiff, white cowboy hats.

Living in a town full of his peers, Cheo had learned a difficult lesson about assimilation. It's hard work, and in a town where it was easy not to mix with Anglos, learning the skills necessary to thrive in Anglo culture sometimes seemed out of reach.

It was a lesson that Miguel Salinas had learned twenty years earlier. Salinas, who was born in Mexico, landed in Gervais when his family found migrant work there. He had grown up working in the fields alongside his father, but one day while working in Gervais, he decided that he was going to do something different. Pulling his coarse work gloves off his bleeding hands, he walked away from the job, found a foster home with a white family, and stayed there for three years, becoming the first Latino to graduate from Gervais High School.

In 1969, Salinas took a position as intern for the Woodburn school district, visiting families with a petition that would help the school district receive federal funding for bilingual education. Back then, most of the Latinos in the area were American families from the Rio Grande Valley. A bilingual program existed—in the form of a single part-time teacher's assistant—but it was for Russian speakers.

After helping Woodburn inch into bilingual ed, Salinas taught, and then he became the principal of Woodburn's Nellie Muir Elementary School before retiring to advocate for Latino kids. Now living close to Portland, he had come to fear that kids like Cheo are not being immersed in English and can avoid interacting with Anglos.

"Woodburn is becoming an ethnically isolated community," he said, "which is a problem if [the kids] want to succeed outside of Woodburn."

Salinas also felt that the Woodburn school district needed to push its kids harder. When the district announced that the high school was outperforming other mostly Hispanic schools, Salinas said angrily that the kids weren't just competing against other Hispanics. For him, the answer to Woodburn's school troubles is dramatic and political. He insists that Latinos in the United States are a modern-day slave class and thinks that no substantial changes will take place in Woodburn until Latino citizens view education as a means of accessing power and pursue it outside of school as well.

"The worst thing we are doing nowadays is giving more to the institution—most people associate education with school, but it needs to be twenty-four/seven," he said. "We need to put resources into the community to aid education rather than just school."

Salinas had many meetings with members of the Woodburn School Board to discuss how the schools could adapt to better serve students. One idea that he had was for each student to have an older mentor, a successful person who would help guide the kid in places where his parents couldn't help. But Salinas felt that his ideas fell on deaf ears, and part of the reason was because the local population in Woodburn did not demand change.

"They said to me, 'The phones are not ringing.' Without external stimulation, you are dependent on the goodwill of the people within the institution who have no motivation to change."

Government bureaucracies may move slowly, but at Woodburn, the number of kids considered English Language Learners grew to the point that the district had to deal with them. In the early part of the immigration wave, administrators weren't sure what to do with kids who didn't speak English. Should they be dropped into classes to sink or swim in a new language? Should they be taught English first, in an immersion program, and then put in regular classes? Should they be taught in Spanish and Russian? Should all classes be bilingual?

Despite decades of non-native English speakers in the schools, classes in Woodburn in the 1990s continued to be taught in English. Spanish speakers who couldn't keep up got half an hour of extra help every day. Because graduation rates and other academic markers had been declining with the increase of non-native English speakers, the district decided it was time to get serious about bilingual education.

Change at Woodburn's schools took on one form as Sherrilynn Rawson, a white linguist who moved to Woodburn from Berkeley in the mid-1990s to work on her doctoral dissertation, ended up becoming an elementary school teacher. While teaching Spanish at Nellie Muir Elementary, Rawson noticed how students who did well in lower grades began struggling as they moved into middle and high school. Many of the kids who spoke Spanish at home couldn't cope with the academic English of high school.

Rawson and others spent eighteen months evaluating different approaches to English as a Second Language (ESL) and bilingual education and sent teams to visit successful programs in other states. The most effective schools all used a similar method of instruction: Two-Way Immersion. In Two-Way Immersion, students start in kindergarten spending about 80 percent of their day speaking Spanish and 20 percent English. In first grade, the percentages shift to about 70 percent Spanish and 30 percent English. By fifth grade, classes are fifty/fifty. Woodburn began its version of Two-Way Immersion—called the English Transition Program—with a single class at Nellie Muir in 1997. By the time the Nellie Muir kindergarteners who participated in the program made it to fourth grade, they were getting noticed. In 2001, the U.S Office of Bilingual Education and Minority Language Affairs named Nellie Muir's English Transition Program one of the top ten bilingual programs in the country.

The change was moving too slowly for kids in the high school, however. Octavio and Cheo spent their first year taking classes in Spanish. When Cheo came to Woodburn High speaking no English, he was also allowed to take the mandatory state test in his native language that first year. But by the second year of schooling, Cheo had only some classes available in his native tongue, and the mandatory tests had to be taken in English. People who favor English immersion over bilingual education point to mandatory tests and a hundred other practical examples as proof of the need for kids to learn English as soon as possible. Proponents of bilingual education point to studies showing that it takes years to become proficient in a second language, especially for kids who don't get any English practice away from school.

For the Woodburn school district, the state test language rule has become an albatross, and people like Principal Laura Lanka insist that if only the state would test her students in Spanish, a huge percentage of the kids who fail state tests would suddenly flourish.

"Imagine if I moved to China, and after one year had to take a college entrance exam in Chinese," she said. "It probably wouldn't work very well. I might be able to get my survival needs across, but I'm certainly not going to know academic Chinese. Or, let me choose an easier language. Italian. I'm certainly not going to know academic Italian after one year. It's just unreasonable to think that you can."

Cheo might have done better with Italian. His command of English grew very slowly, despite his obvious intelligence.

Riding the bus back to Woodburn from his team's most recent victory, singing his songs, Cheo knew that soon high school would be over and he, like all the other kids in Woodburn, would have to work for a living. Not knowing English would mean never getting much of a job. He recognized the stumbling block but he struggled to get past it.

"It is both good and bad," Cheo said about Woodburn. "It's so easy to get by here with just Spanish. That makes it easy to move here. But it also means that you don't have to use English, which makes it hard to leave."

NINE

The Woodburn Curse

We just have the worst luck. Every year we lose in the
playoffs to the team that wins the state championship.
It's the Woodburn curse.

—Martin

On the Thursday afternoon bus ride to McMinnville, Los Perros discussed the upcoming game. Both teams had played five of the eight
regular-season games and neither had lost once. The McMinnville
Grizzlies had been on a tear, and their 7–0 Monday clobbering of
the Newberg Tigers had put them alone in first place in the league.
Woodburn and Tualatin, both with one tie, were in second.

As the coaches and boys discussed the final three games in the
season, they decided that the last two were wins. That left the Mc-
Minnville game as the one real challenge to get through. In the bus,
they figured that whichever team won that night's game would be in
first place and have some good momentum going into the playoffs.

Both teams were based in towns with large Latino communities,
and the McMinnville squad was more than half Latino. If there was
a difference, it was a kid named Frankie Lopez, McMinnville's star
forward, who had already scored twenty-three goals in the season.
As the Bulldogs saw it, the game would come down to their defense
controling Lopez.

Flannigan decided that the key to Lopez was to stick his best
marking back on him and just leave that guy on Lopez the entire
game. He chose Edgar, who had played midfield earlier in the season
before drifting back to defense. Edgar was a quiet, almost diffident
kid off the field, the one senior who had no plans for college and
whose goal in life was to make it as stress-free as possible.

Edgar had been a sharpshooter in junior high when Flannigan

had scouted him, but over the years, it seemed that Edgar's mellow personality had driven him away from the limelight. As a defender he was surprisingly tough, and because Edgar didn't need to be in the middle of the action, Flannigan thought that he might be just the guy to harass Lopez all night long.

The team unloaded the bus on a sidewalk outside of McMinnville High and carried their gear toward a grass field. From the far end of the field came the steady hum of traffic and the boys looked around, spotting their competition, dressed in black with red striping, already warming up near the busy street.

Octavio and Cheo led the team in stretches, followed by a brisk jog. They began to play some keep-away while Carlos practiced deflecting shots to the corners of the goal. Large white clouds blew across the blue sky.

When the game began, it took almost ten minutes before either of the teams gained enough control to make a run at the goal. The ball just seemed to bounce around at midfield, occasionally soaring out to one side before a defender pounded it back in. Then, as Octavio paused on the field near the sideline during a throw-in, Coach Flannigan yelled to him.

"I haven't seen you make your run yet! C'mon, you can do it, you can do it!"

Two minutes later, Octavio drifted to the left side, where he intercepted a pass and dashed with the ball down the sideline, trying to free himself from two defenders. As the three young men closed in on the penalty area, one of the defenders hurled himself forward, kicking the ball over the end line.

Tony ran toward the corner, set the ball down on the right corner, took a few steps back, and looked at his teammates arranging themselves in front of the McMinnville goal. In the background, Tony could hear traffic passing on the street, but he was too focused to pay it any attention. They were twenty-five minutes into the game against the only unbeaten team in the league, and a score here would catapult the Bulldogs into a tie for first place.

From the corner, Tony could make the ball do several things depending on what side of it he kicked. Unless he kicked it straight on, so that the ball didn't spin at all, the ball was going to curve as it flew. If Tony hit it correctly, he could make the ball appear to be going out past the goal before it abruptly shot to the right and into the net. Players who have mastered controlling a ball's curve—David Beckham is one of the best at this—can build a career out of the skill.

The physics behind the often dramatic movement in a soccer ball's path comes from something called the Magnus effect, named after Heinrich Magnus, a nineteenth-century German physicist who studied spinning bullets. What he learned about bullets has been applied to the study of soccer balls, baseballs, volleyballs, and anything else that spins as it travels.

The basic physics behind why a spinning object's flight path bends will be familiar to anyone who knows why an airplane's wing creates lift. As a ball moves forward, air is forced to travel around it. If a ball spins while moving forward, the movement of the air around the outside of the ball becomes uneven. One side of the ball, spinning with the movement of the air, creates less friction than the other side of the ball, spinning against the movement of the air. The difference in friction also means a difference in air pressure, pushing the ball away from the point of greatest drag.

In other words, if Tony kicked the left side of the ball, creating a clockwise spin, the ball would curve to the right.

Tony did just that, the ball leaping away from his foot toward the outer edge of the group gathered before the McMinnville goal, then sliding to the right as it fell, finding Juan at the near post. He leaped up to head the ball, which skipped off his forehead, rolling from right to left in front of the keeper, slipping past two defenders and slowing down in front of Octavio, who lashed out with his right foot. From only ten feet away, it was as sure a setup as any goal can be, but somehow Octavio got his foot too far under the ball and sent it up and over the crossbar. He threw his head back and grabbed his hair, and across the field, near where Coach Flannigan was standing, also holding his head, the bench players collectively groaned.

"Stupid!" Octavio said to himself as he trotted back to midfield. "That was stupid!"

The game shifted back to the middle. For another ten minutes, neither team could put together a run. Then, as Octavio received a pass, a Grizzly came in hard with a dangerously high kick, barely missing Octavio's face. He watched the Grizzly run on, and then he turned to yell at the referee, who hadn't seen the foul. When the referee shrugged his shoulders, Octavio ran after the offending Grizzly and shoved him with both hands, shouting at him in Spanish. They faced off as teammates came running to separate them.

The referee awarded the Grizzly a free kick. The boy aimed the ball toward the left side of the net, exposed behind the Woodburn wall, and missed badly.

Ten minutes later, Octavio stole a McMinnville pass and from thirty yards out, tried a long shot on goal, aiming for the high right corner. The ball whipped between several defenders, over the outstretched arms of the leaping keeper, and continued going over the goal. Coach Flannigan, momentarily motionless while watching the shot, lurched forward in frustration to stomp on the ground and shout to nobody in particular:

"Give us a chance! Dammit! Octavio's going back to his old fieldkicking days!"

Octavio didn't hear Flannigan, but he may as well have. In his mind he began listing all the mistakes he had just made.

As the team's center-midfielder, Octavio's first priority was not to take shots on goal at all. Octavio was supposed to create action. He needed to control the ball and pass it to his teammates. Like most Mexican-born soccer players, Octavio had been trained to play possession soccer, so his passes were low and aimed at the feet, or, sometimes, played to space—aiming the ball at where the feet would soon be. To make an accurate pass, Octavio had to take into consideration the direction that twenty individuals were moving, their relative speeds, the distance the ball must travel, the speed of the grass or artificial turf surface on which they were playing, and the weather. As a midfielder, Octavio usually made passes while running forward, so when he kicked the ball, he had to do so in stride; his timing, as well as his reading of the field and players, must be perfect or the ball would not end up where he wanted it to. In Octavio's eyes, the game was one of perpetually shifting angles: Octavio experienced *fútbol* as geometry in motion.

At times, he got the equation wrong. He pushed too hard, wanting —needing—his teammates to be better than they were, faster, more accurate. The season was half through and he still had not heard from a college coach. He dragged that knowledge around with him like a weight shackled to his foot.

At halftime, Ransom drew Octavio aside and began a gentle but persistent monologue. "*Cálmate, cálmate*," Ransom said, while Octavio stood glaring at the goal in regret. A group of five small boys, perhaps six and seven years old, ran out onto the field, established a keeper, and began scrimmaging in front of the same net that Octavio had recently missed. Octavio looked toward them, listening to Ransom, hands on his hips, nodding his head.

Coach Flannigan gathered the boys around him and smiled.

"Let's start from the back," he said. "I like what I see back there. Carlos is doing a good job of talking, Cheo is doing a good job of positioning, and Edgar, nice work on Frankie. You did such a good job that we were able to free up Luis and Manolo to clog the middle.

"At our midfield, I think we were a little surprised by their speed. They are very fast, so what we need to do is to get quicker touches. They are coming in hard and fast, so if we can do things first touch and know what we want to do once we get the ball, then good things will happen."

Flannigan told the forwards that they, too, needed to speed up their play, and when they got the ball, they needed to look inside.

"They are in a three-five-two formation just like we are. Good teams are like that for a reason; it clogs up the middle. So you'll notice that you don't have much room. That's why, in our offense, sending that center-mid through will help. You forwards and outside mids, if you get through, look back to the middle, there's a big hole here. Let's get Octavio or Cesar coming through on the middle after our forwards."

He stopped and looked over his shoulder at the McMinnville team, also gathered around their coach.

"Listen," he said. "Their goalkeeper is not that good, and you can see from the way they play defense that they know he's not that good. So let's get some shots on him, on target. Make him make the save, because he's not that good. I can live with zero–zero at half, but now it's time. Let's get something going. Keep up the good work, make sure you get some water, and let's go!"

Early in the second half, the game scoreless, McMinnville's star player, Frankie Lopez, was fouled in the penalty box by a Woodburn defender. The bench players stood up to watch Frankie set up his penalty kick. Coach Flannigan stopped pacing to watch; the fans in the stands were silent. In the goal, Carlos bounced up and down on his toes, bent his knees into a crouch, and extended his arms slightly forward, as if he were demonstrating the size of a small fish. Carlos had a theory about PKs. By watching the player's feet just before the shot was taken, he believed he could tell which way a player would kick the ball. He watched Frankie take a few steps back before running forward, and as soon as he saw Frankie plant his right foot, Carlos dove right, trapping the ball between his chest and the field.

Flannigan's arms shot toward the sky; the Woodburn bench players cheered and clapped, and then began to brag about Carlos. He's so good! He might be the best goalie in the state, you know. Frankie stood for a moment staring at Carlos in either disbelief, anger, or admiration, then turned and walked away.

One of the things that Flannigan felt was missing from the team was a true leader. His best players, Octavio, Cheo, and Carlos, were not natural leaders. Flannigan viewed Frankie as an ideal model for a team leader. Frankie was not only the team's best player, he was also its on-field general, cajoling, encouraging, and driving his teammates to perform at their peak. Frankie was also Hispanic and a good student, and he would later attend the University of Portland and play on their Division One soccer team.

Ten minutes later, freshman Jovanny stood on the sidelines with the ball over his head, waiting for a whistle to restart play. Octavio, standing about fifteen yards away in the middle of the field, began to run toward Jovanny as the whistle blew, momentarily leaving his defender behind. Jovanny took two steps and hurled the ball down the left sideline. It bounced once, rolled, and Octavio was there to collect it, a defender on his heels and another coming in fast from the right.

His attention on the ball, Octavio didn't see the second player coming in. Tapping the ball once, he planted his right leg, swinging the left to collect the ball before it rolled out of bounds, meaning to start a run toward the goal. But his left foot never connected. Instead, the player on the right slide-tackled the ball out of bounds and took out Octavio as well. It was as violent as a football hit. Octavio tumbled left, spun in the air, slammed into the grass, and rolled, coming to rest on his back with his hands clasped around his right knee, writhing in obvious pain.

As Octavio lay on the grass, he felt for a moment that he was back on the field in Irapuato, and he knew that the crunch he felt in his knee was not just a minor injury. He was thinking, "No, not again!"

For several minutes, Octavio lay rolling from side to side, clutching his knee, while milling players wandered to the sidelines to get a drink. Laurie and the McMinnville trainer arrived in a golf cart, loaded him into the back, and drove off the field. None of his teammates paid him much attention when he arrived at the Woodburn bench. The trainers prodded his knee and produced a bag of ice for it. But the Bulldogs, who had all seen Octavio go down hurt before, kept their attention on the game. Octavio sat in the cart, the bag of ice cubes plastic-wrapped to his knee, his face twisted in pain.

With Octavio out, McMinnville drove downfield and took a hard shot from the upper-left corner of the penalty box. Carlos took two steps and leaped to meet the ball, knocking it up and over the net. This set McMinnville up for a corner kick. The kicker placed the ball down, took a couple of steps back, and raised his hand to call a play. When he kicked, the ball soared over most of the players to a small group standing near the far goalpost. Carlos slipped, falling to one knee, and the ball slid past him into the net.

Despite several more shots on the McMinnville goal, Woodburn never managed to score, losing the game 1–0. Octavio limped over to the bus on crutches, pulling himself up the steps with a tremendous grimace, looking as though he'd suffered a back-alley beating.

None of his teammates stepped forward to help; most looked the other way.

That night, Octavio didn't sleep. The pain in his knee was too bad for a couple of Advil to help, and when he tried to roll over, it felt as if glass was grinding inside the joint. By morning, his knee had swelled to the size of a grapefruit and was a nasty purple color. His uncle helped him into the car and took him to the hospital.

The X-rays were inconclusive. Nothing was broken, nothing big and obvious was out of place, torn, or otherwise visibly damaged. The doctors recommended that he make an appointment to have an MRI, and Octavio went back home. He knew he was probably not going to play again that season, and the pain in his heart hurt more than the pain in his knee.

For Octavio, the knee injury meant more than just not being on the team. As he limped across campus on crutches in the coming weeks, he knew that his hopes of going to college might be over, for how would he pay for school if not on an athletic scholarship? He began to wonder if he should bother trying to stay in the United States at all. Standing on the sidelines, watching the team practice, he thought about this a lot.

The pull that Mexico—that his family and familiar things—had on him had never left. Since arriving in Oregon, he had thought about returning to Mexico every once in a while, usually when he felt low. He desperately wanted to go back for a visit, but without the right papers, returning to the United States was expensive and risky.

There was another reason for him not to leave the United States. Her name was Anita.

Octavio had first seen Anita when the boys' team returned from an away game his junior year. A varsity girls' soccer game was taking place, and Coach Flannigan urged the boys to head over to support the girls. The boys didn't need to be told twice. As Octavio lined up along the fence with the rest of his teammates, he noticed a particularly cute midfielder, whose hair bounced as she ran. Later, he saw that she was a pretty good player.

Over the next couple of weeks, Octavio learned that this girl's name was Anita, that she was not dating anyone, that she had been

THE BOYS FROM LITTLE MEXICO

born in the United States to Mexican immigrants, and that she was a serious student. He approached his courtship of Anita the way he approached most things. He thought about it for a long time, doubting himself, watching her from a distance. His friends, Cheo especially, encouraged him to talk to her, but he wanted to do it right. He wanted to be a proper gentleman. It was wintertime before he took any action.

Like a nineteenth-century bachelor, Octavio wrote Anita a letter, put it in an envelope, and gave it to a mutual friend to deliver. The friend, perhaps not understanding the importance of the document, passed it off to Anita with a dismissive, "Here," and walked away. Anita opened it, thinking it was from the boy who had just walked away.

The letter said:

Dear Anita:
You look like you are a good person. I would like to meet you and talk to you. Maybe we can be friends or even more than friends. We can meet and just let God decide.
                                                                    —Octavio

Anita, an adorable girl with a bright and easy smile, looked at it carefully. That's really old-fashioned, she thought. Then she thought, who in the world is Octavio?

It took her a moment before she figured it out. For the past couple of months, some friends had been telling her that there was a guy named Octavio who liked her a lot, and she had asked them to point him out. When they did, she looked at him closely, thinking, how does he know that he likes me if he has never spoken with me? Her friends had also told her that Octavio played on the varsity team, which Anita found weird, because she knew some people on the varsity team, and although she couldn't go to all the games, she did see them in practice. She had never even noticed Octavio.

He's not my type, she thought.

However, Octavio had taken the time to write a nice letter, so she wrote back to him, suggesting that they meet and talk some time. A couple of weeks later, the two of them met by chance in the lunchroom and had a short conversation. Soon they were talking and texting every day.

What eventually won Anita over was Octavio's old-fashioned nature, formed out of the stratified and oddly formal life of rural Mexico. He sent her flowers, gave her small gifts, approached her parents to request permission to go out with her. They spoke on the phone often over the summer between Octavio's junior and senior year and by the start of the 2005 fall soccer season, they were dating seriously, and Anita decided that Octavio was her type after all.

Octavio had left a serious girlfriend in Guanajuato when he came to the United States, had broken up with her rather than leave her not knowing when he would come back. He had missed the girl terribly and had not been interested in another girlfriend. Having found Anita, however, Octavio was reluctant to lose her as well. As he moped along the hallways on his crutches and reluctantly watched practices, Octavio's heart tugged in two directions at once.

TEN

Reading and Writing

I think the problem is multigenerational. There are families
who have been in the area for three or four generations.
They need to provide leadership and provide a direction
for the newcomers, but they don't do that.

—Miguel Salinas

In Woodburn, you can almost draw a chart correlating education changes with foreign names in the high school yearbook. In 1955, Fidel and Joanne Gaviola were the only Hispanic faces looking out from the yearbook pages. In 1967, there were only three: Lydia Rodriquez, Rudolph Medina, and Margaret Medina, trying to fit in with a full bouffant hairdo and horn-rimmed glasses.

By 1973, the number of Hispanics had grown to a couple of dozen, although many of the Hispanic students—perhaps even a majority back then—belonged to families of migrant workers and didn't always stick around for the entire school year. By the early 1980s, when onetime *Woodburn Independent* education reporter Michelle Te was a Woodburn High student, the number of Latino students was still low. Te recalled just a handful of Hispanic students who stayed the entire school year. At the time, she said, when people thought about bilingual education, or large-scale immigration, they thought about the Russian families, whose children made up about 15 percent of the student body.

"Back then," she said, "none of the kids paid much attention to the Latinos. I mean, nobody thought of them as a different group. I think there just weren't enough of them. "

By 1986, the year that IRCA passed, the number of Latino students had grown to over 10 percent of the student body. Look at a yearbook from the era and you'll see that names like Smith and Flanders still easily outnumber names like Arellano and Sanchez.

Over the next five years, though, the high school and the percentage of Latino students grew quickly. In the meantime, Michelle
Te graduated, moved away to attend college, lived in another state,
then returned in 1991 to take her first newspaper job at the *Woodburn
Independent*. The changes she saw stunned her.

"Walking down the hallway when I came back, it was completely
different," she said. "When I was there, it was still a quiet little town
and the high school was mostly white kids. I think there were about
five Hispanics when I was in high school, and they were all from
Texas."

But in 1991, she saw that nearly half of the students were Latinos
—and she heard most of them speaking Spanish. The change was so
abrupt that for a while she found it difficult to understand how, in five
or six years, the school could have been so transformed.

"The school didn't have a lot of Spanish-speaking teachers or
staff, so for a while, it was really hard for everybody." Te herself realized that she was resistant to the sudden influx of Spanish speakers, wondering how all these new people would affect her nice, small
town, and wondering if the school should adapt itself to their language needs. Why not just force all the kids to immerse in English?

"I wasn't sure that I liked it, but then I went to a school, one
of the elementary schools, and I saw this little boy crying. He just
couldn't communicate. And I thought, 'How would I feel if this were
my kid?'"

Other people familiar with the high school experienced similar
shock at the speed of the transformation. Hank Vrendenberg, who
taught social sciences at Woodburn High from 1972 to 1995, was one
of those caught off guard.

"The first immigrants we had in any numbers were the Russian
Old Believers," he said. "They came here after they were driven out
of several other countries, and settled all around town. It was hard
to keep them in school. The boys would leave to work on the family construction business or go fishing in Alaska, and the girls would
leave when they were fifteen or sixteen to get married. I remember it
was years and years before we had a female Old Believer graduate."

The Old Believers had arrived as a group in the 1960s, all at once, so their transition was dramatic. But the number of Latinos grew slowly, a few more each year, until the 1980s. Then, suddenly, it seemed to Vrendenberg, he looked around the campus and there were Hispanic kids everywhere.

As Hispanic students began to arrive in higher numbers, Vrendenberg also saw the first community resistance to the kids. When he had started teaching in the 1970s, there were so few Latino kids at the high school that nobody felt threatened enough to pester them. But going to a soccer game in the early 1980s, before the team was very good, Vrendenberg was surprised to hear a steady stream of racial slurs coming mostly from the opposing team's parents, and he recalled a basketball game played away, during which the kids from the other team wore sombreros and lined up to taunt the Bulldogs coming off the school bus.

Years later, Vrendenberg was knocking on doors to gather support for an upcoming school bond vote. He was in Senior Estates, a large retirement community on the western edge of town that—being full of old, white people—had a large number of active voters and was the city's political powerhouse.

"No bond could pass without their backing," he said. "And it could be really hard to get people to vote on school bonds. They didn't want their money going to help Hispanic kids. I remember talking to a guy at his door, and he said some of the most racist comments I have ever heard. I was shocked to find out that people still thought that way."

The rapid immigration had other effects. Vrendenberg, who left teaching for the athletic director position in the mid-1990s, estimated that even in 1996, a quarter of all the kids he oversaw playing sports were new every year.

"Back then, they were still mostly migrant workers and would go home over Christmas; a lot of times they'd be gone January and February. Russian students would be gone during all of their saints' holidays." In other words, due to cultural issues, kids were missing large chunks of their school year.

Then there were the parents. One of the missing ingredients in Woodburn High's educational environment was parental participation. Unlike previous groups, most of the new Latino immigrants didn't take part in the traditional school support system: bake sales, car washes, PTA meetings. And since parental involvement pops up in study after study as one of the biggest factors driving student success, administrators realized that unless they could get parents involved, it didn't matter what else was done in the school district.

When Michelle Te had her own children, she considered not sending them to the Woodburn school district, although she lived in town. She knew other people who sent their kids to North Marion, the neighboring district, because they didn't think Woodburn's schools would give their children a good enough education. On the other hand, Te wanted to support the public school system, and she liked the idea of her own kids growing up bilingual.

As white parents often do, she started a parent group as soon as she had her kids in school. "The school is like seventy percent Hispanic, so I tried to get some Hispanic parents, but it was really hard to get anybody to show up, and when they did show up, it was really hard to get them to say anything." Despite her years of covering education and living with Latino neighbors, Te found this frustrating. "It seems like they just don't care about education. I know they do care about their kids' education, but they don't do anything about it."

It was a classic cultural misunderstanding. In Mexico, schoolteachers are treated with great respect and given a wide degree of authority and autonomy in their treatment of children. What U.S. school administrators expect—the busy parent who wants to know exactly how Johnny spends his day and what the teachers are going to do to get his grades up—was not what the parents of Woodburn High's new students felt comfortable doing.

Principal Laura Lanka put it more kindly:

"I think parents are totally fish out of water here. In Mexico, they would never let their kids stay out late, never let them get away with what they do here. But here the child and parent become totally mixed up. The kid can speak English, the parent can't. They have to rely on their child to do all this stuff for them. It's a total mix-up, and the kid begins to not respect the parent. I saw it all the time in my office where a child would be so disrespectful to their parents. It was just a surprise. The parent would say to me, 'In America, you just allow all these things to happen.'

"The perception many of our kids' parents have is that this country is out of control. This country doesn't make their kids do homework, this country doesn't . . . I would always sort of be in shock when they would say the United States is so easy, high school is so easy. I would be sitting there thinking, 'Your child is flunking. How can you tell me that high school is so easy?' I think what they were saying is that in Mexico, the school would have laid the law down. The teachers in Mexico would have laid the law down. As parents, they lay the law down about social things. But for them, everything is mixed up in this country."

In 2006, the Chalkboard Project, a nonprofit organization aiming to improve Oregon schools, surveyed low-income parents across Oregon. They found some interesting and some surprising results: Hispanic parents volunteered an average of three days a year at school while white parents donated thirty days in a school year. On the other hand, while nearly a third of Hispanic parents helped their kids with homework five nights a week, a little more than 10 percent of white parents did the same.

Not only were Hispanic parents not involving themselves in their children's school and not making demands of teachers, they also seemed to have different expectations than white members of the community. Hispanic and Anglo parents had a completely different view of adulthood, for example. By the time a kid made it to high school, many Hispanic parents seemed to feel that they were old enough to take care of themselves. Coaches saw this on the soccer field. In elementary school, in middle school, parents showed up to watch games and signed their kids up for club teams. In high school, those same parents stopped going to games, and their kids stopped playing club sports.

Octavio's girlfriend, Anita, observed that high-school-age kids were old enough to make their own decisions about homework. "When you're in elementary school, your parents do have a large part in making sure you do your homework, but when you are older, when you're in high school, it becomes your responsibility."

José Romero, whose own family had lived in a small southern California town for many generations before he became the first kid to go to college, feels that not only do Latino parents have different expectations of their children than do white parents, they also don't feel comfortable challenging state institutions, especially schools. He saw such discomfort in his own parents before he moved to Oregon and began teaching at Colegio Cesar Chavez, a tiny college near Woodburn that recruited students heavily from local farm workers in the 1970s.

"Sometimes parents write themselves off as the generation that is lost so the next generation won't be lost. White parents won't put up with any mistreatment of their children. They will demand a meeting with the principal and the teacher and call the board member that they know from the Rotary Club. But Mexican parents don't want to make waves, so they will ignore it, tell their kids to suck it up.

"They can be ashamed of themselves and of their appearance. They don't want to come. Only have one car, who's going to take care of the kids, etc. They don't have the time to do those things. Especially if you are working at a factory and have no control over leaving in the middle of the day."

Then there are attitudes about gender roles. Latino men are less likely to graduate high school than Latinas, who are also more likely to go to college than their male peers. Although college attendance rates for both black and white men has increased since the early 1980s, for Latino men it hasn't budged, hovering around 18 percent for decades. Hispanic women, on the other hand, have increased their numbers in college, today earning over 60 percent of all degrees by Hispanics. That gap appears to be widening.

Not only are Hispanic boys not succeeding as often as Hispanic girls, they are not even reaching for the same opportunities. For example, teacher Jaime Escalante, the true-life subject of the 1988 Hollywood film *Stand and Deliver*, taught courses in advanced calculus in an impoverished neighborhood in Los Angeles. The students in his classes were a self-selecting group—that is, they chose his class after completing work in feeder courses, knowing how demanding he was and how dedicated they would have to be. The majority of his students were female.

Perhaps a reason for this is that Latino males have different expectations and responsibilities at home, and they are more likely to drop out to work and support their family than girls are. Whatever the reason, teachers report that young Latinas are more involved in their classrooms than young Latinos. Marty Limbird, a community college soccer coach and instructor in nearby Salem, said he sees this regularly.

"In the classes that I teach, Spanish-speaking females are much more likely to ask questions or ask for help, just in general. It seems very segregated by sex, very different between males and females. I notice that a lot on our soccer team. It took a long time for the guys to open up to me as a peer rather than just a coach. I think I have a better relationship with them now where they will open up to me, where before a lot of the guys would hide if they are having issues or not want to talk to me about it. I think they really try to shield their shortcomings in classes."

At Woodburn High, poor performance by Latino kids translated into a failing school. By 1999, when Laura Lanka took over as principal, Woodburn High had an almost 10 percent dropout rate (an improvement from almost 15 percent in 1996–97), and only a third of the students—mostly the white third—were taking the SAT in preparation for college. In 1998, the school had received a Low rating from the state Department of Education, meaning that student performance on statewide math and reading tests had actually declined in the previous four years.

Lanka, a former French teacher who lived in upscale Lake Oswego, came in with big plans, the quintessential bleeding-heart liberal. She began making promises to kids about getting them into college that she soon found she couldn't keep. And for a while, she felt adrift at the school.

"There was so much when I came on as principal that I didn't know. I felt that I had come into a school that didn't have a college-going attitude, and not just the kids, but the parents, the teachers, everybody. That seemed strange to me. I wanted to know how come we don't have college prep courses here, how come the only college we talk about for our students is community college? How come, for our best and brightest, we only think about two state schools?"

Lanka had never been in a school like Woodburn before. She didn't speak Spanish, and she came from an upper-class white culture that had completely different values than the kids she was now in charge of. For one thing, she hadn't considered the consequences for her students of being born outside the United States.

"At first, one of the things I told students was that, if you are prepared, I will find a way for you to go to college. There are so many scholarships available, especially to Hispanic students, that if you are ready, there are loads of schools that would be thrilled to have you. But my home school contact came to me and said, 'You don't know what you are saying.' It was like two worlds not communicating."

"She told me that not all Latinos have the right to go to college. I didn't understand this whole undocumented business."

It was a wake-up call for Lanka. She decided that if she could not get more of her qualified kids into even a state college because of their documentation status, then she would change the law.

In 2003, Lanka began by finding two sympathetic Oregon legislators, Peter Courtney (D) and Billy Dalto (R). They crafted a bill that would allow any graduate of an Oregon high school to attend an Oregon state university for the cost of a state resident, regardless of the individual's legal status in the United States. The students had to attend high school in Oregon for at least three years and declare their intention to become U.S. citizens.

As Representative Courtney pointed out, most of the undocumented immigrant children living in the United States were there because of decisions their parents made.

"As a politician, I would hope that people wouldn't hold my children accountable for something their dad did."

Representatives of the Oregon University System, which has seven campuses, estimated that the bill would bring in an additional 20 to 250 students per year, out of a total of nearly 80,000 students.

In other words, the impact on the system would be next to nothing. However, a legislative accountant came up with a completely different number: $800,000, the amount the bill would drain from the university system in lost tuition.

Lanka thought that this was absurd, especially since the students hoping to get a degree under the potential new law wouldn't go to college unless they paid in-state tuition. The bill wouldn't drain a dollar—in fact, it would add income.

The legislation, House Bill 10, was immediately opposed by the group Oregonians for Immigration Reform, which insisted that not only would the bill force the state to lose money, college slots would be stolen away from citizens and given to people who shouldn't even be in the country.

Courtney and Dalto pressed on, arguing that many other states, including California, Utah, New York, Texas, Illinois, Oklahoma, and Washington, all had passed similar laws. However, the bill failed in committee and was replaced by a watered-down version that gave in-state tuition to legal residents who had graduated from an Oregon high school even if their parents were not legal residents.

Despite the weakness of the new law, many people in Oregon remained resistant. Representative Jeff Kropf, a Republican, said, "When they have obtained American citizenship, let them then have the full rights and privileges of American citizenship. This should not be granted just because they are here as a student, as a resident alien."

If HB 10 had passed, one of the first students who almost certainly would have benefited from it was Octavio. With his grades and desire, he likely would have received an academic scholarship to pay for most of, if not all, his education at the University of Oregon or Portland State University. Without HB 10, however, a kid like Octavio, even with a scholarship, would need to pony up the difference between $3,000 a quarter in tuition and $13,000, the difference between in-state and out-of-state tuition.

Unlike many previous Woodburn soccer teams, all but one of the 2005 varsity seniors were applying to college. Octavio, Cheo, Ramon,

Javier, Betos—all applied to local Oregon colleges such as Portland State University and Western Oregon University. Even Cesar, who worried that going to college would make his family suffer financially, sent out applications. Only easygoing, sweet-smiling Edgar, whose solution to pressure was to glide around it like water around a rock, had no college aims. In early 2006, when the other seniors were waiting anxiously to hear back from college admissions, Edgar attended one class and wondered when to apply to an apprenticeship program through the local plumber's union.

Cheo and Octavio applied to several schools together, but the one they really had their eye on was George Fox University, a private Quaker liberal-arts school with a Division Three soccer team. At George Fox, as at other Division Three schools, admissions were based strictly on academics. Students accepted to the school could then try out for a team. Having no athletic scholarships to offer, Division Three soccer schools often recruit locally and pay more attention to high school teams than Division One universities.

Manfred Tschan, a Swiss native who had coached at George Fox for eighteen years, recognized Octavio and Cheo when they called to set up an appointment.

"Woodburn has had a good program for a long time," Tschan said later. "I've gone to a lot of games. We've always contacted kids who have stood out, but we've only had one kid from Woodburn on the team before. We've had interest in others, but a lot of them didn't show enough interest when they found out that we didn't have athletic scholarships. Or they didn't make it academically."

Going to visit had been Octavio's idea. As a junior, he had received a letter of interest from Tschan. The two boys had met with the coach and walked around campus. It was a rare clear day in February. The campus, a small, quiet set of buildings surrounded by native firs and cedars, excited Octavio and Cheo. It seemed like a calm place, a good place to study. They thought the coach was nice. He seemed patient and sincere in his interest in them.

Tschan had a similar impression of the two boys. He was also thrilled with their soccer knowledge.

"Both are skillful and both have a natural quickness and love for the game that is hard to match. They have a savvy about the game, an understanding of it at a different level than American students, just from being from a soccer country.

"Everything American kids do is structured. They have always played with coaches and always against kids of the same age. They don't have casual games. These guys grew up with pickup games, developing their skills against adults. For prototypical college players, they're kind of small, but that's more than made up for by their savvy."

Although he hadn't guaranteed a spot for either of them, Tschan felt confident that both boys could succeed on the team. And he also felt confident that they could be successful students.

Cheo echoed his feelings. Unlike his best friend, Cheo's identity wasn't tied up in being a good soccer player. He was willing to go to whatever school took him, even Portland State University, which didn't have a men's soccer team.

"I want to play, but at the same time I want to study. If we go to George Fox, then I think it's the best, because I can play, but my main goal is to study. To get a career. You can play at the age of thirty or something like that. I want to study because it is my future. I have all my life to play soccer."

ELEVEN

Playing Rough

We've had some kids go on to college and do well, but not
enough. We'd have kids who would say, "I can't play. I don't
have shoes," so we'd buy shoes for them. I think it's a cultural endemic that these kids don't get the support. If they
got the support, just think how successful they could be.

—Coach Brian Flannigan

The loss to McMinnville dropped Woodburn into third place. Mc-
Minnville sat alone in first, trailed by Tualatin. The top four teams
from each league go to the playoffs, so with only two games left in
the regular season, against Tigard and longtime rival Canby, the
Bulldogs suddenly faced the very real possibility that they might not
make the playoffs for the first time in twenty years.

With Octavio out from his injury, the Bulldogs tried fitting different players into the center-mid slot. Against Tigard, Flannigan
used Martin, Juan, and Cheo. The team still lost 1–0, the players
trotting off the field to slump onto the grass near their bench, staring
blankly at nothing while Flannigan told them how disappointed he
was. After the Tigard loss, with a single game left, Woodburn and
Forest Grove were tied for fourth place, the lowest possible playoff
berth. Woodburn had the tiebreaker, so if both teams won or both
teams lost, Woodburn would still advance. However, if Forest Grove
won its final game and Woodburn lost, the playoff streak would end.

Coach Flannigan approached the final regular season game
against Canby with an ambivalent attitude. Canby's record was poor;
the game should go to Woodburn. However, Canby was the team's
fiercest rival, partially because the two towns were only ten miles
apart, but also because the Canby coach, Scott Enyart, was another
ex-Woodburn player who had been the assistant coach when Mike
Flannigan played.

Back in 1987, when then–head coach Greg Baisch quit his coaching job, Enyart applied for but lost the job to Brian Flannigan, Mike's uncle and adoptive father. According to Brian, Enyart had nursed a grudge ever since.

"They tend to play rough with us," Brian Flannigan commented at practice. "They would love to knock us out of the playoffs."

Woodburn's sudden fall in the standings also started to chew away at the boys' nerves. Following the Tigard game, everybody seemed on edge. During one scrimmage, Carlos sat on the bench, annoyed. He saw everybody making obvious mistakes, not passing well, not thinking, not playing as a team. Finally, he began to yell at whoever had the ball.

"Pass it, *güey!* Pass it!"

On the field, Tony started to get irritated. It seemed Carlos wouldn't stop yelling, and nobody was telling him to shut up.

Flannigan blew his whistle, putting the bench players in and sitting the others. Tony watched Carlos run downfield with the ball. Still annoyed, he shouted for Carlos to pass it every time he received the ball.

"Pass it, *güey!*"

"Shut up!" Carlos finally yelled back.

Tony didn't.

At the end of the scrimmage, Carlos walked directly and aggressively toward Tony. Some of the other players turned to watch. Carlos had forty pounds on Tony and the body of a full-grown man. He stopped a foot away from his friend and stared at him hard. Tony returned the glare.

"Don't you ever yell at me again," Carlos said.

"Then don't yell at us!" Tony snapped back.

Carlos cocked his right fist, his body twisting slightly as if preparing to throw a punch. He stood there for a moment, then dropped his arm, turned, and stalked away.

Coach Flannigan knew that Carlos didn't want to fight other kids on the team, especially Tony, who was probably his closest friend. It was not the first time they had had this kind of falling out. Both boys had tempers and easily triggered feelings of injustice. But the coach thought that it seemed less like a personal problem between Tony and Carlos and more of a sign of the team's frustration.

"They had high expectations early on," he said. "The first meeting we had as a team, some of the guys came right out and said that they wanted to win league, and wanted to win state. I thought, Great, I'm glad they want it. But it also made me a little worried. I wasn't sure if they realized just how much work they were going to have to put in to get there. I think we never fully recovered from losing Octavio, and by the end of the season, guys were just getting on each others' nerves."

Carlos regretted his threatening action later. Tony had been one of the first boys to befriend him when he started playing for Omar, when they were freshmen and Carlos and his brothers were living with their foster family in a mobile home at the end of a short gravel road next door to a Russian Christmas tree farm. Still being new to Gervais, Carlos didn't have many friends at the time.

One of Carlos's favorite memories was the first time he went out with the guys who were on Omar's team, the guys who now made up his circle of friends—Juan, Tony, Martin. It was during the annual Fiesta Mexicana and the boys were cruising the grounds, stopping to talk to girls. Carlos, normally a confident, outgoing kid, felt a little out of place. But he was pleased that the group had accepted him—it was almost as if getting on Omar's team had given him a new family —and he didn't want to ruffle any feathers. It was just nice to walk around and belong.

Being on Omar's club team had given Carlos a door into another world where he was surrounded by friends and had adults who were dependable and whom he could talk to. After discovering this, he began to try and spend as much time as possible in this new world, away from the Gervais foster home.

It wasn't that his foster parents were cruel. They weren't. But they also weren't *family*. They were just paid caretakers, and the more time he spent away from them, the more he resented them.

In 2003, after four years of frustration with his foster parents, Carlos finally reached an emotional dead end. He came home from school, walked straight to his room, and locked his door. His foster parents knocked on his door. He didn't answer. When he left the room, he ignored their questions.

He spent the evening in bed with earphones on, listening to hip-hop and staring at the ceiling, thinking about leaving. He did the same the next night, and the next. After about two weeks, he decided. It was around ten thirty at night. He got out of bed and stood up. Running away was easy: pull open the window, climb into the backyard, hop the fence, and walk across a fallow field to the train tracks. He knew from friends that a steady jog down the tracks would get him into Woodburn in about fifteen minutes. He pulled on his sweatpants, his sweatshirt, and his sneakers, hesitated, and then sat down on his bed, thinking, Shit, I'm going to do this.

But he didn't. His caseworker, a young woman he trusted enough to share his runaway fantasy with, had told him that leaving the foster home would hurt his ability to negotiate with DHS and make them less likely to grant requests, such as paying for his soccer dues. So he sat there, paralyzed by the implications behind staying and going.

His plan was to run to the Mendozas' house. Pat had offered him a place in their home a couple of months before, telling Carlos that she and Omar would be his foster parents if he wanted. But he had responded the way Carlos responded to any inquiries about his needs. He waved it off, saying, "Nah, I'm okay."

For all his impulsiveness and his inability to sit still, Carlos was not self-destructive. He didn't drink or smoke or take drugs. He had his eye on his future, on playing soccer in a Division One school, maybe UCLA, and after that, going pro. That night, he fought back the desire to run and the need to leave. He lay down with all his sweats still on, the darkness outside the window still tugging at his feet. Eventually, he fell asleep.

After a few more days of the silent treatment from Carlos, Carlos's foster father called Omar and asked him to talk to Carlos, to find out what the problem was. Omar drove his green pickup over to get him. They went inside Omar's dark, trophy-strewn ranch home and sat down in the living room to watch television. As Carlos recalled it, Pat came out and settled in beside them.

"I hate it over there," Carlos said. "So, if you're still serious about letting me move in, I'd like to do it."

"Okay," said Pat immediately. "We'd like that."

Carlos nodded.

"Hang on," Omar said. "Are you sure you want to live with me? I mean, you know I can be an asshole. You think I'm any different at home?"

"I don't care," said Carlos. "I don't want to go home. If you don't want me, I'll run away and go someplace else."

"What about your brothers?" asked Omar.

"I think they should stay," said Carlos.

"No way," Omar said. "If you're moving in, they're coming, too."

Two days later, his caseworker came to his school and listened. They talked for thirty minutes, and before leaving she told him that she would start the paperwork immediately. His current foster family wouldn't have to know anything until the move happened.

About a month later, the caseworker called the Gervais foster parents and explained that Carlos and his brothers were leaving. Carlos wasn't home when she called, so his brothers found out from their foster parents that they were leaving, not from Carlos. Carlos had been afraid that they wouldn't be able to keep the secret. The next day, when Omar and Pat came to pick them up, Carlos and his brothers were playing basketball in front of the house, their belongings piled up by the curb. Their foster parents were at the DHS office protesting the switch.

Tino and the Mendozas' son O.J. were graduating from eighth grade that evening, so the entire unwieldy group headed to the mall to buy clothes before dropping Alex and Carlos off at their house. Carlos spent his first evening at Omar's watching TV with his brother. It felt wonderful. At Omar's, Carlos thought, *good things are going to happen.*

By the time the Canby game arrived, the fight between Tony and Carlos had blown over, and the two boys kidded each other as they dropped their backpacks near the team bench. Coach Flannigan walked by them, heading over to shake hands with Coach Enyart from Canby, feeling awkward.

Coach Flannigan expected the game to be rough. Woodburn needed to win, and should win, but he didn't want to tempt fate by thinking that. His anxiety about the game had shown up in the locker room in the no-nonsense speech he gave that focused on the players' mental states.

"See yourselves coming out, not just the first five minutes, not just the first ten minutes, but the entire game, playing at the highest level of intensity. If you get tired, we've got guys to come in for you. The problem is, you haven't been getting tired because you haven't been playing hard enough to get tired. So give it everything you got, all right?" he said. "Let some guys on the bench show what they're worth.

"Today I'm going to make sure that I get substitutes in so that you can play with that intensity. So get out there, get the goal early, play our style of soccer. Let's take care of business. Remember, this is Canby, a team we've had circled on our schedule all year long!"

After describing the formation, Coach Flannigan praised Cheo as an attacking center-midfielder in front of the rest of the team, hoping to light a fire under his players.

"He's going to do a great job for us. He's fast, he's going to make those runs for us, and he's got a killer instinct. He's probably the most intense player on the team, and I want to put that most intense player in a place where he can help us.

"I think O.J. is probably the second most intense player on the team when he gets fired up. I don't know what we have to do to get him fired up. I know his dad would say to grab him by the back of the hair and shake his head, Carlos would say to call him a pussy—I don't know what it's going to take. But get fired up! You're a better player when you're a bit on edge. I wouldn't say that about everybody, but O.J., sometimes I think you respond better when you're a bit on edge. I wouldn't want anybody to kick him in the nuts or anything, but let's see what you can do."

He went on in the same vein: intensity, intensity, intensity. Play your hardest, give it your all. He sounded like Octavio.

"This is a game where it doesn't matter if we lose by one goal or five goals. I'm ready to pull the trigger on any sub today and to do anything we can to win. That's where I'm coming from today and hopefully you will as well. And hey, we're at home. We should have some good fan support. So let's go out there today and protect our field. Remember, this is a team that played dirty against us last year, talked bad about us in the paper, knocked us out of first place last year—this is a team that you should have a lot of motivation to play hard against."

When Flannigan finished and offered Coach Ransom the opportunity to speak, Ransom stepped forward, rubbing his chin, and cleared his throat.

"Okay," he said. "I'll just tell you guys a story. When I was young, I used to be skinny and fast and I would play out here," he indicated the midfield on the white board where Flannigan had drawn the day's formation.

"I remember this one game I was playing. I was young and I was confused. I was playing with a guy, a really good player, named Dimas. And I came running in and he had the ball and I was just standing there kind of twitching, and he yelled at me, 'Go!' He was mad at me. And this happened a few times and he kept yelling at me, 'Go! Run!'

"Finally, I said, 'But I don't know where to go!'

"And he told me, 'It doesn't matter! Just go! Just run!'

"That's what I was thinking about when I was watching you guys in practice yesterday. We're not getting away from the ball. It doesn't matter where you go. Just run away from the ball. Running away from the ball makes things happen! Just move, move, move. Even if you don't get the ball, you are pulling guys away, maybe you're opening things up for other people. So run! Run run run run run! Okay?"

Coach Flannigan stepped forward again.

"Okay. How are we going to play this game?"

"Intense!" shouted Carlos.

"That's right. Intensity! Play this like it's the last game you will ever play. All right. Let's go out on Intensity."

"Intensity!" they all shouted.

As the last regular-season game of the year, it was also Senior Appreciation Night, and Coach Flannigan busied himself around his seven seniors like a little old lady fussing over her cats. He had the boys in a row on the sidelines in front of the Bulldog bench, talking to them, straightening their collars, making jokes. Behind the seniors, the younger players chortled and spoke with mock seriousness about the occasion. The seniors all looked uncomfortable and embarrassed as they stood waiting to cross the soccer pitch.

Athletic Director Greg Baisch was talking into an underpowered portable PA system on the other side of the field, and to the players sitting on the Woodburn bench, or standing beside it, it sounded as if Baisch was on a bad long-distance connection. The stands were unusually full, for this was the one game that the seniors' parents (and, sometimes, families too) would all show up for. The parents and the boys' brothers and sisters sat on the aluminum bleachers across the field, watching the seniors intently.

Baisch, holding a microphone in his hand, began to talk, and the words that screeched from the PA system sounded like destinations crackling from a broken speaker in a Greyhound station.

"Seegarruk!" the boys heard.

The seniors looked at each other with furrowed brows.

"Cee mo fraik grin brackle!" Baisch insisted.

Coach Flannigan pushed Cesar forward, and the soft-spoken young man walked slowly toward the fans, who began diligently clapping.

"Ho the jrg grim prow!" Baisch said, and Flannigan gave a nudge to Cheo, who briefly looked back at the underclassmen behind him, now giggling like schoolgirls.

One by one, the broken syllables boomed forth and Coach Flannigan indicated which of the boys was to walk forward: Ramon, Betos, Javier.

Baisch gurgled, and Coach Flannigan nodded to Octavio, now standing stiffly and self-consciously with his crutches tucked under his arms, a blue foam brace around his knee, his bright red jacket gently waving in the breeze. Coach Flannigan pushed him, smiling, and Octavio swung the crutches forward onto the grass, lifting up his right leg so that his foot skipped over the tips of the grass blades. He swung forward once, twice, then turned to see Edgar stroll past him, feeling himself slow-moving, no longer the athlete who had recently played four complete *fútbol* games in a single day without feeling tired.

A sudden flash of anger hit him, the way it always did, as if a switch had been turned on, and he threw the crutches to the field and continued crossing with a defiant hobble. To people who didn't know Octavio, it was a melodramatic gesture. His friends, such as Coach Ransom, just shook their heads. Octavio joined the other boys in the center of the field, where they were handed bouquets of roses and treated to a standing ovation by the crowd of families in the stands, and by their classmates, who stood shoulder to shoulder at the fence. Greg Baisch said something else indecipherable—was it "Congratulations" and "Good luck"?—and then the group of seven seniors trotted back to their team with Octavio limping behind.

Moments later, after the other Bulldogs finished teasing them for having roses, most of the seniors took the field for the start of the game. Octavio stood a few paces away from the bench, his reclaimed crutches tucked under his arms, feeling more comfortable as the crowd's attention left him. His knee throbbed and he clenched his jaw, watching his teammates and watching the referee put the whistle to his mouth. One more win and his team would make the playoffs for the twentieth year in a row.

Coach Flannigan moved Cheo to center-mid, a position that he played well, slid Angel over to sweeper, and put Vlad and O.J. up front. Chuy was starting on the wing. Thirty minutes into the half, Cheo chased a ball out of bounds, scooped it up, and turned for a throw-in, finding Tony straight down the sideline. With the ball just beyond the tips of his shoes, Tony cut inside around one defender,

plunged forward two steps, and, seeing nobody between himself and
the keeper, tried a shot from the far corner of the penalty box. The
ball wobbled as it sped forward, the result of kicking it without spin,
and for a moment it looked like the ball would skim over the crossbar.
The keeper leaped for it, but the ball took a final lurch downward and
plunged into the net for Woodburn's first goal.

A minute later, Tony scudded a pass to Cheo, who was racing up
on the left side of the field. Cheo tapped it to Juan, whose short pass
found O.J. on the right side of the penalty box. O.J. gathered in the
ball, slowed down to create space and crossed a pass to Vlad, alone in
front of the goal. One dribble and Vlad let loose, scoring the team's
second goal.

As Vlad was running back with his hands in the air, he heard a
whistle. The play had been called offsides, prompting the usual argument about referee incompetence from Coach Flannigan.

"I don't think they really understand the offsides rule," he insisted.

But Canby was not waiting around for explanations. As soon as
the referee restarted the game, they hit a long pass into Woodburn
territory. Angel challenged their forward, taking him out with a rough
slide tackle. Another whistle blew, this time signaling a free kick.

Woodburn built its defensive wall while a Canby player rested
near the ball. At the sound of the whistle, he kicked. The ball arced
over the line of Bulldogs and bounced once, surprising Carlos. He
ran forward, then quickly spun around to leap for the ball going over
his head. Too late. It thumped down behind him and bounced into
the goal.

Woodburn 1. Canby 1.

"We need this win, guys," Coach Flannigan muttered on the
sidelines.

The ball was brought back to midfield, and once again, Canby
took control and worked the ball quickly into Woodburn territory, using long passes over the Bulldogs' heads. Just two minutes
after their first goal, Canby got off another shot. This time Carlos
grabbed it.

The Bulldogs appeared shaken. For a moment they were gun-shy, reluctant to make a pass, taking too long to set up a play. For the next ten minutes, the ball was banged around impotently in the middle of the field.

Then Juan collected a pass around midfield and dished it left, to Cesar, out in the middle of the field thirty yards from the net. However, the keeper had crept forward, and Cesar, settling the pass as a Canby defender ran toward him, tried one of the longest goals of his life.

From Coach Flannigan's perspective, it was hard to tell if the ball was on target, it was traveling so far. He watched it curve up and then plummet down. He saw the keeper running fast, trying to get back, and leaping as the ball seemed to burn the ends of his fingertips before hitting the upper-right corner of the net.

"Yeah, Cesar!" the coach shouted, flinging his arms into the air, and he turned to look at the players beside him, all of whom were standing in various attitudes of amazement.

"That's more like it!" he said.

Cesar quietly smiled and let his teammates smack him around in their joy.

Suddenly Woodburn seemed to feel confident again. Cheo took a shot off a Tony assist, missing wide right. Two minutes later, Tony slipped in another pass to O.J., who one-touched it straight to Luis, who knocked it in low and left for the third goal. Canby retaliated with an attempt of their own just before halftime, which Carlos caught and then returned with a long kick to O.J., who passed to Martin in the center of Canby's penalty area. Martin's shot made an abrupt bend, hit the right goalpost, and ricocheted out of bounds.

Martin came off the field at halftime and fell onto the bench, pulling at his shoe. He held it up to show that the sole was peeling off.

"No wonder it curved like that!"

"I thought that was a much better job of getting runs," Coach Flannigan said at halftime. "We're faster than these guys, and we're getting everybody involved. Martin, you've had some great shots. You keep getting those things low and wide like that, one of them is going to go in. I can live with that much more than kicking them over the top."

The first half had shown the coaches that the Bulldogs could beat Canby if they kept the pressure on. Coach Flannigan had seen a worrisome trend, however: the boys were pulling back after scoring, protecting their goal, not pressing forward to hassle the Canby defense. The passes, which had been quick one-touch or two-touches in the first half hour, had deteriorated. The intensity Coach Flannigan wanted was waning.

"A two-goal lead is not enough with these guys," he said. "I want another goal. Listen. I'm not talking about being disrespectful, but going out there and playing hard and being aggressive. Playing hard and being aggressive. All right?"

Ransom reminded the boys to make quick passes or to back it up and swing to the side. As he finished, Carlos spoke up.

"C'mon guys, we better not let up."

"Keep up the pace," Ransom agreed. "Now, I'd kind of like to hear what Octavio has to say. He's been standing there watching the game."

"We need to play smart," Octavio offered. "We can beat these guys if we keep the pressure up and think about where our passes are going."

"*Piensa, piensa!*" repeated Carlos. Think, think!

As the second half began, so did Omar's frustration. In the stands with his family, Omar had been trying to will the Perros to victory. As a Canby player raced down the near sideline, Omar shook his head.

"They're stabbing!" he said. "Look at that!" O.J. had thrust out a leg at his opponent and missed, allowing the Canby player to run by.

"They would never do that if I was the coach. Not to take anything from Flannigan. I think he's a good coach. But he's asking these guys to think on the field. I know these guys. They're not thinkers."

As he watched, a long pass to a Canby forward drew Angel out of position, leaving a hole in front of the goal. The forward passed the ball quickly, a delicate tap to a teammate outdistancing his Woodburn defender. The Canby attacker hacked at the ball awkwardly,

Carlos dove, and then the entire Canby squad was leaping up and giving each other high-fives on the sidelines.

Omar groaned.

"I know these guys!" he repeated. "You can't let them think!"

With the score now 3–2, Coach Flannigan decided that he had seen enough. He pulled Cheo out of the midfield and put him back into his usual position at sweeper. The Bulldogs' defense immediately tightened up.

With three minutes left, a careening ball slapped a Woodburn player's hand, and the referee blew his whistle.

Coach Flannigan shouted, "It bounced up and hit his hand! It wasn't intentional! That's a first-grade call!"

He began to mock the man in a high, mincing voice, "I saw it hit his hand so I call a handball. I don't know what I'm doing!" But not loud enough for the referee to hear.

The free kick was taken from about midfield, too far away to be very dangerous, but Carlos nervously watched it come his way. He could not afford to let a shot get by him or the game would go into overtime with the momentum in Canby's favor.

The kick landed short, and Cheo booted it aside.

In the last two minutes, Canby took shots from all over the field, hoping for a lucky bounce or to catch the Woodburn defense already celebrating. But their shots didn't even make it to Carlos. Instead, Cheo seemed to be everywhere, stripping the ball from Canby forwards, intercepting long passes, punting the ball out of bounds. Every player on the Woodburn bench stood up to watch, and as the game ended, they cheered and ran onto the field to meet their friends jogging toward them.

It was only Woodburn's fifth regular-season win, but it was enough to squeak them into the playoffs. In the league's other important final game, Forest Grove handed McMinnville their only loss of the season. If Woodburn hadn't won, their season would have been over.

As the boys hugged and shouted, Brian Flannigan scooted around with his camera, clicking away, his teeth glinting in the overhead lights.

"We didn't break the twenty-year streak! You guys did it!" he said again and again.

Octavio, who had watched the game from the sidelines, swung forward on his crutches, reluctantly joining in the pictures.

Omar and Pat came down from the stands to congratulate O.J. and Carlos, and stood with all the friends and girlfriends on the edge of the field bearing smiles, waiting for the photo shoot to end.

Coach Flannigan shouted over the boys' excited voices, gathering them together into a tight group.

"Hey, give yourselves a hand, you kept the streak alive!"

"The what?" asked Martin.

Coach Ransom, somewhat exasperated, said, "The streak. Making the playoffs for twenty years straight, you didn't blow it."

"Oh," said Martin, as if it was the first he'd ever heard of it.

"You'll have another chance of ruining it next year," Ransom commented and the boys laughed.

"All right," said Coach Flannigan. He nodded toward Ransom. "Coach reminded me earlier today that some of our best seasons have been when we were fourth seeds. And don't get me wrong, I would love to have the league title, but at this stage, when we're still figuring things out, that extra game will help us. We're doing some good things but I think we also have things to work on. We took a step forward offensively today but we took a step back defensively. As well as our defense has played all year, they deserve to have a game off, but it's a good thing we scored three goals."

With the next game only a couple of days away, Flannigan announced a short and mandatory practice the next morning.

"Listen," he said. "I don't want to hear stories about how your sister made me go sign some papers, my dad made me go to work with him. None of that shit is going to fly with me tomorrow. Show up or sit on the bench."

He looked around. Nobody spoke.

"All right," he said, and turned to Ransom with an upraised eyebrow.

Coach Ransom, looking stern, cleared his throat.

"You guys played well in a pressure situation today. However, I think in the second half, when they scored that second goal, you guys started to think, 'I don't know, we might lose.' I felt it here," he said, tapping his chest. "I saw it in you guys. The only way to get rid of that feeling is to live through a couple of these games. You panic, you survive. So next game, let's stay calm, we'll get through it.

"There are no easy games left," he said. "They are all going to feel the same way."

Even as Ransom finished his sentence, Cheo started talking in Spanish.

"We need to play hard," he said in a low rumble that his teammates could hardly hear. "It doesn't cost us anything to play hard. We need to play with more heart."

"We need to play like we did today, at the beginning." Tony added.

"We need to give more," Cheo insisted. "We need to all get back after a goal, and get back quickly. We need to pressure more, not just play defense. They scored on us today because we stopped attacking them. We scored a goal and then we hung back and played defense. We need to keep attacking, keep trying to score, make them play defense."

He was into it now, waving his arm and looking at his friends with all the heartfelt passion of a Baptist preacher. He had let his friend Octavio do the talking all year, but now the words and the feelings poured out of him.

"We were winning today," he went on, "but we stopped playing hard. We need to play *con ganas*, we can't just let another team come and attack us! If we play with everything that we have it won't be like this next time. We just need to push and pressure and never let the other team have a chance to breathe!

"We have to play harder. All of us together!"

For a moment nobody spoke. Then the team began to applaud and cheer.

"I like it," said Coach Flannigan, who had understood only a handful of the senior's words. "It's the last game of league, Cheo, but there you go!"

POSTSEASON

TWELVE

The Fourth Seed

A lot of people discriminate and say, "Go pick your berries, get out of here." Players and fans say crap like that. It
doesn't matter. It doesn't affect me in any way, just pisses
me off. My freshman year, some tall, big white guy would
start saying crap and I would just stop playing and go up to
him. It brings my game up. He thinks he can take me. I'll
show him.

—Chuy

Octavio approached the field slowly, walking with two crutches,
wearing his puffy red jacket against the crisp fall chill. He gave a
sad, embarrassed smile and ducked his head while his teammates approached him. He had been absent at practices while rumors spread
around the team that he was still in bed, his leg was broken, or he was
avoiding them. Coach Flannigan had wondered why Octavio didn't
make an appearance, had even been disappointed that the boy hadn't
come by. It seemed as if Octavio was running from his responsibilities to the team.

"Have you been to a doctor?" Flannigan asked him.

Octavio explained that he had received X-rays, but he still needed
to arrange an MRI.

"Get that done," Coach Flannigan encouraged. "Let's find out
what's wrong. You've got insurance."

Octavio nodded obediently, but not convincingly. Coach Flannigan had seen this before—a reluctance in some of his players to
get help. He assumed that it was a cultural thing, but it annoyed him.
Why not just go see a doctor?

After staying home for about a week, while the swelling in his
knee slowly went down, Octavio entrusted his knee to a man in Mc-

Minnville whom he claimed was an amateur *curandero*, a kind of un-trained herbal doctor. The man massaged the knee, but it was too painful, and he told Octavio to return after the swelling died down. Octavio had managed to get by without seeing a doctor the last time his knee was injured. Why not now as well, he thought.

As the coach and other players dispersed onto the field, Octavio stood alone on the sidelines, looking unsure. He brightened up when Coach Ransom approached him with a smile, and for a while the two conversed in Spanish. Then Ransom returned to his coaching du-ties and Octavio stared dolefully at his teammates. His head swiveled around and he smiled insecurely when people looked his way.

When Octavio was a child, his father's ancient tractor broke down. Like most farmers in rural Mexico, Octavio's father did not have much of an education. He did not have a manual for the tractor; he did not have money for a mechanic; he had a limited number of tools. But, like farmers everywhere, Octavio's father was a practical man. He began to take the tractor apart.

Over the next few weeks, as time permitted, the vehicle's motor shrunk and the pile of parts scattered around the shed began to grow. Eventually, the tractor was in nearly as many pieces as their field had stalks of corn, and Octavio wondered how his father knew what went where, and how to put it all back together again.

As Octavio remembered it, rebuilding the tractor took months. His father inspected and cleaned each piece, fitted it in place, then moved methodically to the next part. At times he was stumped, clutching in his hand a part that didn't seem to fit anywhere. He walked around the tractor silently, seeming to imagine the piece, to fit its shape against the shape of the half-assembled motor. Often Oc-tavio saw him deep in conversation with a brother or cousin, trying to solve the tractor's greasy riddle. Sometimes a piece was put in the wrong place, and metal parts that had been replaced had to be re-moved again. When the engine finally was rebuilt, Octavio watched his father start it, and he saw a dense cloud of black smoke billow from the exhaust. His father shut down the tractor and began to take it apart again.

Then one day, Octavio came home from school to see his father seated atop the rumbling and smoke-free tractor, and he ran across the rancho in his excitement. He became sure that his father could do anything. Years later, and three thousand miles away, Octavio's boyish enthusiasm both dwindled and deepened. He now knew that his father was a poor man living in a poor part of a poor country, a man who rarely read a book and who sometimes had to leave his family to work in another country just to make enough money for food and clothing. He also knew that his father was a hard worker, and he thought of the tractor's repair as an example of his father's patience, intelligence, and curiosity—three virtues that he wanted for himself.

Since he had come to the United States, Octavio had come to think of himself as somebody who, like his father, was good at pursuing goals, somebody who was a long-term thinker. He did this daily, carefully blocking out his time for school papers, spending his weekends working, taking classes that were hard even for native English speakers.

He thought about the tractor because as he watched his teammates warm up, he felt doubt creep over him. Was he the kind of person who could pursue a difficult, long-term goal? What if he was just kidding himself? What if he didn't have what it took? Or worse, what if he worked hard, nose to the grindstone, and chance circumstances prevented him from reaching his goal? Isn't that what had happened with his knee? The season, which had started with so much promise, seemed to be falling apart around him. Instead of playing his best soccer, chatting with college coaches, and looking over scholarships, he was standing on the sidelines doing nothing.

What had seemed like the beginning of a new chapter in his life now seemed like the end of one. It would be the end of his education, and he would be left with the life his father had warned him against, a life of hard physical labor. Octavio still thought of America as a meritocracy, but if that was true, then what was he? No scholarship, no papers, no team—wasn't that proof that he didn't warrant any prizes? That he was just another dumb Mexican unable to make it playing the white man's game?

Octavio didn't like to involve other people when he was feeling low. He had his family, his aunt and uncle with whom he lived, his phone calls to Guanajuato, and he had Anita, who still beamed when she saw him and held his hand when they walked down the street. But he didn't tell her about his feelings. He didn't tell her how he thought about home—not the turf farm—but home, far away, a bittersweet pain. He wanted badly to go there, just to see his mom and dad, to smell the air that he had grown up with, but if he crossed the border, it might be years until he could come back—if he ever got the chance again. He had broken up with one longtime girlfriend to come here. Would he break up with Anita to go there?

He also had practical concerns. Was Guanajuato safe? Since he had moved to Oregon, his Uncle Pedro, with whom he had lived while playing for Atlas, had been shot and killed. At first, it seemed like a random act—a rich man caught in the wrong part of town. Then Octavio's father called and told him what actually happened. Pedro, it turned out, was involved in a drug cartel—was perhaps even the leader—and had been murdered by members of a rival cartel. Octavio had been shocked, not only because Pedro had seemed like a nice man, but also because he had stayed in the man's house and had seen nothing to suggest that his uncle was a criminal.

But now, the violence that Octavio read about and saw on the news had entered his family's home. What if he returned to Mexico? Would he be in danger because he had lived with his uncle? Or would he just get caught in the crossfire?

The practice ended and Octavio wandered off to wait for Cheo outside the locker room, alone in the darkness.

In Oregon high school soccer, before the first round of playoffs begins, the fourth-seeded teams play a sub-round game against each other, a kind of pre-playoff game. These games occur before the rest of the playoffs. The winner of the sub-round, still considered a fourth seed, is then scheduled to play a number one–seeded team from another league in the state. The Bulldogs had been a fourth seed once before, had won their sub-round game, and then lost to mighty Jesuit, the team that went on to win the championship.

The Bulldogs' fourth-seed rival in 2005 were the North Medford Black Tornadoes from the Southern League. Medford is a city of about 75,000 located in the hot and dry Rogue Valley, a short drive north of the California border. Like Woodburn, it began as a railroad depot set amongst small farms. Unlike Woodburn, Medford's Hispanic residents made up less than 10 percent of the town's total population. Almost 90 percent of the city was white, including the soccer team and its coach. The team had one Hispanic player.

The North Medford game took place on a brisk evening in late October. Many North Medford supporters had made the four-hour drive north to Woodburn to watch the game, and the bleachers were unusually full.

Coach Flannigan expected a win. The Black Tornadoes played in a weaker league than Woodburn and had a worse record, and the Bulldogs were the home team. He decided to keep Cheo at center-mid and brought in some extra players from the JV squad—Rambo, a burly forward, and Jorge, a JV sweeper who would fill in at the wing.

It had rained for two days, and a dark sky menaced that morning, but by midafternoon, a cold, cutting wind blew the endless black clouds to the southeast, smoothing and softening the clouds into gray wisps. As the Bulldogs began their usual warm-up routine on the baseball field, Octavio arrived to watch, still looking hangdog and miserable. He wore white pants and a crimson jacket and stood awkwardly just inside the baseball diamond, leaning against a tall, chain-link fence.

Martin, always looking for entertainment, saw Octavio standing there and walked over. Octavio smiled at him in greeting. Martin said hello, smiled, and then quickly stepped forward to grab Octavio's face in both hands. Before Octavio could react, Martin kissed him on the cheek loudly, then let go and ran away, laughing. Octavio turned red and looked around, embarrassed and uncertain.

The team finished their warm-ups and headed to the field where the Black Tornadoes were already working on passes, their goalkeeper alternately blocking kicks from the left and right. As the Bulldogs began their own practice kicks, the sky darkened and a thin drizzle oozed onto the field.

A few minutes before the game started, Coach Flannigan gathered the Bulldogs in front of him and gave a short speech. The wind blew the sleeves of his coat backwards, toward the high school building, and the players, many of them standing in shirtsleeves, held their arms close to their sides and bounced up and down. Coach Flannigan raised his voice to speak.

"Okay, gentlemen," Coach Flannigan shouted. "You did what you had to do to get here. You got to the playoffs."

He paused and took a couple of steps to the left. Behind him, the aluminum bleachers were filling with spectators.

"Now it all starts fresh. Now everybody is zero–zero. So let's take care of business and win at our home."

The team came together in a huddle, hands stretched toward the middle. Octavio, who had been lingering on the outside of the group, stepped in.

"Woodburn!"

On the first drive, the Bulldogs slipped two quick passes through the defense and got the ball to Tony near the sidelines. As Tony raced forward, he lost control of the ball, which rolled out of bounds. A North Medford player, wearing his black road uniform, trotted forward for the throw-in. North Medford was not a huge team, but they had a tall, blond midfielder named Lars who, rumor had it, was a Danish exchange student. The Bulldogs had taken one look at the kid and christened him "The Viking." After a short run and a long pass to the top of the penalty box, the ball ended up at Lars's feet with no defenders between himself and the Woodburn goal. But before he could set up for his kick, Carlos came barreling out of the goal at top speed, sliding into the ball before Lars could chip it over him. Carlos jogged back to the goal, shouting at his defenders. Coach Flannigan let out his breath and glanced at his center midfielder. If Cheo were playing sweeper instead of Angel, Carlos never would have needed to come out so far.

Despite the Dane's initial penetration, Woodburn re-formed its defense and began to methodically strip the ball from every North Medford player. Half an hour into the first half, Woodburn got its first shot at goal when Chuy sprinted down the right sideline and made a difficult running cross into the middle of the penalty box, right in front of the goal. Two Woodburn players were in a group with three North Medford defenders racing for the ball, as was the North Medford goalie, who dove on top of it.

Uncharacteristically, it was Chuck Ransom who began yelling at Chuy, disappointed about the inaccurate pass.

"What are we doing?!" He shouted. "Play to feet! Play to feet!"

Cheo was tackled from behind just outside the penalty box. The Black Tornadoes set up their wall in front of the goal and the Bulldogs set three players around the ball, Cheo, Juan, and Cesar. With three players able to approach the free kick, the number of directions that the ball can be sent becomes difficult for a defending team to cover. The ball could be kicked straight over, or through, the defensive wall. It could be sent to one side of the wall or the other toward a Woodburn player, who would turn and one-touch kick it into the goal.

The whistle blew. Cheo ran to the ball and over it; Juan, coming from the other side, did the same. As Juan jumped over the ball, Cesar ran forward, curving the ball over the right side of the wall and down into the bottom-right corner of the net, slipping it past the keeper's prone body.

Woodburn 1. North Medford 0.

Less than three minutes later, North Medford sent a long and clearly offsides pass into the penalty box. There were no defenders to slow down the receiving forward, who sent the ball past Carlos and into the far side of the net. As soon as the whistle blew, Carlos charged the referee.

"Sir!" he complained. "That was offsides!"

Coach Flannigan, sensing a potential penalty card against his talented goalkeeper, began to shout.

"Carlos, get back!"

Carlos opened his mouth as if he was going to say something else, either to his coach or the ref, but then he spun around and ran back to his spot in goal. As the cluster of North Medford fans cheered in the stands, Coach Flannigan began arguing with the referee.

"That's why we didn't use you against Corvallis!" he shouted as the ref jogged by. "It's over your head! Too difficult!"

"That's enough!" the ref shouted.

"You can overturn it!"

Brian Flannigan added, "We've got it on tape. We'll be appealing the decision."

"That's enough!"

Ransom put his hand on Mike Flannigan's shoulder, and the coach turned his head, letting the ref jog by.

"Let it go," he said. "We can't do anything about it now and we can still win this game."

Coach Flannigan bit his lip but nodded.

The ball was put back in play. Cheo took it forward, sending a pass to O.J., who ran about ten yards with the ball at his feet, a defender pacing him on his right. As he approached the goal, the keeper came forward and O.J. delicately tapped it past him, toward the left side of the goal. As the ball rolled, slowing in the tall grass, the North Medford sweeper slid in aggressively, his outstretched leg catching the ball and knocking it away from the goal.

The first half ended in a 1–1 tie. The boys came off the field, drank some water, and took a moment to sit down. Carlos complained about the lack of an offsides call. As they rested, the clouds passed by and the night became noticeably colder, the wind blowing in from the north, a cold blast down from Canada.

As the second half started, Coach Flannigan turned to his father and said with a smile:

"I'm going to try a more positive approach in the second half."

Brian chuckled and said, "Yeah. Well, that will let them referee better."

Coach Flannigan put Cheo back in as sweeper, giving up some speed in the middle but making himself feel more secure. At center mid he put Martin, whose goal attempt earlier in the game—a header off a cross from Tony—had gone straight to the keeper. Martin liked to juke and fake his opponent when he had the ball, his arms swinging up and down as he did so, as if he was shaking a castanet in each hand.

Coach Flannigan was unsure about putting Martin in the center —Martin had been a forward and could hog the ball—but he did well, making deft passes and aggressively challenging his counterpart, the Viking.

Flannigan kept Juan and Vlad as forwards, and early in the second half, the two of them came down the field playing give-and-go, challenging the keeper together. Vlad, the ball at his feet, tried a kick from close in, but he was tackled by the keeper, who also took down Juan, earning Woodburn a penalty kick. Juan's PK was low and to the left, a very efficient blast that the keeper had no chance of stopping. About five minutes later, Juan received a Tony cross and kicked the ball in again, almost hitting the same spot in the net.

Woodburn 3, North Medford 1.

On the Woodburn field, both the home and away teams sat on benches on the same side of the pitch, the side across from where the fans sat or stood. They were separated by the midfield line, about twenty yards between the two groups, enough room to prevent the boys from talking to each other, but close enough that the coaches, who often wandered away from their benches, could speak to each other on occasion. After Juan made his PK, the North Medford coach looked across the space toward Coach Flannigan and said, "They're helping you out."

There it was. Coach Flannigan knew that people really believed this—that they thought referees sometimes favored Woodburn, especially if the referee was Hispanic, as this one was. It drove Flannigan crazy.

"Sure," he said sarcastically, "like they always are."

"That's right," the North Medford coach replied with certainty.

The two glared at each other for a moment, thought better of a confrontation, and walked away.

"He's just mad they're losing," Brian said, as Coach Flannigan walked back to his bench.

"If anybody's been helped, it's their team," Flannigan said sharply, recalling North Medford's goal. "That offsides call was bullshit."

With twenty minutes left in the game, North Medford earned a free kick about forty yards from the Woodburn goal. They ran in most of their team, determined to take advantage of the height difference, and sent a long ball into the scrum in front of Carlos's goal. About six boys jumped at the same time; the ball careened off the head of a blond player, the Viking again. The ball bounced oddly, probably not where the player intended, crossing the face of the goal, bouncing off Manolo's shoulder and past the startled Carlos into the net.

Carlos immediately heard two noises: the North Medford fans cheering and his coach, halfway across the field, shouting, "What was that! You've got to own that goal, Carlos!"

Manolo felt so upset by the own goal that he asked Coach Flannigan to take him out. Manolo sat on the bench staring at the ground while his teammates told him that he shouldn't blame himself. After a couple of minutes, he lifted his head and turned a broad smile to Martin.

"Well, at least I scored," he said.

With fifteen minutes to go, a big North Medford defender shoved Vlad aside before going up for a contested header. The big guy came down, took a step, and put his foot into Vlad's back. The maneuver brought Juan running to complain to the ref, insisting that the defender had purposefully injured Vlad—who still lay prone on the grass, clutching his side, knees drawn to his chest—and demanded that the referee toss the other player from the game. The referee disagreed loudly, and the two stood chest to chest for a moment before the ref's hand shot into the air holding a yellow card.

Within seconds, other Woodburn players surrounded Juan and moved him away from the ref before he could make matters worse. Juan was known to have a short temper, and it wouldn't have been the first time he refused to back down, possibly damaging his team's future chances. On the sidelines, Coach Flannigan was shouting to make a substitution, wanting to get Juan off the field for a moment.

After Juan cooled off, he returned to the field, replacing Luis, who limped off with a cramping hamstring. A few plays later, Juan took the ball down the left side, spotted Vlad approaching the top of the penalty box with no defenders around him, made a feint toward the goal, then stopped himself and the ball abruptly. His defender put on the brakes, but it was too late. Juan turned, delivered a low pass to Vlad's feet, and Vlad took the shot without hesitation, straight to the bottom right corner of the net.

Woodburn 4, North Medford 2.

Five minutes later, Vlad drilled a second ball into the left side of the net on a short pass from Cesar, putting Woodburn up three with only eight minutes to go.

Coach Flannigan was delighted, arms thrust in the air, and as Vlad came off the field, Coach Ransom grabbed him in a bear hug. "Vladi!" he shouted. "I've been waiting all season for you to kick like that! You're back! You're back!"

But North Medford hadn't given up. With four minutes left, they booted another long pass into a group in front of Woodburn's goal, Carlos crouching and following the ball intently. It disappeared into the tight knot of black and white uniforms, and then the ball shot from the scrum like soap out of a hand and squirted past Carlos for the Black Tornadoes' third goal.

They tried again, but this time Carlos shoved players aside, leaping to catch the incoming pass. The clock ticked off the remaining time and the Bulldogs slowly trotted back to their places. With a minute remaining and the win almost within reach, Woodburn's fans began to chant. "Bulldog power! Bulldog power! Bulldog power!" As the game ended, the Woodburn bench jumped up and began to hug each other, and the stands erupted in screams. One game down. Win three more and they were in the state championship.

The win over North Medford felt good, but Flannigan knew that the real test would be the next game, against a big undefeated team that the Perros would play away from home.

THIRTEEN

This Dream

Soccer's the best sport in Woodburn High School. You
talk to anybody about Woodburn, the first thing they're
going to say is soccer. They'll say Woodburn's got a good
soccer team, every year. I don't even know why we've got a
football team. They haven't won a game in two years.

—Juan

After seeing too many players climb on the team bus to an away game
clutching nothing but a cup of instant soup, Flannigan insisted that
the team meet early Saturday afternoon to eat. Standing beside a
table in the cafeteria watching the boys slap together turkey-and-
cheese sandwiches, the coach felt confident. Not only had the Bulldogs performed well in their first playoff game, Flannigan thought
that he might have hit on a solution for the hole in the middle of the
field created by Octavio's injury. Martin, who had played so poorly
at forward, had protected and passed the ball well as the center-mid
during the past two games. Although he didn't have Octavio's stam-
ina, Martin was a good ball-handler and capable passer. Flannigan
was also surprisingly pleased with Rambo, the JV forward he brought
up to fill Martin's spot. Rambo wasn't fast, but he was strong and had
a willingness to shoot the ball that many other players lacked.

The boys' voices echoed off the ceiling of the cavernous cafeteria. Taped to the lockers lining the walls were handmade posters:
"Ramon #12," "Go Bulldogs!" "Vlad #7," "Beat South Eugene!" The
players sat at two tables, laughing and talking, while the coaches sat
at a third, picking at turkey scraps and eyeing the clock. When all
the food was gone, Flannigan sent the team into the locker room to
change while he walked into his classroom to finalize the roster.

Nearly two dozen players were crammed into the little blue
locker room, squeezed together on the benches, sprawled on the

floor, or standing, leaning against a locker, when Flannigan and Ransom entered. Tony shut off his MP3 player, and the group watched as Flannigan removed the top of a blue pen and began to draw the starting lineup on the room's whiteboard. Ransom stood off to one side, filling up the doorway. When Flannigan began to talk, Carlos shifted on his corner of the bench, his headphones on, a tinny plinking wafting out of them and into the pauses between Flannigan's words. The coach stopped and looked at him. Reluctantly, with studied slowness, Carlos reached into his jacket pocket, turned off his CD player, and plucked one of the earphones out, leaving it dangling on his leg.

Flannigan capped his pen.

"Okay, now, I'm going to tell you a story. For the last couple years, we've had guys at these big games who have come up and said, 'I had a dream about this game, it was a bad dream.' . . . So, let me tell you about this dream that *I* had last night."

He barely paused. He had practiced this all morning in his head, and he wanted to get it right. Adding some energy to his voice, he continued.

"Oh, I had this dream! I tell you what, I dreamed I was at this concert, it was Destiny's Child."

The boys murmured approval. They sat or stood motionless, watching him.

"And as I'm standing there in the first or second row, Beyoncé did this to me."

Flannigan curled his finger, mimicking the singer beckoning to him. He raised his eyebrows and the team chuckled.

"I'm there," he said with a smile. "We go backstage, in her room, and man, we are hitting it!"

The team burst into laughter. Carlos threw his head back. Cesar spun around and pounded on his locker.

"So, what I want to know," the coach continued, "since I had this dream, is it going to come true?"

Lots of shaking heads and smiles.

"Probably no," he said. "Actually, being a loyal married man, there's no way in hell it's going to happen. So, I don't want to hear these stories after the game, guys saying, 'Well, I had this dream so I

THE BOYS FROM LITTLE MEXICO

just knew that we were going to lose and so that's why we didn't have a very good game.' Okay? That's a bunch of crap, all right? So, I don't want to hear anything about, 'Oh, I had this vision come to me,' or, 'I rolled the dice and they came up all sixes.' *That's* not what is going to decide the outcome of the game, all right? It's you guys playing hard, playing intense, playing Woodburn-style soccer that's going to determine the outcome of this game. Is that understood?"

A chorus of yeahs.

"Okay, and if I get it on with Beyoncé Knowles in the next couple of months, I'll tell you, 'So much for that theory. Believe your dreams.'"

"Even wet dreams?" Angel asked, as everybody laughed.

"I did have to change my boxers afterwards," Flannigan lied. Then he stepped back and let Ransom talk.

Flannigan hadn't dreamt about Beyoncé. But as he told Ransom afterwards, he knew that he would have to address the superstitious nature of the team. On every Woodburn squad that he had coached, Mike Flannigan had heard, directly or indirectly, about a player who predicted the outcomes of games based on messages from the spirit world. On previous teams, some of these players had spooked themselves so badly that they had been nearly unable to play. Two years earlier, Luis's cousin Henry dreamed of a playoff loss and came to the game shaken and seemingly determined to lose. Halftime found him standing off the field by a chain-link fence praying and burning herbs to lift the game's curse.

So Flannigan knew he had to discuss it. However, as the team filed out of the locker room toward the waiting bus, Ransom sidled up next to him. Cheo, the team's most prolific dreamer, had not understood the nature of Flannigan's lesson. As his teammates ventured into the rain, he explained to Ransom that Flannigan didn't need to worry, that he had already dreamed that they would win, 1–0 on a penalty kick from Juan.

As the bus pulled out, Ransom and Flannigan had to admit that they had their own superstitions. Ransom had picked up a softball-sized rock during the first game of the previous season and had carried it to every game until their loss to Lakeridge in the playoffs. As the bus rolled south on I-5, the noise from the wind and rain making conversation difficult, Flannigan copped to his own superstition. He sat up front with his head tilted to hear the blustery radio broadcast of a University of Oregon football game. When U of O won during overtime, Flannigan sighed and leaned back with a big smile.

"Last year," he said, "when Lakeridge beat us, Cal was playing Oregon the same day and had to come from behind to get the win. So, since Oregon came from behind to win in overtime this year, maybe that's a sign for us."

By 4:00 p.m., it was already dark. The first large winter storm had blown in from the Pacific, and forecasters were predicting up to two inches of rain over the next twenty-four hours, centered over the Eugene area. Inside the bus, it sounded as if rocks were being thrown on the roof. Rambo fished out a bag of hard candy and began throwing pieces to his friends, which began the usual shoving and wrestling matches in the back of the bus. After a while, though, the players settled down into their usual roles, calling girlfriends, listening to music, and talking with each other.

Ransom sat silently, thinking about the game and the upcoming conversion of the high school into four small schools. Ransom had applied for a position as principal at one of them. If he got the job, he would not be allowed to coach next year, his first time not working with a youth sports team in ten years. As the bus rumbled south, he wondered if this game would be his last as a Bulldog coach.

The bus arrived at South Eugene High School an hour before game time, a girls' playoff game still taking place. The South Eugene pitch was a short artificial-turf field with uncovered bleachers on one side and two sets of benches—one set for each team—on the opposite side of the field. There was no sign of the South Eugene players as the Bulldogs splashed through puddles toward the team benches, dropped their bags on the high ground around a storage shed, and huddled under the various coaches' umbrellas to watch the girls play. The wind blasted through the chain-link fence surrounding the field, swirling under pant legs and turning ears painfully red.

Everybody was cold and wet by the time Flannigan found the

South Eugene athletic director and sent the team onto an unlit, muddy field to begin warm-ups. The coaches continued to watch the girls' game, and as it neared the end, Brian Flannigan started moving some bags, hoping to claim the better of the two covered team benches. A few minutes later, Coach Flannigan turned to the athletic director and commented on the South Eugene girls' win, "Hopefully this is a good sign. One win for you is enough."

As the girls' teams left, the Bulldogs got their first look at the South Eugene Axemen. Many of the boys knew nothing about them, which some players, like Chuy and Tony, preferred. The Axemen were a tall team that had gone undefeated in league play. Two years earlier, Ryan White, their star midfielder, was the only player from Oregon to make the U.S. Under-16 National team. As he started to warm up, they saw him for the first time. At six-foot-three and over two hundred pounds, he already had the muscular build of a professional athlete. He wore a hinged metal brace on his left knee, which had been sore lately, the aftereffects of an old ACL tear. The Axemen wore white; Woodburn wore blue.

A few minutes before game time, Coach Flannigan gathered the team together on the sideline and gave a short speech. He had, he felt, already done what he could in the locker room. Now it was up to the boys. The team gathered around in a tight huddle and Flannigan made it simple:

"C'mon guys, this is what we play for! We win today, we go on! If we lose, we go home. So let's go!"

He stepped back, and Octavio limped into his place. The team gathered in a tighter group as Octavio began his usual rapid-fire urgings:

"¡Con ganas, cabrones! ¡Con todo, cabrones! ¡Aquí no hay mañana, hay sólo hoy!"

"Now," said Chuy, "now, make it happen, baby!"

They barked. Throughout the season, there had been occasional calls for barking in the huddle, but many of the players felt self-conscious about it. They had barked against North Medford, however, and it seemed unlucky not to continue. The sound started quietly, as if nobody was certain that the other players would join in.

Then it rose as the huddle began to bounce up and down in time to the shouts: "Ark, ark, ark, ark, ARK!"

Members of the South Eugene team glanced at them. Then, with a final "ARK!" the huddle broke up and the bench players raced back to find a spot under the rain awning, elbowing each other out of the way. Betos, a huge grin on his face, snatched the single blanket and draped it over his lap. The starters took their habitual spots on the pitch, dropped onto one knee, and waited for the whistle. Juan put his hands together to pray for a good game. Martin stood opposite Ryan White, his head barely clearing Ryan's shoulders. Tony, aware of his sore lower back, tried to stretch as he waited. In the stands, two crowds sat apart from each other, the Hispanics on one end and the Anglos on the other. Besides the close friends and family members, about twenty Woodburn students had taken advantage of a second bus to come down and watch the game. As usual, right in the middle of the crowd sat Omar and Pat Mendoza.

As soon as the game started, it was obvious that the teams were well matched but playing noticeably different styles of soccer. Woodburn, with its ball-handling and short, quick passes, moved downfield with patience, as if each player were a relay-runner, assigned to guard *la pelota* for a brief distance. South Eugene tended to make long, penetrating passes, moving forward in quick rushes, taking advantage of their height to head the ball farther along. Flannigan paced in front of his bench, simmering and commenting on the decisions of his players and the referees to nobody in particular. Ransom stood near the midfield line, legs placed wide, as still as a rock. The rain slowly lightened until only a vague mist dripped onto the field like a slowly falling cloud.

After ten minutes, O.J. collected a pass thirty yards in front of the Axemen's goal, put his head down, and began to run with the ball, a defender stuck to his hip. As they jostled, the South Eugene player pushed him: a foul. It was Woodburn's first scoring opportunity. O.J. set the ball down carefully, stamping the turf between the ball and his foot, while six Axemen lined up in a defensive wall between him and the goal. O.J. took a few steps back, the ref blew his whistle, and O.J. stepped forward, kicking the ball over the wall into a mixed group of players in front of the goal. The Woodburn bench players leaped to their feet; for a moment, none of them could see who had control. The crouching South Eugene keeper shifted his weight from foot to foot as the ball was batted around before a Woodburn player kicked it out of bounds to the right of the goal. The Woodburn bench sat down again, and the keeper kicked the ball deep into Woodburn territory.

Ten minutes later, Chuy slipped the ball past a defender and bolted down the right sideline, sending a pass toward the front-right corner of the penalty box. Vlad dashed after it, but the ball kept rolling, the artificial turf quicker than the Woodburn players were used to, and Vlad was unable to reach the ball before it went out of bounds.

"Dammit!" Flannigan hissed.

Ryan White received a long pass, took two steps, and then turned his head, giving Martin a moment to steal the ball. White spun around to chase him, shouting at one of his teammates. What Flannigan had said earlier seemed to be true: the Axemen were not expecting such good play from a fourth-seeded team.

Even caught unawares, White remained a dangerous player. With seventeen minutes left in the first half, the Axemen's strategy finally worked, and one of their midfielders found himself with nothing but grass between the ball and Woodburn's keeper. He kicked it, a high volley headed for the top-right corner of the net. Carlos dove toward the ball in desperation, his arms stretched, and knocked the ball out to the right of the goal. In the resulting corner kick, Ryan White showed his value, jumping a head higher than any defender and heading the ball straight toward—and over—the net.

On the sidelines, players from both benches sat back down, shaking their heads.

A minute later, White again threatened to score when he captured Carlos's incoming kick and sprinted down the middle of the pitch, dishing the ball out to the left wing when pressured. The Axemen took it down the left side and attempted a shot from twenty-five yards out that Cheo intercepted and booted forward. Three minutes later, South Eugene pressured near the top of the Woodburn penalty box and tried a shot that went out of bounds to the left.

For the last five minutes of the half, the Bulldogs looked tired and overwhelmed as the Axemen pressed forward again and again, sending long passes over the heads of the Woodburn players. Twice Cheo had to chase down and slide-tackle the ball out of bounds to prevent a wide-open shot on the goal. When the whistle blew, the Bulldogs jogged off looking tense and winded. Tony trotted off feeling the soreness in his back with each step. The score was 0–0.

"I'll take that," Flannigan said as the team dropped to the field around him. He felt happy with the team's defense and told them so, warning Cheo and Carlos to be aware of the Axemen's tendency to send both forwards to one side, setting up the potential for another player to break free into the open area on the opposite side of the pitch. "We've got to make sure nobody's coming through on the weak side," he said.

Flannigan's other concern was the Bulldogs' tendency to imitate the opposite team's style of play. In this game, it meant that the Woodburn players were taking too many long passes down the middle, where the taller Axemen could usually win airballs. He continued:

"The more we shoot long balls down the middle, the more we play into their hands. Let's get the ball out wide more often. Our best attack against these guys is on the outside."

There were other problems. Woodburn, used to playing on grass, still hadn't adjusted to the speed of the ball on turf and had mistimed nearly a dozen passes. The forwards were starting their runs too late and the midfielders were passing too soon.

Omar had come down out of the stands, too caught up in the game to sit any longer. He was also concerned by the mistimed passes and the occasional defensive lapses. For the most part, however, Omar felt that the boys looked focused and determined. Separated from the field by a short metal fence, Omar paced back and forth, wishing he were on the sidelines.

Halftime ended during a break in the storm. The wind gently but persistently yanked on the reserve players' warm-up jackets as the starters ran on to the field. When the game restarted, Woodburn made more runs down the sidelines and got several shots on goal, but the South Eugene keeper, a tall lanky kid with a quick leap, seemed to swallow up any balls that went near him. Woodburn also continued to mistime its passes, causing Flannigan to swear and stomp back and forth.

The game was at times overwhelmingly defensive. In one sequence, Martin stole the ball, lost it to an Axeman who lost it to Edgar, who lost it to another of the Axemen, who dribbled it a few paces before losing it to Cesar. The possessions were held so briefly that often the game's observers didn't have time to get excited. In the middle of the half, the game bogged down, neither team able to break out of the midfield.

With eighteen minutes left in the half, Flannigan walked over to the rooted Ransom. The two stood side by side in their thick jackets, fogging the air as they spoke.

"So, with ten minutes left, do we play for overtime or do we play to win?" Flannigan asked.

Ransom answered with a shrug, "We're playing well enough to win right now."

Flannigan walked away, mulling over his options. Playing for overtime was the conservative choice, leaving the team as it was. He could, however, pull Carlos from goal and stick him in front as a third forward. The danger was that Betos, the backup goalie, was not as skilled as Carlos. The improved offense meant a weaker defense, and Flannigan hated a weak defense.

As he considered this, the ref blew his whistle, calling a foul on a South Eugene player for a high kick near Juan's face. Flannigan shouted, "Four! Four!" a play that called for two players taking turns pretending to kick the ball, then a third kicking it wide of the defensive wall to a waiting player. But Martin and Juan, setting the ball up in front of the penalty area, didn't hear him, and ran their own choice, a play that resulted in the third player kicking the ball over the defensive wall toward the goal. Cheo took the shot, a beautiful arcing ball that barely skimmed the averted heads of the defensive players and curved down toward the net, and straight into the goalie's arms.

Flannigan erupted. "That's not a four! Dammit!" and stalked down the field yelling at Martin and Juan.

Martin heard him, but pretended not to. Ever since Octavio's injury, when Martin had returned to a starting spot on the team, he had felt his old self again. There had been times during the beginning of the season when he almost quit because he played so poorly. And it seemed like Flannigan was always on his ass about something. He thought Ransom was all right. Ransom calmly explained how to play better, but Flannigan yelled. This was the first time Flannigan had singled him out him in this game, and Martin decided to just ignore it and concentrate on scoring.

On the next play, he got his chance. Taking a long pass, Vlad turned and flicked the ball to Tony, who dashed down the left sideline, head down. Tony paused just long enough for a defender to rush past, and then he cut in toward the goal. He spotted Martin wide open about twenty yards from the goal and sent him a low, fast ball that skipped over the surface of the field like a hockey puck. Martin dribbled once and took the shot, a hard, high kick to the left side of the net. The Axemen's goalie dove, hands extended, and engulfed the ball with his long arms.

Martin turned and hung his head; on the bench, the Bulldogs cheered his shot. Damn, he thought. It was a good shot—not like the ones he had taken during league play, all of them going wide or over the net—but still not good enough. His knee was hurting too, the repaired meniscus probably inflamed. He paused to rub it the way the physical therapist had shown him. After all those games sitting on the bench, he was not going to ask for a substitute.

A couple of minutes after Martin's shot, the Axemen took a corner kick, getting the incoming ball and heading it toward the Woodburn goal, over the top post and Carlos's upraised hands. A few minutes later, when the clock finally ran out, the score was still tied 0–0.

Flannigan gathered the team around him, aware of the game's uncanny resemblance to the Lakeridge game that had ended their last season.

"Okay," he said. "Listen. The game's going into two ten-minute overtimes. This isn't sudden death. We play all ten minutes of both overtimes. So if they score, the game's not over. If it's tied at the end of both overtimes, then we go into penalty kicks."

Flannigan was impressed by their keeper and didn't want the game to go to penalty kicks, but he didn't say that. Instead, he shrugged and said, "Look, I'm happy any way you win this thing. Let's go."

After the first overtime ended, the long night began to take its toll. In the five-minute break between overtimes, Tony's hamstring cramped up enough that he asked to be taken out of the game, and he lay on his back grimacing into the renewed drizzle as O.J. helped stretch his leg. Cesar lay in the back of Brian Flannigan's truck, his face tightened in pain, the trainers taping up his ankle, which one of the Axemen had landed on. Martin's knee throbbed. After ninety minutes of nearly continuous, grueling play, all the starters were exhausted.

But the game was also taking its toll on the South Eugene team. They stood in a dripping circle around their coach, and something in their body language showed that they were tired and uncertain. It had, no doubt, come as a surprise that Woodburn, a number-four seed, was even competitive. Ryan White, possibly the state's best player, had been unable to keep the ball for any extended period of time, and apart from a couple of headers on corner kicks, had not been much of a threat.

Jovanny pointed this out to the coach, and after Flannigan let the boys get water and a few minutes of rest, he called them into another huddle.

"Listen," he said. "These guys did not expect this. These guys have not played a game this hard since the preseason. They are not used to having to play this tough. They are *tired.* I've already seen a couple of their guys cramp up. So let's play hard."

He paused. "You're not tired, are you?"

"Hell, no!" Carlos yelled, and the rest of the Bulldogs joined in loudly. Octavio limped into the middle of the circle and rattled off in staccato time exactly what they knew he would say: play hard, play with guts, play with your heart, *con ganas, con huevos, con todo, con todo!*

Anybody watching from the sidelines could have seen the difference between the two teams returning for the final ten-minute overtime period. While South Eugene slowly jogged back onto the field, the Woodburn players ran to their positions.

Omar paced the sidelines, unable to stay seated.

The Woodburn fans, perhaps sensing the difference, began to stamp their feet and chant, "Let's go, Woodburn, let's go!"

The game started again. Despite the Axemen's weariness and the Bulldogs' apparent vitality, the game continued to be a midfield battle, the ball rarely controlled by one team for more than ten seconds before a hard-charging defender stripped it away. Just after the first minute, a South Eugene player broke free from a cluster of three Woodburn defenders and blasted a kick from the top of the Woodburn penalty box, cursing and clutching his fists when it went out of bounds to the right of the net.

A couple of minutes later, Martin stripped the ball clean and headed toward the midfield, dribbling around two defenders, his arms flapping as he shifted his weight from foot to foot in a flurry of fakes before passing the ball to Vlad, running from midfield toward the left corner. The Woodburn fans jumped out, shouting in unison, "Olé!" Just before the top of the penalty box, a South Eugene player slide-tackled Vlad, who rolled into the box clutching his right ankle. As the Woodburn bench bolted to its feet, the referee awarded Woodburn a free kick. Vlad slowly got to his feet, limping toward the goal.

The bench chatter silenced and the Woodburn fans began to pound the bleachers with their feet, creating a low, rumbling thunder. Juan prepared the ball, took a few steps back, and then struck it over the defensive wall toward the top of the net, where the keeper met it, jumping to punch the ball high. No goal, but with only four minutes left, Woodburn had a corner kick coming.

Flannigan quickly called for a substitute, bringing in Jovanny from the left wing. For a freshman, Jovanny had been surprisingly good, but with little time remaining, Flannigan knew that this could be the Bulldogs' final chance for a goal. He turned to Tony, his most dependable and accurate corner kicker. Tony, hamstring cramping, back aching, stripped off his jacket and started jogging in place to warm up. When Jovanny arrived, Flannigan asked him if he felt confident taking the kick. Jovanny shook his head; Flannigan turned to Tony and nodded.

"Number one," he said.

The play called for Tony at the corner, O.J. at the near post, and Vlad at the far post. The idea was to kick the ball to O.J., who would head-flick the ball backwards to Vlad, who would head it into the goal. They had successfully performed this in practice, but never on the field. Flannigan called the play out of deference to the South Eugene keeper's skill. The only way to get the ball past this guy, he thought, was to commit him to defend one corner of the net and then hurry the ball to the other corner.

Gripping a low fence that bordered the field, Omar turned to a South Eugene parent standing next to him and shook his head.

"Great game, huh?" the other parent said.

"Yeah," Omar agreed.

Tony set the ball down, raised his arm, and waited for the ref's whistle. His kick was nearly perfect, coming down about ten feet in front of the near post. O.J., leaping up to flick it back, misjudged the ball's speed, and it hit him between the shoulder blades and bounced up again. In a crowd of players leaping for the second header, Cheo won the ball, shifting his head to send it over the keeper and into the goal. Instead, the ball fell short, just to the left of the keeper, about three feet in front of the goal, right at Luis's feet. Two paces away, Vlad was already swinging his leg forward to kick when Luis stepped forward and poked at the ball with his toe, and the ball rolled, almost gently, right between the keeper's legs, nestling into the back of the net.

Woodburn 1. South Eugene 0.

Flannigan stabbed his fist into the air, shouting, the cold and wet and wind replaced by a sudden sharp joy. Behind him, the bench players were leaping up and down and hugging each other. The Woodburn fans began screaming. In the stands, it was hard to tell who had kicked the ball, but Luis's older brother, Francisco, insisted to his family that Luis had scored. He stood clapping and shouting, wishing he were back on the pitch again. Luis was mobbed briefly before the teams retreated. There were still almost three minutes left to play.

With their playoff lives on the line, South Eugene spent the last few minutes of the game attacking, sending long passes into clusters of players at the top of Woodburn's penalty box. Twice they earned corner kicks, but each was defended successfully, and when the whistle blew at the end of the game, the Woodburn bench players, coaches, friends, and family members poured onto the field to embrace the team. Octavio limped over and grabbed Cheo in a bear hug. Flannigan was so excited that he embraced a reporter, tears in his eyes. Somebody's father shook everyone's hand, grinning like a cat. In the middle of the crowd, Tony forgot about his back and leg pain. He was surrounded by players and their friends and family when he saw his brother, Isidro, running across the turf toward him. They grabbed each other and Isidro lifted Tony off the ground.

Pulling himself from the arms of his wife, Flannigan forced himself to concentrate on the customs of the game. The South Eugene team was already forming into a sad line, and Flannigan began shouting over the happy voices, lining his team up, and tacking himself onto the end of the line, trying to hold back some of the joy he felt as he solemnly offered his hand to the players and coaches from South Eugene.

Freshman Manolo burst up from the pool of plastic balls, an ecstatic smile creasing his face. Flannigan and Ransom paused to watch him toss the balls in the air around him, Daffy Duck swimming through gold coins in Ali Baba's cave. Flannigan chuckled; Ransom shook his head.

"One minute they're serious adults, the next minute they're kids again."

Ransom followed Flannigan to order pizzas for the hungry team. Manolo, Angel, and some of the other younger Bulldogs stayed in the restaurant's play area for a few minutes, climbing a plastic structure and chasing each other. The juniors and seniors were already in the back room that had been reserved for the team. A college football game was showing on televisions scattered throughout the restaurant, and while the coaches and other adults sat down to watch, the Bulldogs, still dressed in their blue away uniforms, tossed balled-up paper napkins at each other and replayed, over and over, Luis's game-winning goal.

Luis reddened as his teammates congratulated him, or threw an arm around his broad shoulders, or playfully slapped his head. When the season had started, he had figured that he should score three times, and South Eugene had been number three. Fulfilling his promise made him as happy as scoring the game-winning shot, and as all the positive attention came his way, a huge, almost beatific smile curved across his face.

The coaches were feeling good, too. Both felt that the boys had shown them some grit in the South Eugene game that they hadn't seen before. Coach Flannigan, who didn't typically let himself think games ahead, briefly let his mind wander. The Bulldogs could go far in the playoffs, maybe build on that for the future. His team was so close to being the dominant force they should be. Could he afford the time to organize a club team, keep these boys playing together until next year?

He had contacted parents before, told them that the high school athletes needed a club team, but so far nobody in the community had taken it on. He heard various reasons—they didn't have the money, they didn't have the time—and he knew they probably didn't. But it was twenty years since he and his brother had taken Woodburn to the state finals, and more than anything, he wanted to get his team back there again.

This team had shown him strength in adversity for the first time. Could they keep it up?

FOURTEEN

Just a Game

I used to be a thug, a little thug wannabe. Then I started
playing soccer. If it wasn't for soccer, I probably would
have dropped out by now.

—Martin

With a couple of days to prepare for the upcoming game against
Westview, Flannigan decided to watch the Lakeridge–North Salem game. The winner of that game would play the winner of the
Woodburn-Westview match, and Flannigan liked seeing the opposing teams play as often as possible. He invited the entire team to join
him, but only Carlos accepted the offer. From the high school, they
stopped at Flannigan's house and switched into his wife Lynn's new
Ford Explorer. Lynn drove. By the time they were on the road, it
was rush hour and the lines of cars, headlights on, were backed up at
every light. It was early November, dark, cold, and windy, but thank-
fully not raining.

The game was a surprise. Neither of the two teams, Lakeridge
nor North Salem, was in the Pac-9 league with Woodburn, but the
Bulldogs had a connection to both. There was bad blood, of course,
with Lakeridge after last year's game; and North Salem was probably the team in Oregon most similar to Woodburn. It had a lot of
Hispanics, represented a working-class part of the state capital, and
played an entertaining, possession style of soccer. Flannigan wasn't
sure which team he wanted to meet more. Playing against North Salem would be fun, he thought, with both teams playing Latin-style,
but playing against Lakeridge would be Woodburn's chance to get
revenge.

As the reigning state champions, Lakeridge was the highest-
ranked high school soccer team in the state and the seventh-ranked
team in the country. North Salem wasn't even listed in the national

rankings. Yet North Salem got started early, scoring twice in the first half and then holding on to allow only a single Lakeridge goal in the second half. Later, the Bulldogs looked at the score and nodded—we would have beaten Lakeridge this year, they said. That night, several other top-seeded teams were eliminated: Corvallis, another favorite to win it all, and Lincoln, league champs in Portland.

They returned to the SUV together, and as Lynn steered through the departing cars, Mike turned around to talk to Carlos. He knew little about Carlos's personal life except that his goalie was a foster child living with O.J.'s family. He had met Carlos three years before, during the kid's freshman year, when Carlos and Omar showed up during a practice to talk about Carlos transferring from Gervais High School. Carlos had just left his previous foster home to move in with Omar, and both he and Omar not only wanted Carlos to go to a closer school, they wanted him to be able to participate in a winning soccer program.

Flannigan liked Carlos's abilities in the net, but he also felt close to Carlos because of their shared experiences. Carlos was one of the few players on his team who seemed to take soccer seriously, as a long-term commitment. After all, here was Carlos in the car with him, the only kid who had wanted to come scout their potential op-position.

Sitting in the darkness, the lights from oncoming cars shining on his face, Flannigan decided to open up to Carlos. From a pure soccer-skills perspective, he thought the boy was the one player on the team most likely to turn pro, and he wanted to do what he could to help Carlos reach his dream.

"Listen, Carlos," he said, "I don't really know what you've gone through. I mean, I have heard a bit, but I wanted you to know that you're not totally alone. I don't know if you know this, but I lived with foster parents, too."

He described some of his upbringing, and Carlos, a little uncomfortable at his coach's sudden openness, tried to listen. Something had to really hold Carlos to make him sit still and look somebody in the eye. Coach Flannigan's story did that.

The conversation between the two lasted only a few minutes,

ending when Carlos didn't volunteer any information. He was too busy trying to process his coach's newfound vulnerability. He understood that Mike had lived in foster homes, but it slipped past him that Brian was not Flannigan's father. It would be months before he understood all that Flannigan told him. Lynn drove on through the rain while Carlos and Mike sat quietly.

Carlos was not naturally introspective; he didn't feel comfortable poking around in his deeper feelings. In fact, he dismissed any suggestions that his upbringing made him vulnerable. He knew people assumed that foster kids were depressed or needed to talk—state workers had mentioned it enough times.

When he first got into foster care, they made him talk to a counselor who told him he needed to express his feelings. Carlos thought, "What the hell is he talking about? What do you want me to say to you?" Then his social worker would tell his foster parents that he wasn't cooperating.

Carlos felt that the whole thing was stupid, a game he was supposed to play to make other people feel useful. They wanted him to say his heart was broken, to struggle, to confess to secret fears. But Carlos thought, "That's just all in the head. You don't think about it, you don't do it." His mom pissed him off, but he didn't dwell on it. He never even thought about it.

Carlos knew that a lot of kids did struggle with foster care, and when he stepped back, he could empathize. He knew that some foster kids were beaten or molested or just ignored. He figured that the reason he didn't struggle was because with Omar, he had landed in a good home. He thought that he was just lucky. It wasn't worth pondering why.

Carlos and Mike Flannigan had that in common, probably more than either realized. They both found homes with strong father figures who had lifted themselves out of their own morasses: Omar, who lived in extreme poverty and dropped out of school at eighth grade, who relied on mechanical aptitude, hard work, and keeping his eye focused on long-term goals; and Brian, who saw his brothers go to jail and rejected that path, and who depended on his athletic aptitude and hard work to secure his family's first college degree. Omar and

Brian both knew the kind of pitfalls that young men fall into, and both decided that the solution lay in sports.

Mike and Carlos, a generation apart, their ancestors from two different continents, were two people who, given slightly different circumstances, might have wandered into some kind of hopeless lifestyle. Mike could have become isolated and withdrawn; Carlos could have lashed out in violence. Sports had saved both of these men, but because they were men, they couldn't talk about it.

It had started raining regularly the Saturday they played at South Eugene. By Thursday, the grass field at Westview, where the Westview football team also played, was a mud pit. Flannigan fought to have the game played at Woodburn, where the tall grass would slow the pace of the ball and deny Westview a speed advantage. His argument was this: they had played one playoff game at home and one away—50 percent home games. Westview, on the other hand, had played one game at home—100 percent home games. His argument was rejected, and the game was scheduled for the artificial-turf field of a neutral high school.

When the Bulldogs arrived, they walked onto a field already occupied by a practicing football team. Reluctantly, the football coach gave up half the field, which the Woodburn and Westview teams shared during warm-ups. This sort of treatment drove Mike Flannigan nuts: football gets everything, and soccer scrapes up the crumbs.

Standing on the turf, bundled into a thick black jacket, Flannigan got on his cell phone to Athletic Director Greg Baisch. Flannigan and the Westview coach had agreed to extend the warm-up an extra half hour so they could use the full field once the football team left at 4:30. He stood with the phone pressed to his ear, air fogging in front of his mouth, the sound of traffic in the background. When he reached Baisch, he asked him to call the Westview athletic director and clear the change with him. Baisch agreed, but then, after talking to the Westview athletic director, he decided to start the game at the original time.

"Goddammit," Coach Flannigan said upon hearing this. "Baisch is a pussy." He slapped the phone closed.

The Westview Wildcats represented an upper-middle-class neighborhood in Beaverton, a sprawling Portland suburb. The high school had a large number of minority students, but most of these were the children of software engineers at Intel or one of the other computer firms in the area. Only about 7 percent of the student body were English Language Learners. Westview wasn't quite Lakeridge, but it wasn't far off.

This would be the last time the two teams played. In 2005, Oregon had four conferences, the largest schools playing in 4A, which is why Woodburn, with 1,300 students, ended up playing Westview, one of the largest high schools in the state, with 2,300. Obviously, this kind of size difference meant a vast discrepancy in talent pools for athletic teams, and many smaller schools had complained. In 2005, the Oregon Student Athletic Association decided to create two new conferences, hoping to promote greater parity among school size. Starting next year, Woodburn would play in 5A and Westview in 6A.

Jesuit High School, with 1,100 students, had announced it would opt up and play the powerhouses in the 6A division, and Flannigan wanted to follow suit. However, every other team in the school would have to opt up, too—softball, volleyball, track and field, and, of course, football. The Woodburn football team hadn't won a game in two years, so over Flannigan's objections, Woodburn soccer would stay in 5A.

The advantage to this was that Woodburn's chances to go to the state championship in 5A were considerably higher than if they were in 6A. Flannigan didn't want to be too bold, but he felt certain that in 5A, a state championship would come soon. On the other hand, Omar Mendoza insisted that it wasn't really the state championship if you weren't playing the best teams in the state, regardless of the size. Some of the Bulldogs objected to this reasoning, pointing out the disparity in school sizes. Flannigan felt torn. He thought the team probably would do very well at 5A, maybe even dominate the state, but he also thought that Omar was right. Jesuit had fewer students than Woodburn, and they won more games than anybody. So, if 2005 was Woodburn's last chance to play the biggest and the best, then he wanted to win it all.

To the left of the Westview goal, the sun sunk low over the horizon, casting long, freakish shadows of the players and of the three-story steel-frame building at the construction site between the field and the road. The late afternoon sky was a dark, rich blue. Despite the cold, the traffic, and the banging that came from the skeletal structure, it was a lovely evening. As the football team cleared the field a few minutes early, both soccer teams began more intense warm-ups. The sun dipped lower, and pink seeped into the bottom of the clouds. A half moon lay on its back farther south.

Carlos stood in goal, unsmiling, knocking practice balls away and feeling unhappy with his warm-up. He refused to look people in the eye and answered in monosyllables. Omar stood watching him as the Woodburn fans began to arrive and take their seats. Despite Carlos's behavior, Omar felt good about the game. He knew many of the Westview players from club games and felt that his boys would be able to stand up to them. He also thought the team could handle Westview's star midfielder, Ryan Fitzgerald, so long as they hit him hard—literally collided with him—on every possession.

Woodburn JV Coach Levi Arias had missed the South Eugene game so he could scout Westview's first playoff game. He came back very impressed by Fitzgerald, particularly his speed.

"He's very fast," Arias said. "You don't want him to turn. The other midfielder, who is fast, feeds him."

Hearing the click of cleats, Omar turned and saw Juan leaving the bathroom and reached out to stop him, give him some advice. Three Woodburn students walked by. They were white kids wearing T-shirts with handmade blue lettering. The back of one said, "They Are Our Brothers." The back of another said, "I Wish I Was Mexican."

In the middle of the field, Chuck Ransom walked over to Flannigan and said with a smile:

"Well, Cheo says not to worry. He had a dream, and we're going to win two–one."

"I hope he's got a time machine and that's right," Flannigan said.

Both teams rushed through an abbreviated practice before the ref cleared the field and called the captains over. Cheo and Cesar walked to the middle of the field, Octavio watching from the sidelines. Brian Flannigan stopped straightening up the players' backpacks next to the bench and began watching the introductions closely. Each team was allowed twenty players. Westview had twenty-one. It was the sort of minor rule-breaking that the Woodburn team had become very sensitive to, feeling that they were punished for such small infractions when other teams were not.

"That's twenty-one," Brian kept saying. "They've got twenty-one." He pulled out his camera and photographed the extra player on the field. "We've been cheated before; at least we'll have proof," he said.

The pressure of the game didn't seem to have affected many of the players besides Carlos. Angel was smiling; Jovanny looked relaxed. Only Octavio, enveloped by a huge blue-and-white jacket, looked serious and worried. He paced back and forth on the sidelines, wishing he was on the field. He no longer used crutches, but his knee still hurt when he walked. After his initial doctor's visit, he had been dealing with the injury at home, never returning for the recommended MRI.

When the sun finally dropped below the horizon, Octavio took a few more steps to the side until he was standing in front of the players' backpacks. As the starters returned from the introductions, Coach Flannigan gathered them into a tight huddle and spoke briefly. He was sticking to the team that had ended the North Medford game: Martin at center-mid, Cheo at sweeper, Carlos in goal, Vlad and Juan up front. They stopped talking, and Octavio moved forward to hear the coach.

"Okay, listen. We have to come out hard. We have to go out there more intense than they are. Match them stride for stride and let's take it to another level. *Take it to another level.* We've got subs if you need them, okay? So go hard, and we'll take care of you."

That was it. Ransom had nothing to add, and the players went into their huddle as Octavio once again stepped forward to give his rapid-fire, intense speech, urging them to play hard, to play intense, to play with heart, to play with feeling. The huddle broke and the starters took the field.

The game started evenly, with both sides making runs into the others' backfield. Jovanny was surprised by how fast the other players were.

"They looked fast when you watched them from the sidelines," he said. "But when you got out there and ran with them, you realized how fast they really were. I thought, 'Whoa, I am going to have to run in this game.'"

With a little over five minutes gone, Woodburn took the ball the length of the field, Martin dribbling around two players into the penalty box, where he was pushed from behind. He took the free kick with a good, low ball that skimmed the turf but was kicked wide at the last minute by a quick Westview defender.

Then Westview got its chance. Ryan Fitzgerald broke free down the right sideline, sending a low cross to one of the Westview forwards, who took advantage of a brief opening to take a shot from the top of the box. It sailed high. Carlos leaped, and the ball passed just over his fingers, hit the crossbar at the top of the goal and bounced back to the left, toward another Westview player, who kicked it in over Carlos's desperate dive.

Westview 1. Woodburn 0.

Two minutes later, Westview got another shot off that went wide and Ransom, feeling that Carlos was playing tight, worried about making a mistake, shouted, "Carlos! Wake up!"

Woodburn's next chance to score came soon after. Tony drove the ball down the left sideline, slipped around one defender, then had the ball stripped and kicked out of bounds by another. On the throw-in, he spotted Cesar wide open at the far post and hurled the ball deep into the penalty box. Cesar stopped it, turned, and found himself about ten feet away from a wide-open goal, the keeper still running back from where he had positioned himself closer to Tony. The Woodburn bench leaped to its feet and Cesar kicked the ball hard. It rocketed from his foot and soared almost straight up and over the goal. The groan from the Woodburn bench was audible in the stands.

During the rest of the half, both teams had scoring opportunities that they could not capitalize on. Carlos made several good saves, once leaping high to snatch a ball aimed toward the upper-left-hand corner of the net while a Westview player practically embraced him. Minutes later, Tony got off a splendid free kick from forty yards out that landed in front of the goal without any Woodburn player near enough to tap it in.

Flannigan watched the ball bounce out and felt his anger rise. He waved his clipboard around in the air like a man trying to flag down a taxi.

"Somebody's got to want that ball! That's two times now! Somebody's got to want that ball!"

With ten minutes left, Vlad went down, gasping for breath, while the game moved on and Flannigan shouted for the referee to notice and stop the game. The player defending Vlad had hit him hard in the neck with an elbow—intentionally, Vlad thought—and for a few minutes he was scared, having a difficult time just getting enough air to breathe. Vlad came off slowly, hand held to his throat. It felt as if his windpipe had crumpled. Then, as the air came easier, his throat burned and each breath hurt. Later, he would try to even the score when the ref's attention was elsewhere, but his elbow would thud harmlessly into the player's back.

With two minutes left in the half, Westview attacked down the right side, their forward pushing the ball hard into the box toward the goal. Juan, running alongside the Westview forward as if their thighs were glued together, knocked the ball out of the box, unfortunately right toward Fitzgerald, who again rushed in before Cheo appeared and booted the ball out of bounds.

Flannigan turned to Ransom. "Where was Carlos?" he asked.

Ransom replied, "Carlos is playing scared." He said it calmly, without judgment, as if describing the weather conditions.

Coach Flannigan was not happy. When the half ended, he gathered the team and took a moment to figure out how to address the problem, the same problem the Bulldogs had all season. They didn't know how to finish. The team had created opportunities, had taken shots on goal, but the balls either went straight to the keeper or missed the net entirely. Why couldn't his players shoot with more control?

The boys collapsed on the field in front of him. Flannigan, his words clouding the air in front of his face, spoke deliberately.

"Now . . . we knew we had to come into this game and score some goals. We saw early on in this game, I saw us playing with confidence, I saw us control the ball. They got that early goal, but we had a great chance as well. They finished theirs; we didn't. Really, you look at the shot chart, it's eight-seven. This is an even game.

"A little worry we had as coaches is our inside midfielders, as the game went on, slowly started to hang back more, hang back more, hang back more. If we're getting tired, let me know, we'll get some subs, all right? But we cannot have our two attacking center mids hanging back on defense. Yes, we want you to get back when they have the ball, but we also want you to get up. There were a couple times where they put the ball in and their midfielders were there to pick it up and all of our midfielders were sucked in on our back line, all right?

"Defensively, I don't have a lot of problems. One mistake, all right, one time we let that guy get by us, and they made us pay. It wasn't the initial shot, it was us reacting slow to the second shot, all right? If Carlos doesn't make that save, we need to respond quicker. We have the ability to score on these guys. That goalkeeper, they're taking a little bit of a gamble on his long punt. He does not cover his posts, he's slow getting off his line. So let's get some shots on this guy. He's given up a lot of goals this year.

"I see us taking those long kicks, getting the ball in the air, making it a fifty–fifty ball. That's not our game. Our game is right to feet, right to feet. All right? They scored that goal, we got a little bit scared, a little bit panicky, we started hanging back."

He then described a few plays he had seen, what he felt the players were and were not doing. Coach Ransom watched impassively. He had seen this team doubt itself before. The team didn't have much confidence in its ability to score, and rather than pressing the attack, the Bulldogs tended to collapse on the ball when it was taken by the other team. When that happened, players acted less as a group and more as individuals, each trying to beat the other team alone. This meant the Bulldogs stopped talking to each other.

"And listen," Coach Flannigan continued. "The longer this game goes without us scoring, we gotta pick up the intensity. Five minutes go, we haven't scored, pick it up. Ten minutes go, we haven't scored, pick it up. We need a goal. This is it! We need a goal!"

The second half began with Rambo taking Vlad's place at forward. Early on, Westview earned a corner kick, and as the ball came down near the net, Carlos charged into the field, leaping high to punch it wide. Moments later, Rambo stole the ball at midfield, dribbled in, gave a quick give-and-go pass to Juan and tried a shot from the middle of the box that a Westview defender blocked. Martin took a foul kick from the thirty-yard line that was headed back to him; he took the second shot straight toward—and over—the goal.

Then O.J. went down, a hand to his face, and came off the field, blood seeping through his fingers.

"They're throwing elbows," he said angrily, Laurie the trainer hovering around him with a towel.

Then, with fifteen minutes gone, Woodburn lined up to block a Westview free kick. The ball soared around the wall to a Westview player at full run, timed perfectly to avoid an offsides call. As the Bulldogs broke up their wall to chase the ball, the Westview player headed it in for a goal.

Westview 2. Woodburn 0.

There it was. Anybody who had observed the Bulldogs that year, who knew their body language, could see what was happening. The slumping shoulders, the hanging heads, the lack of quick decisions. As the game restarted, the Bulldogs collectively protected the ball, second-guessed themselves, became reluctant to commit to the attack. The second goal broke Woodburn's spirit. The team that had trouble scoring, that prided itself on its defense, *knew* that they would not come back against Westview if down by two. The Bulldogs had seen several of their shots—good shots—rejected, and several other scoring opportunities sail over or around the Westview net. The Bulldogs had never come back from being down in a game all season. After that second goal, it seemed it wasn't meant to be. It was the Woodburn curse. They were not going to make it to the finals.

Even from the sidelines, it was easy to see the change in the players' attitudes. Luis's cousin Henry, sitting in the stands with Luis's brothers, felt a spike of disgust. This team lacked intensity, he thought. They were too friendly, too willing to play and have fun. They had been down three times this season and they had never come back to win. "This game," he thought, "is over."

In the last twenty minutes, Coach Flannigan moved some of the boys around to try and find a way to pull off the upset. He moved a midfielder forward to give him three shooters. A few minutes later, Ryan Fitzgerald turned with the ball, saw an opening, and blasted in Westview's third goal. Even as Carlos dove, he knew he was not going to reach the ball. "That guy's a finisher," he said.

With that goal, Flannigan gave up on defense and put Betos in, moving Carlos into the central forward spot. Carlos tossed Betos his gloves and ran into position.

With only five minutes left, Carlos got his chance. A long pass reached him after he had turned and sprinted past the final defender, leaving him in a one-on-one with the Westview keeper. The Woodburn bench jumped up, eyes wide, arms upraised. A thought flitted through their communal consciousness: get this goal, play hard, maybe get two more quick ones for a shift in momentum that would take them to overtime feeling confident. Carlos judged the distance and chipped the ball over the goalie, a short shot that sent the ball up and down quickly, with little forward momentum. But the ball flew a bit too far, landing on top of the net before rolling to the ground behind, and the bench players collapsed with a groan.

Carlos jogged back to the center of the pitch, cursing. "Flannigan should have put me in sooner!" he thought savagely. "It's too late!"

. . .

With three minutes left, Tony came off the field, stripped the tape holding his shin guards on and fell back on the turf, his feet pointed toward the field, his head near the line of backpacks. He closed his eyes and arranged his black warm-up pants over his face. Lying that way, he missed the shot Westview took on Betos, a rocket the backup goalie blocked, and then chased from the box and kicked out of bounds.

Omar shook his head. The game was deteriorating and the boys were no longer playing as a team. He had watched two previous high school seasons end like this, and he still wasn't used to it. Flannigan had been too cautious from the beginning, he thought. Then he wondered how to turn the loss into a lesson for all the boys who would no doubt soon be at his house, downcast and dejected.

In the last thirty seconds, Westview tried again, working into the Woodburn penalty box. Cheo, fueled by frustration, aimed a vicious kick at the ball, and for the first time all year, he mistimed it so badly that his foot missed the ball entirely and the momentum of his effort spun his body around 180 degrees. Another Westview player ran forward and took a shot that went out of bounds to the left of the goal.

The clock ticked down the seconds: 4, 3, 2, 1, 0.

With another game scheduled on the same field that evening, both Woodburn and Westview were hurried from their benches and off the pitch. They had quickly taken care of the necessary rituals—shaking hands with opposing players, offering their congratulations—before reluctantly walking away, the coaches behind them. The Bulldogs carried their backpacks dangling from their hands like cold, wet towels and slowly collected in a corner where they would be out of the way.

As he followed, Flannigan felt that he had let the team down. Not because of the score, but because he had failed, once again, to give his boys confidence. It was all their expectations, he thought. They fall behind and they think "Shit, we're going to lose this and then we're not going to win the state championship and I'm not going to go to college. I'm going to be picking berries for the rest of my life."

To Coach Flannigan, the boys on his team had never experienced much success and had never been around it, so when they were suddenly supposed to be the best soccer team in all Oregon, they didn't know how to deal with the pressure.

Chuck Ransom walked beside Octavio, thinking of the game as a series of missed opportunities. If the Bulldogs had scored on one of those early attempts, he thought, the mental game would have changed. We would have planted a seed of doubt in our opponents' minds, and we would have been confident. Our guys thought the gods were against them.

Flannigan found four reporters converging on him. A bit impatiently, he asked them to wait until after he had spoken to his team. As he approached, he could see that jerseys were already piling up in the middle of the seated circle of players in a sad blue-and-white pile. Tony had stripped off his jersey and was wearing a gray hoodie; Cheo had pulled on a white Tommy Hilfiger hoodie over his T-shirt.

Some players hung their heads or stared at nothing. The older players took it harder than the younger ones. Octavio, who hadn't even played, was probably the most upset. He leaned against the fence silently. Manolo, however, was already smiling and joking. A freshman, he had three more years of varsity play to look forward to, and he was already a starter, perhaps destined to be a star.

Flannigan stepped close to the circle, dropped his bag, and gestured for the team to close in.

"Gather round, guys," he said. "Get close; I don't want anybody else to listen to this.

"Quick analysis of this game. I don't need to say much. But, I mean, we look at the score, we see three–nothing. But how different could this game have been? We had three, as I see them, great opportunities. I'm not pointing fingers at anybody because I think that goalkeeper came up with some big saves, okay? He impressed me. When I scouted him, he did not look that good. He came up with some huge saves.

"But what we need to realize, when we were that close, is that we make one or two of those shots, and who knows? Another overtime . . . a shootout . . . who knows? So don't let that score make you feel like they kicked your ass because it was inches away from going in our favor. We knew we had our work cut out for us. We knew, coming in as a four seed, that it would be tough.

"But what makes me so proud of you guys is I never heard anybody, this whole time, doubt yourselves. You guys took this head on and said, bring it on and we're going to do it. All right? At least we can walk out of the state playoffs with two wins. There's not a lot of teams in the state of Oregon that won two state playoff games."

For once, Flannigan wasn't pacing as he spoke. There wasn't room, with the players close around him, but also, he wanted to concentrate on what he said. He wanted to make things better.

"This never feels good; it hurts. But it makes you stronger, all right. And you seniors, I just want to say, I really like the senior class. I don't know how we do it, but every year we put together a great senior class, and this year, you guys are just as good, if not better, than any other senior class. And to lose Octavio and for you guys to rally and to put us in the position we are . . . Most teams, if they lost one of their best players, would have folded, and you guys stuck together. Cheo, you really became a leader after that. Cesar stepped up. Edgar, who never wants a leadership position, really became one of the better players on our team. So, I think this was a team led by seniors and I'm very proud of you. Juniors and sophomores and freshmen, you get another shot."

Flannigan told the team to meet the next day at the locker room, where they would have a final debriefing and turn in uniforms and backpacks.

"Okay, captains, how about a word?"

The coach turned his head to look at Cheo, Edgar, Octavio. None of them spoke. The rest of the team looked at them, and then looked away.

"C'mon," Coach Flannigan said. "I know this is tough, but you seniors should say something."

Octavio shook his head. Cesar shrugged and smiled. Finally, his coach's eyes on him, Cheo said, "We'll win next time."

The coach let that sit there for a moment, saw that he wasn't going to get anything else from them, and gestured for the team to stand up.

The boys rose and put their left arms out, spokes in a wheel, closed fists, standing in a tight circle. Flannigan turned to Octavio, who had his hands thrust deep into the pockets of his jacket, the white hood of his sweatshirt flared out behind him.

"Octavio," Flannigan said, "What do we got?"

Octavio spoke so softly that, at six feet away, his voice couldn't be heard.

"Team," he said.

Together the entire group shouted: "TEAM!"

Octavio and Cheo climbed aboard the bus silently. Many of the other boys lingered by the field, as if reluctant to acknowledge the end of the season. Two other teams were already warming up, and some of the boys greeted players they knew from club soccer.

As Octavio climbed aboard, he noticed a single Woodburn player already sitting, by himself, at the very back of the bus. It was Betos, the reserve goalkeeper, who had taken over for Carlos when Flannigan moved him into the forward position. He was bent forward, his head in his hands, body shaking slightly. Octavio heard the sound of crying.

Octavio and Cheo approached Betos, and sat down on the seats one row before his. Betos looked up and saw them smile.

"It's okay," said Cheo, "It's just a game."

"You will feel better tomorrow," Octavio said.

Betos nodded, smiled slightly, and tried to hold back the tears. He didn't argue, but he wasn't feeling upset that the team had lost. He was thinking about how he would never play with the Bulldogs again, and as a graduating senior, probably never play organized soccer again. He was thinking that this game, where he was brought in for a brief stretch at the end and made two saves, may be the last time he set foot on a soccer field. He was looking forward to graduating and going to college, but he also didn't want high school to end.

"I'm okay," he said, as the rest of the team began to climb on the bus. "It's all over."

FIFTEEN

Game Over

I thought we could take it all the way. I think everybody
thought that. But we lost because of inexperience, our defense, and the fact that a lot of our players didn't know what
to do against people who had been playing club soccer their
whole lives. Next year. Next year. It's always next year.

—O.J.

The season ended on a Tuesday night. In previous years, Coach
Flannigan had asked his kids to turn in their uniforms the night the
playoffs ended. They would walk or ride back to the locker room
and change, a sullen, silent experience that the coach loathed. As the
Bulldogs entered the playoffs, Coach Flannigan suddenly realized
that there was no reason to turn in uniforms immediately after the
game. They wouldn't be used for nine months.

So the boys turned in their uniforms on Wednesday during private exit interviews held in the coaches' office. The exit interviews
represented another new way of doing things, meant to give the players a moment of reflection. For Flannigan, the exit interviews were
the team's version of the "reframing" he did with his English classes
throughout the year. He didn't want his players to end the season
feeling as if they had lost, or hadn't tried hard enough, or that they
were destined to fail. He wanted to sit with them and explain, the
way he explained the meaning of *Julius Caesar*, that there was another
way to look at their experience—that, in fact, they could decide how
to view it.

"We sit down with each one," he said, "to try and get them to realize that even if they lost the game, it's not the end of the world, try
and reframe what happened for them. It's taken me a while to realize
that we don't have to win it all to be successful."

Like the boys on his team, when Flannigan started coaching, he was gunning for the state championship. However, after years on the sidelines, he had come to believe in the power of simply being on a team. Being successful, he now thought, wasn't just about winning the big game—despite what some parents might say—it was about getting on the field and busting your ass trying. It was about working together toward a common goal. He sometimes winced inwardly at the clichés, but they were true.

Some of the meetings with players went well, especially with the starters who had performed well. Some of the boys didn't want to hear his ideas about how to improve. Ramon, who never had agreed with Flannigan's decision to bring him off the bench, felt hurt by some of the coach's comments, and afterwards he turned his head away from the coach when they met in the school hallways.

Coach Ransom saw the loss to Westview through an even narrower lens. Los Perros had a couple of chances to put the game away early and didn't. He didn't know if the lack of scoring came from nerves, from some deep internal desire to lose, or just plain bad luck, but he knew that missing those first couple of goals changed the entire tenor of the game.

Ransom had seen the change in his team's attitude after Westview scored the first time. He had felt it. The Bulldogs knew that they had never come from behind, and they began to think that they couldn't come from behind. With each goal, he had watched Westview's confidence rise and Woodburn's plummet. He had found it pretty painful to watch at the end.

Ransom was a big believer in self-esteem. In his mind, what the kids of Woodburn needed most was to feel that they were capable. Then it would be a self-fulfilling prophecy. He didn't think that he could raise the boys' self-esteem in three months of soccer, but as he spoke with each one in turn during exit interviews, he also hoped that just by being in the boys' lives, he might help, one small interaction at a time.

A month later, on the last day of school before the December holidays, the team met at Coach Mike Flannigan's house for a party. Several cars arrived simultaneously in the darkness, and the boys lingered on the sidewalk in a group, each reluctant to go in first, not sure of the etiquette of entering their coach's house. Although it was around 5 p.m., it was already dark, the temperature in the high thirties, windy and wet.

Flannigan arrived with a huge pot of spaghetti sauce and urged the boys inside, where they stood around uncomfortably until somebody mentioned the video games upstairs. Only a handful of players were absent, including Cheo and Octavio. Coach Ransom said that they were probably on their way after work, together—the two of them were always traveling around together.

A month is an eternity for teenage boys, and by the time they gathered at Coach Flannigan's, the painful loss to Westview was behind them. Westview had beaten North Salem to advance to the state finals, where they had lost to Jesuit, 1–0.

As the first few boys began loading piles of steaming spaghetti onto their plates, Ransom's cell phone rang. He looked at the number —it was Cheo. The reception was poor, and he stepped outside into the cold to try and make sense of the call—he assumed Cheo was calling from somewhere rural—but he got the gist of it.

The boys had been in a car accident. Cheo's car was totaled, and they weren't sure what to do. Ransom was unable to understand exactly where they were, but he knew the road they were on. He left the party and drove out to find them.

On their way out of Woodburn, Cheo and Octavio were driving a familiar rural road at fifty miles an hour. They hit a small rise, and as they dropped into the swale below, saw brake lights close ahead. A car was slowing to make a left-hand turn in the darkness, a large SUV close behind it. Cheo hit the brakes hard, and the wheels locked up. They careened downhill toward the other cars, out of control. It happened so quickly that neither recalled much later: fear, speed, disorientation.

They slammed into the back of the SUV, their seat belts digging into their shoulders. Octavio's head snapped forward, and then flopped back against his seat's headrest. The noise was deafening and confusing.

They crawled out of the car slowly. The SUV's driver emerged, shaken but unhurt. For a while, all three of them looked at Cheo's wrecked 1991 Honda Accord, wedged under the SUV almost up to its windshield.

"You boys are sure lucky," the SUV's driver said.

By the time Ransom arrived, the two boys were thinking more clearly and feeling very cold. They waited for the police in Ransom's car. It took about twenty more minutes before the first cop, a state patrolman, showed up. Thinking back on it later, Ransom couldn't remember the patrolman's name, but from his accent alone, he was clearly Russian. That meant he probably lived in Woodburn.

After checking for injuries, the officer listened to Cheo describe the accident, Ransom helping to translate. He asked for Cheo's license and insurance, and Ransom felt sure the cop was disappointed that the young man had both. Then he went off to interview the SUV driver.

About this time, a second policeman showed up, a sheriff's deputy. He was very friendly, and he told Cheo that they could leave once the police knew where to have the car towed. However, the state patrolman returned with a different attitude.

"I'm afraid that I'm going to have to write Cheo a ticket," he said. "I'm charging him with reckless driving."

Ransom realized that the two policemen, each viewing the same scene, had come to opposite conclusions. The deputy had blamed the collision on road conditions; the state patrolman, on operator error. As Cheo started to protest, Ransom asked the patrolman if he was including the road conditions in his report—in particular, the black ice.

"I don't see any ice," the patrolman replied.

Ransom turned his flashlight toward the road. "See that glittery stuff?" he said sarcastically. "That's ice."

When the other officer began to gently take Ransom's side, the patrolman told them that there was no ice, and to prove it, he asked the deputy to re-create the events of the accident.

"I couldn't believe it when he said that," Ransom said later. "I've never heard of re-creating an accident. It was dark, there was clearly ice on the road. I thought he was nuts."

Ransom took Octavio and Cheo far enough off the road to feel safe. When the deputy's cruiser came roaring past, Ransom could hear the antilock brakes clicking. But the state patrolman turned to them and said, "You see, his car didn't skid." Even when the deputy emerged from his car, confirming that only his modern brakes had kept him from a skid, the state patrolman didn't change his mind. He gave Cheo a ticket for reckless driving and then got into his patrol car and left. Ransom didn't know quite what to think of the patrolman's behavior.

"Clearly he was going to give Cheo a ticket regardless of the road conditions. I argued at first, I even knocked some ice up with my foot and shone my flashlight on it. But he still said that he didn't see ice. So I backed off and told Cheo to plead not guilty and that I would testify."

The deputy assured Ransom that he would appear on Cheo's behalf if necessary, and then he too drove off. Ransom loaded the boys into his own car.

"I asked them what they wanted to do. 'Do you want to go to the party?' But they both said no, they wanted to go home."

Octavio's aunt and uncle had gone to Mexico for the holidays, so he went to stay with a cousin for a little while. Although he hadn't sustained any serious injuries, he spent a few weeks trying to stretch out the pain in his neck and back. The first three days after the accident, he didn't even leave the house. "I was feeling very scared," he said. "I just stayed in the house thinking about it."

The boys stayed in Woodburn for winter break, Octavio living alone at his uncle's house. He spent Christmas with Cheo's family and called home to talk with his own parents. When Cheo finally received his insurance check, he bought another Honda and he and Octavio started going to work again. They had found jobs as house painters, both hoping to save a few thousand dollars to pay for college. Cheo had been accepted to the private Quaker university George Fox; Octavio hoped to attend Portland State University, which had offered him a partial academic scholarship. Although both planned to live in Woodburn and commute, the universities were in opposite directions. They weren't going to be called twins anymore.

Over the next few months, Cheo occasionally came to Ransom's office with some new piece of paperwork about the legal case that he didn't understand. When the case finally went to court, the state patrolman failed to show up, so Cheo's reckless driving charge was dismissed. Looking back on the event months later, Octavio and Cheo shrugged their shoulders and turned their palms up to the sky. After all, it was over, and what could they do? But Ransom, although philosophical, retained some anger at the way the cop had treated them:

"They got in the wreck and they called me—help, get us out of this. Their parents would help, but they're looking for somebody who knows the system. What do I do? How do I plea this? What's this form mean? You've got to walk them through it. They'd be able to do it fine the second time—heaven forbid they should have another accident—but it's not just the language issue that stops them from knowing what to do. It's the system."

Since the 2005 season ended, the town of Woodburn has gone through a few dramatic changes. Just months after the loss to Westview, legislation was proposed in Oregon to issue drivers' licenses only to people who could prove legal residency. Hispanic communities across the state held protests, and in Woodburn, many of the students marched in support, including most of the varsity Bulldogs. A later protest, also attended by students, railed against a proposed law to ban bilingual education in the state. The law failed to pass.

In 2008, Woodburn briefly appeared on the national stage when then–presidential candidate Barack Obama stopped for lunch at Luis's Taqueria. Obama was joined by his brother-in-law, Craig Robinson, who had recently been hired as the head basketball coach at Oregon State University. They ate *carne asada* tacos and talked with an excited crowd.

The economic collapse that hit the United States in 2008 propelled Oregon's unemployment rate from about 6 percent to over 12 percent. The Woodburn city government managed to keep from laying off employees, but all raises were postponed. County unemployment hovered close to the state average in the spring of 2009, although the town received federal money for fixing roads and buying new buses and other equipment. Property-based crime, which had been decreasing steadily for years, continued to go down, but other types of crime increased, much of it domestic violence charges. In 2008, violent crime rose 40 percent over the previous year, including a December bomb attack on a bank that killed two police officers and injured the police chief.

The Woodburn school district continued its expansion of bilingual language courses. At Nellie Muir, still under Sherrilynn Rawson's guiding hand, state test scores soared, leading the Oregon Department of Education in 2006 and 2008 to give Nellie Muir awards for closing the achievement gap between minority and white students. Fresh from this success, the district came up with a new idea—why not aim to have every student, regardless of native tongue, graduate bilingual? That plan is in the works.

In 2006, the high school successfully divided into four Small Schools plus the Success Academy, designed for kids who otherwise might fail high school. That first year of Small Schools didn't prove anything useful—standardized test scores at the high school level dropped below the scores reached in 2005. The following year, however, test scores jumped back up, and for the first time in a decade, some test scores in middle and elementary schools actually surpassed the state average.

The switch to Small Schools also seemed to have a profound and immediate impact on dropout rates. In 2005, the year I followed the team, the high school's dropout rate was almost one in ten. The first year of Small Schools, that rate was cut nearly in half, to 5.1 percent. It continued to get better until 2009, when new guidelines were created to define graduation. No longer able to count kids who went to an alternative school, who took five years to graduate, or who got their GED, the high school's collective graduation rate plummeted dramatically.

Beginning in 2006, the newly named Oregon School Activities Association reclassified the number of conferences (based on school size) from four to six. In 2006, the Woodburn Bulldogs swept through their league undefeated, giving up far more goals than the 2005 team, but scoring far more as well. Led by their core of experienced seniors—Carlos, Tony, and Juan, with Carlos now playing forward exclusively—Woodburn reached the semifinals before losing to Bend, the eventual state champion.

In 2007, the team again went undefeated through its league before losing to Glencoe, the eventual state champion, in the quarter-final round. In 2008, ranked number one in the state, still carrying two players from the 2005 team, the Bulldogs swept their league for the third year in a row, and then again lost to Glencoe with thirteen seconds on the clock, a heartbreaking defeat that left some of the boys sprawled and weeping on the chilly grass field.

In 2009, the Woodburn Bulldogs made it to the playoffs for the twenty-fourth consecutive year, and lost in their first game.

Despite these losses, the Bulldogs' twenty-four consecutive years of making the postseason set a new state record—the longest continuous streak of playoff appearances for any Oregon high school team. Going back to 1986, when the young Mike Flannigan was stationed between the goalposts, no Oregon high school soccer, baseball, football, or basketball team had made the playoffs every year except for Woodburn—a noteworthy feat that has gone nearly unnoticed.

Finally, the front of the team's warm-ups no longer reads "Bulldogs." Instead, the boys of Woodburn wear the name they have called themselves for years: "Perros."

Coach **Mike Flannigan** quit coaching JV basketball after the 2005 season ended and witnessed the birth of his first child, a boy. He won Coach of the Year awards for soccer in 2007 and 2008. Coach Flannigan was assigned to teach at the Small School he had helped design, but in the first year of the new school, Flannigan became more and more frustrated by the lack of organization.

In a move that surprised many people, Coach Flannigan announced his retirement from coaching Woodburn soccer after the end of the 2008 season. Busy with teaching and his family, Coach Flannigan planned to take some time off before looking for other opportunities to coach at a club or college. His departure opened up the job of head varsity soccer coach at Woodburn for the first time in over two decades. The new coach, Luis Del Rio, is an ex-semipro player from Mexico who has coached local club teams. The Bulldogs are his first high school team.

By 2009, Coach Flannigan felt that he was beginning to see positive changes in the classroom that he could attribute to the Small School. He is keeping his fingers crossed that the minor league soccer team in Portland, the Timbers, will be replaced by a new MLS team in 2011. In the fall of 2009, with Portland City approval and the backing of a wealthy owner, it appeared that his hope would come true.

Mike's father, **Brian Flannigan**, who had said he would quit coaching when Mike did, did just that, leaving the school where he had coached since 1984. Always busy with family and projects, Brian hopes to follow his son to wherever Mike coaches next.

Assistant Coach **Chuck Ransom** left the team after the end of the 2005 season to pour all his energy into organizing the switch to Small Schools. Before the 2006 school year began, Ransom suffered a minor heart attack, but he recovered to accept a post as principal of the Academy of International Studies. He can still be seen at games, wandering the sidelines keeping an eye on the crowd and the game, staying in touch with all the students who wander up to him for those brief but important reunions.

Omar Mendoza focused on coaching club soccer and began to receive a small stipend for doing so. As busy as ever, Omar and Pat took the whole family on a trip to south Texas to visit family, and they continued to show up to watch every Bulldog game in 2006 and 2007. They also fostered two more of Carlos's half-siblings, the last as an infant. Then Omar and Pat decided that they had been in Oregon long enough; it was time to return to Texas. They sent both O.J. and Carlos to live with family in Texas while they put their house on the market, just in time for the 2008 housing crunch. They continue to live in Woodburn waiting for the economy to recover so they can sell their house and move back home.

O.J. moved to south Texas, where his father grew up, and attended the University of Texas–Brownsville as a freshman, when he was on the university's soccer team. Then his girlfriend became pregnant. To save money, O.J. spent his sophomore year at Texas State

Technical College in Harlingen. He plans to return to a four-year university as a junior.

Martin took a trip to Mexico with his old club teammate Dario, and both tried out for Segunda División teams in Guadalajara. Neither was offered a spot. Back in Woodburn, Martin began coursework to become an X-ray technician while working with a drywall crew. Then he took a full-time job answering phones at a nearby corporate office. He is toying with the idea of becoming a private investigator.

Chuy did not play on the 2006 team. He took up mixed martial arts, and in 2007 he won his first—and so far only—fight. He got a job painting houses with his cousin. He is working sixty hours a week, saving his money, and wondering what to do with his life.

Ramon went to Western Oregon University, where he is majoring in education. He plans to graduate in the summer of 2010.

Angel moved to Corvallis to attend Oregon State University. He is studying Human Development and Family Services and plans to be a probation officer. Angel is already using academic language to describe the kids he wants to work with, kids like himself, "growing up in low-resource areas."

Cesar graduated with a good GPA and high SAT score, but he was too busy studying for his contractor's license and launching a roofing business with his father to apply for college. His business went well for two years, and while working full-time, he finished some community college coursework. But trying to balance full-time school and full-time work took its toll, and his grades suffered. Then his roofing business was cold-cocked by the economic collapse. His father found another job while Cesar struggled to keep work coming in. He hopes that work will pick up so he can save enough money to get an engineering degree.

Juan graduated in 2007 and moved to Mexico with his mother to wait for the completion of his residency papers. He returned to Woodburn six months later and began attending Warner Pacific College in Portland, where he plays on the university team and studies business administration. He hopes to become a sports agent.

Moved out of goal to play forward, **Carlos** led the Perros in scoring during 2006. At the end of that season, Carlos was voted

first-team All-State as a forward, having won the same award as a
goalkeeper the year before. Despite these achievements, no college
teams courted him. During the winter break of his senior year, he
sent out applications to the local state colleges.

After graduating in June 2007, Carlos was accepted at George
Fox University, where he was a starting forward on the soccer team
and studied social work. Living in a dorm, away from his family,
Carlos lost focus on his schoolwork, partied too much, and got poor
grades. He felt frustrated by the poor play of his college team, saying
that he had to work harder at Woodburn than he was ever asked to
work at George Fox.

His birth mother once tried to contact him at the college. Carlos was in his dorm when he got a call from the college's information desk. When he was told that his mother was on the campus, he
thought of Pat at first. But Pat knew his dorm, knew his cell number.
When he realized that Beth was there, he blew his top. Refusing to
even meet with her, he told security to take her off the campus. Since
then, he has only seen her in court, whenever she shows up to try
and regain custody of Carlos's younger sisters, now living with him
at Omar and Pat's.

After one year at George Fox, Carlos took a Greyhound bus to
south Texas, where he joined O.J. on the Brownsville campus. Arianna, his girlfriend, followed him. Carlos tried out for the university
soccer team, but because of his poor grades at George Fox, he was
deemed academically ineligible to play.

When Omar and Pat were unable to leave Woodburn, Carlos
returned to help take care of his sisters. In 2009, as a junior, he joined
his friend Juan at Warner Pacific, where they once again are on the
same team. Carlos still wants to be a social worker. With Carlos and
Juan both playing, the 2009 Warner Pacific Knights won their first
ever Cascade Collegiate Conference Championship. "Finally," Carlos said. He had found a school that knew how to win. The team then
drove down to California to play in a national tournament and lost
their first game.

Octavio graduated and began working full time. His knee slowly
healed. Unable to accept either of his college scholarships because

of his nonresident status, he began taking a few classes at a local community college. He and his girlfriend, Anita, who was attending a four-year college, were married. Then Anita got pregnant and dropped out of school. She had a healthy baby boy, and they made new plans: both would attend community college part-time.

Then, something unexpected happened. Chemeketa Community College, in nearby Salem, Oregon, decided to start a men's soccer team, the Storm, as part of a move to increase student enrollment, especially Latino enrollment. Chemeketa had a history of reaching out to the large Latino population in the Willamette Valley. The school offered financial assistance to the children of seasonal farm workers, brought over high school students from the Latino-heavy schools at Gervais, North Salem, and Woodburn for tutoring, and offered a fifth-year program through Woodburn High that allowed students to finish high school classes while they started college.

The Chemeketa team's new coach, Marty Limbird, found out about his new position in the spring of 2008, long after the high school soccer season had ended. Unable to scout local schools, he asked high school coaches to pass the word around to their graduating players, and he held an open tryout. Octavio, a young man whom Limbird had never heard of, showed up and wowed him.

"Octavio stood out almost immediately," said Limbird, "although I didn't know how good he really was until we started the season. I can't put my finger on it—he's not the fastest kid, he's not the biggest kid, it's more the way he moves on the field, his anticipation, the way he controls the ball. He never makes a mistake."

Getting on the team at Chemeketa meant that Octavio needed to study full time to stay eligible for both soccer and his athletic scholarship. He also needed to commit to attend the school for two full years. He would have to work days and go to school nights—an arduous routine—but he jumped at the chance.

"He was so excited," said Anita. "He was really happy to be playing soccer but also happy because they would pay for his school, which meant he could finish sooner."

Other players from Woodburn tried out as well, many of them having graduated years earlier. Among those who made the cut and became starters on the new team was Octavio's best friend, Cheo. **Cheo** had accepted a scholarship to George Fox University, but he dropped out before the end of the first semester because, he said, his English still wasn't good enough to understand college-level coursework.

Tony, the quick and dependable winger, struggled academically, eventually leaving the regular high school to attend Success Academy, from which he graduated. He worked part-time at a retail job with no real direction in life until the 2008 Chemeketa soccer team accepted him. He moved into an apartment in Salem and began taking classes. However, poor grades forced him off the 2009 team, just as Chemeketa accepted **Luis**, **Jovanny**, and **Manolo**. Including Juan-Carlos, Luis's older brother and another ex-Bulldog, nearly one-third of the 2009 Chemeketa team were from Woodburn. **Vlad**, also a young father, attended Chemeketa through its fifth-year program, although he didn't try out for the team.

Octavio did well his first year, finishing with a 3.5 GPA, the second-highest on the team, while simultaneously holding down a full-time job painting houses. He went to school at night, and while his wife and son slept, he stayed up late at night or woke up early in the morning to complete his homework.

The Chemeketa Storm, made up mostly of Hispanic players from the Willamette Valley, was exceptionally skilled right away. Even before his squad had played a single game, Coach Limbird knew that other teams would have difficulty matching up against them. He was right. Although Limbird had never before coached a soccer team, the Storm took first place in their division and cut a swath through the early playoff rounds, making it to the regional championship in Seattle.

There, Octavio and his teammates faced the league's top-ranked squad, from Walla Walla, Washington, whose community college had fielded a soccer team for thirty-four years without winning a title. The game was tied 2–2 at the end of regulation play, sending it into overtime. Unlike high school, overtime for soccer in community college ends in sudden death, and five minutes into it, Walla

Walla scored a golden goal, sending the Chemeketa players home in silence.

Octavio took the loss hard. Coach Limbird hadn't realized it, but a lot of the players from Walla Walla were talking trash during the game, while the Chemeketa players had always let their play speak for itself. Losing against a team that talked trash, that hurt.

Nobody spoke on the van ride home for almost two hours, then a player sitting on the back seat with Octavio and Cheo blurted out, "Fuck it, guys, we'll beat them next year."

The 2009 Chemeketa team basked in its league status as leading championship contender, ending the season in third place. The team's final loss came when a handball was called on Octavio inside the penalty area. Despite the team's arguments that the handball was unintentional, the opposing team scored on their PK, and the Storm never equalized.

Octavio was a starter on the team, but to Coach Limbird, he was also important because of his attitude about education. While many of his teammates lost focus outside the soccer season, Octavio was a scholastic metronome, never letting up on his trips from school to work, school to work. As the season had progressed, Limbird came to rely on Octavio as a positive role model for the other players.

"I really want to see him succeed so I can point to him in the future. I hope that he can ignite something."

Like the teachers and administrators at Woodburn High School, Coach Limbird seemed to need some of his players to succeed, as if he was looking for proof that the world is the way he hopes it can be, a place where all one needs to do is work hard and walk straight, a place where the American Dream really can come true. For all the well-meaning Anglos around him, Octavio provides a concrete home for those earnest fantasies while his teammates bring teachers and coaches back down to reality.

"I don't know if things would have been different if we would have won the championship," Limbird said, "if more guys would have come back. To get that close and not to get it, they saw all the aspects of our league play, the playoffs, how it's run, all the way up to the championship game, getting into the stadium. I wanted them to experience all of that. I can really see us getting back there next year, but you know, soccer's a funny game, anything can happen."

The last time I had lunch with Octavio, at the restaurant where he first courted Anita, he sounded confident about the future and grew excited as he talked about the possibilities that college brought. "I just want to keep learning," he said. "I want to take classes and just keep learning new things. Get my master's degree, maybe get a PhD. Why not? I can teach for most of the year and go to college part-time in the summer."

Octavio's fantasies of success took a step closer to reality because he married Anita, a U.S. citizen. As a legal resident, Octavio would qualify for financial aid and his university bills would drop. Where he could look for work would also change. In fact, Octavio already has a job offer. As soon as he gets his degree, he can begin work as a substitute teacher at one of the Small Schools at Woodburn High.

However, marriage alone can't change his immigration status. Because Octavio entered the country without permission, his application for residency will be automatically denied, and his next step, to plea that his absence will create an unreasonable hardship on his wife and child, may be denied as well. If that happens, Octavio will be refused entry to the United States for ten years.

In the winter of 2009, after much discussion with his family, Octavio decided to take that risk. He returned to Mexico alone and applied for residency. As yet, he doesn't know which direction his future will take.

ACKNOWLEDGMENTS

Many people were indispensible in the reporting and writing of this book—my sincere thanks to all of you: Michael McGregor, Roberto DeAnda, Matt McGowan, Allison Trzop, Mark Hyman, Howard Bryant, Dana Brigham, Alejandro Ruvel-Caba, Brian Flannigan, Laura Lanka, Greg Baisch, Pete McCallum, Miguel Salinas, Chuck Ransom, Michelle Te, José Romero, Pat Mendoza, Everardo Castro, Loreto Castro, Nicole Holmes, Antonio Ramos, Hank Vrendenberg, Francisco Ibañez, Henry Estrada, Jack Reeves, Sherrilynn Rawson, and Marty Limbird. Thanks to Lisa Sibbett, Dan Deweese, and the revolving members of Dan's writing group for comments on drafts. My wife, Cathy, was very patient with all those trips to Woodburn—thanks, honey.

I owe an extra heaping of appreciation to the staff and all the varsity athletes on the 2005 Perros team, who put up with me and my endless questions with grace and wit. I had a great time spending the season with you. Finally, I want to thank the four men who made so much room in their busy lives for this project: Omar Mendoza, Mike Flannigan, Carlos, and Octavio. Best of luck to all of you.